Contents

Alternatives to Grading Student Writing

129628

Alternatives to Grading Student Writing

Edited by

Stephen Tchudi
University of Nevada, Reno

NCTE Committee on Alternatives to Grading Student Writing

National Council of Teachers of English
1111 W. Kenyon Road, Urbana, Illinois 61801-1096

Manuscript Editor: Robert A. Heister/Humanities & Sciences Associates
Production Editor: Jamie Hutchinson
Interior Design: Doug Burnett
Cover Design: Loren Kirkwood

NCTE Stock Number: 01305-3050

Library of Congress Cataloging-in-Publication Data

Alternatives to grading student writing / edited by Stephen Tchudi :
   NCTE Committee on Alternatives to Grading Student Writing.
      p.   cm.
   Includes bibliographical references.
   ISBN 0-8141-0130-5
      1. English language—Composition and exercises—Ability testing—
   United States.   2. English language—Composition and exercises—
   Study and teaching—United States—Evaluation.   I. Tchudi,
   Stephen, 1942–   .   II. NCTE Committee on Alternatives to Grading
   Student Writing.
   LB1576.A6157   1997
   808'.042'071—dc21   97-10157
                                                                        CIP

Introduction: Degrees of Freedom in Assessment, Evaluation, and Grading

Stephen Tchudi
Chair, NCTE Committee on Alternatives to Grading Student Writing

One of the highlights of my week is a trip to the neighborhood grocery/deli with my fourteen-year-old son Chris, to indulge in a couple of doughnuts and a shared reading of the *Weekly World News*. For those unfamiliar with this tabloid, you'll find it at the checkout counter next to the *National Enquirer* and the *Star*, papers that Chris and I regard as mere scandal sheets. *Weekly World News*, to our way of thinking, is more serious journalism—though not in the league of the *Washington Post*. The *News* entertains us with stories of possibly true and certainly odd happenings from around the globe.

For example, we read of a math teacher from Herford, Germany, who was "fired for making kids eat night crawlers!" (30 Jan. 1996: 4). It seems that William Enbeck used "sadistic" assignments to let students raise their grades. He gave a girl thirty points "for pushing a peanut around the classroom with her nose for an hour"; he awarded a passing grade to the lad who "submerged his head in a bucket of cold water for 45 seconds." Another kid went up the grading scale while eating "half a pound of long, fat earthworms." At the hearing called by irate parents and administrators, Enbeck defended himself by claiming that these were character-building exercises that demonstrated students' "guts and willingness to take risks—qualities that will take them much farther in life than basic math."

As Chair of NCTE's Committee on Alternatives to Grading Student Writing, I have to confess that I found Enbeck's alternatives quite interesting. He articulated clear goals; he set specific assignments with obvious criteria for evaluation; and if the students did the work, they got the reward. His grading scheme seemed a lot simpler and in some ways no more arbitrary and subjective than those devised by many of us more conventional elementary, secondary, and college writing teachers. Now, I don't think I'll be having my students eat worms, though some might say that my assignments are just as unpleasant. But hyperbole aside, the Enbeck story dramatizes the dilemma of grading that prompts this book: the arbitrariness of grades, the use of grades to coerce students into performance, and the irrelevance of grades to the sort of authentic assessment one experiences in life.

My personal quest for alternatives to grading student writing began more than thirty years ago, during my first year of college teaching. At Northwestern University, I was teaching an undergraduate course called "Practical Rhetoric." In the spirit of the then recent Dartmouth Conference, I had turned this traditionally analytic course into a writing workshop with an emphasis on the process of composing, from prewriting through editing. I graded the first round of papers by conventional standards: C = OK, B = Better, A = Excellent. I had no complaints from the students, who mostly received B's and A's, thanks to the possibility of revision through writing workshops. But for the second round of papers, I hit a snag. Student Julie, who had received an A on her first paper, complained about the B I gave her this time. I explained and justified the grade to her: I thought that the second paper lacked the verve and voice of the first and that it showed some signs of hasty revision. In words that are echoed in an essay by Jean Ketter and Judith Hunter elsewhere in this collection, Julie said, in effect, *"This is the best I can do; it's my very best!"* I suggested that she might do further revision, but I might as well have asked her to eat night crawlers. She did C-level work for the rest of the course and seldom talked to me. This experience was something of an epiphany for me. To this day, I blame the grading system for poisoning my teacher/ student relationship with Julie, and since that course, I have never again put a letter grade on a piece of student writing.

I have sought alternatives. For a while, I used a "recommended" grading system, where students would do self-assessment and justify or argue for a grade. The scheme left me uneasy, however, especially when a colleague accused me of making the students do what I, myself, was unwilling to do: reduce a range of achievements to a letter grade. I've tried a variety of contract- and performance-based systems; I've worked in pass/fail and nongraded systems; and I've used holistic as well as analytic scoring of portfolios. Each of these schemes offered me certain degrees of freedom to assess and respond to student writing, and each had certain drawbacks, restrictions, and problems. Always problems.

Each semester, as I'm preparing my syllabi, I agonize over the grading criteria. What will it be this semester? Contracts? Achievement grading? A point system? Portfolios? Negotiated grades? Self-evaluation? In what combination? I find myself in the absurd position of rearranging course content in order to accommodate the demands of the grading system. I've been known to develop several alternative syllabi, carefully saved in the computer, and to make my final selection of a grading system only at the last minute, when forced to photocopy the syllabus for those students who will show up an hour later and want to know, "How do I get an A out of this course?" or "How can I get out of this course with a C?"

I'm almost phobic about this aspect of my teaching, and that's why I accepted the invitation to chair the NCTE Committee on Alternatives to Grading Student Writing. We were charged by the Executive Committee of NCTE

> to investigate all alternatives to giving students grades in writing so that progress can be evaluated in ways sensitive to the needs of students as well as universities, colleges, and school districts; to organize the results of that investigation through manuscripts that help teachers and others in elementary, middle, and secondary schools and in colleges and universities to understand the theory and practice of alternatives to grading; to set a timely schedule for the gathering of information and the submitting of a prospectus and manuscript to the NCTE Editorial Board.

I saw chairing this committee as an opportunity to learn new approaches and alternatives, and maybe even to find pedagogical salvation: the Perfect Grading System that would be true to the research on grading, consistent with current writing pedagogy, fair to students, and productive in moving students toward being highly motivated, highly skilled writers.

Well, the committee *hasn't* found that *perfect* system, although the readers of this book will learn about some very powerful alternatives to grading student writing. I have personally learned a great deal from the members of the committee (listed in the front matter of this book) and from the contributors to this volume. I have experimented with the grading schemes described here and have found that they produced a good deal of peace of mind, though not complete salvation. Actually, none of the writers has found or claims to have found that perfect system, but everyone represented in this book is working at it constantly, as, I suspect, are the readers who pick up this volume.

We're a community, we searchers for alternatives to grading student writing.

The committee is convinced by the research presented in Part I of this book, which shows quite clearly that grading writing doesn't contribute much to learning to write and is in conflict with the new paradigms for writing instruction. As a committee, we would unanimously love to see grades disappear from education altogether so that teachers and students can focus on authentic assessment, but we realize that in the current educational climate, that's not likely to happen. Although a few schools and colleges are experimenting with nongraded systems, and although a growing number of school systems do not grade the youngest students, the vast majority of English/language arts teachers will, throughout their teaching careers, be faced with the periodic need to sum up students' work by some set of criteria and to translate that performance into a grade that goes on a report card or transcript. From the outset, we wanted this book to be theoretically sound but classroom practical, supplying genuine alternatives for teachers who work under the shadow of grading systems.

We think it is useful to conceive of the problem by adapting a concept from math and science: "degrees of freedom." Both numbers and molecules have constraints on their freedom to move, to vary. Changing parameters or restrictions often opens up new areas of freedom, but just as often results in the loss of other directions of movement. So it is, we think, with grading. The aim of this book is to help teachers increase their freedom to explore alternatives in assessment.

Figure 1 shows our interpretation of this concept and will help the reader understand the structure and philosophy of this book. The figure represents the tension between what research and teacher instinct tell us—to broaden the range of possibilities for assessment and reaction to student work—versus the pressures to place a single grade/symbol on the final product.

The committee thinks it important to distinguish among four interrelated terms and concepts shown in Figure 1: *response, assessment, evaluation,* and *grading.* From top to bottom, these represent *decreasing* degrees of freedom in reacting to and evaluating student work. Response to writing is, we believe, at the heart of the process. As Lynn Holaday says in her essay in this volume, *"Writing students need coaches, not judges." Response* is so important, in fact, that the committee wanted an entire section of the book (Part II) devoted to response strategies, without any reference to grades. Response to writing has the greatest range of freedom because it is naturalistic, growing direct-

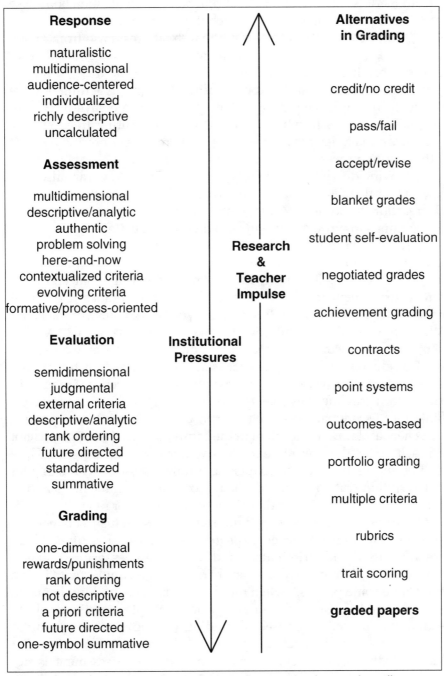

Figure 1. Degrees of freedom in assessment, evaluation, and grading

ly from readers' reaction to a text. Somebody loves it; somebody else hates it; a third person wants to punch the writer in the nose.

Although most teachers agree that "real" response from "real" audiences is desirable, there are some reasons to make certain that response is productive and civil (unlike a punch in the nose), which is why we teach writing in classrooms rather than simply letting novices pick it up through the school of hard knocks. The essays in Part II, then, suggest ways in which, without unduly limiting freedom, the teacher can make response to writing an increasingly productive part of the writing process.

Moving down the left-hand column of Figure 1, we are also persuaded that there is a need for what we'll call "instructionally calculated" reaction to student writing—peers, teachers, parents, or others saying things to writers that will help them write better.

Assessment in writing is a bit more limited in its degrees of freedom than response. Assessment asks broadly: "How did this project turn out?" "How is it turning out?" "Are you getting what you want from your audience?" "Can I suggest a few possibilities that might make this thing work better?" "What do you think your work needs?" "What are your ideas about how to make it more successful?" Assessment certainly incorporates reader response (to drafts as well as finished products), and it is often focused on practical, functional concerns: "What do I have to do to make this paper *work?*" Frequently, criteria for assessment evolve *as* one writes: "How do I know what I think until I see what I say?" The purpose of assessment is very much in the here and now, rather than in the future; that is, the concern is not so much "How do I get to be a better writer in the future?" as "How can I be successful with this paper right now?" Assessment uses a lot of description (rather than judgments) of readers and writers and is "formative" or in-process rather than "summative" or final.

We think it is especially important to distinguish between assessment and the next level, *evaluation* of writing. Too often, these terms are used indiscriminately and are sometimes even conflated with "grading." I regularly hear teachers say, for example, that "I have to evaluate some papers," when they will, in fact, be grading them. Or, as the committee heard on several occasions, people sometimes falsely assume that if you're opposed to grading writing, you're refusing to evaluate or assess, just accepting any old thing a student writes. For clarity of discussion, then, it's important to say "assessment is not evaluation is not grading," although the three are clearly linked.

To distinguish from the broader term, assessment, we argue that *evaluation* implies fixed or a priori criteria rather than evolutionary or constructed values. To "evaluate" means to compare work with some sort of marker, benchmark, or standard. Unfortunately, many students see evaluation as essentially punitive: "No, James, this paper is not up to par." However, the best evaluation can be constructive: "I think this paper moves beyond what you were doing in your last one" or "Yes, I think this paper is just about ready for publication." Where assessment criteria tend to be developed within the rhetorical context of a project, evaluation looks to established criteria: "This paper does/doesn't have a clear sense of purpose" or "The language is/is not gobbledy-gook" or "Your spelling is/is not up to standard." Evaluation also tends to be comparative—using phrases like "better than" or "worse than"—and it lends itself to rank ordering: "top to bottom," "upper third," or "90th percentile."

Both evaluation and assessment are a natural part of the writing process; writers assess and evaluate constantly, from idea to printed page. The committee (supported by the new paradigm in writing) believes that assessment, along with cultivated response, is the most useful kind of information that writers can receive. Evaluation, although more restricted in the range of commentary it can offer, seems a natural enough element in writing, for we all want to know "How'm I doin'?" and "How can I do better?"

But then there is *grading*, the fourth term in our model. As Leisel O'Hagan shows us in the next essay, very few people have anything nice to say about grading. Grades are extremely limited in their degrees of freedom, for they take a vast array of data and condense it into a single symbol that, in itself, doesn't communicative very much. Grades are one-dimensional, and they tend to be based on a priori, even Platonic, notions of "good" and "bad." As a result, grades stereotype, pigeonhole, and rank order students and their writing. Any grade less than an A destroys student morale to some extent, and even the prized A falsely implies that the student has reached a kind of perfection. Above all, grades fail to provide descriptive information of any significance—what, after all, does a C or an A tell you about how people responded to your work or even what you might do with the next piece you write? Furthermore, grades reduce students' degrees of freedom to internalize advice about writing: Why should you pay attention to what the teacher or peers said when all that matters is that grade?

The focus of Part III is on practical alternatives to grading student writing, systems and techniques that maintain many degrees of freedom in reacting to students' work while still satisfying the institutional need to derive a grade. As summarized in the right-hand column of Figure 1, the papers in the collection explore systems ranging from pass/fail (with very high degrees of freedom) to rubrics (which increase degrees of freedom over traditional grades though careful delineation of criteria). In between, the reader will find essays that deal with such approaches as collaborative evaluation, contract grading, achievement grading, outcomes-based assessment, portfolio grading, and total quality evaluation.

In addition, sprinkled among these "how to" essays, the reader will also find some statements we call "Interludes," gleaned from the committee's discussion folder on NCTENet. We think these brief statements offer some provocative thoughts about grading issues and offer further techniques and strategies being tried effectively by teachers all across North America.

Part IV closes the book with a set of outlines for faculty workshops in alternatives to grading student writing. Although virtually all of the grading alternatives described in Part III can be done by the individual teacher in his or her own classroom, there is both safety and the possibility of increased curriculum coherence in numbers. If grading alternatives are to achieve their true potential for helping students and teachers think differently about writing, response, assessment, and evaluation, faculties need to work together systematically to develop, implement, and evaluate new approaches. The workshops are designed with that in mind and are intended for use by small clusters of like-minded teachers or by entire school buildings or districts. The workshops were developed by members of the NCTE Committee on Alternatives to Grading Student Writing and were field-tested at the NCTE Annual Convention in San Diego.

Finally, I want to close this introduction by appealing briefly to potential readers of this book who may *not* be sold on the whole concept of alternatives to grading student writing or who are in systems that specifically require letter grades to be placed on individual papers. In our work as a committee, we have heard from articulate teachers who argued that the problem is not with grading, but with *how* teachers grade. We have also heard from teachers who would like not to use grades but explain that "the principal has mandated it." The committee members want to share our belief that even in such cases, there are bad, good, and better ways of going about grading writing—

fair and unfair; equitable and inequitable; destructive, constructive, and highly constructive. There's certainly no support in the professional literature for arbitrary grading of the "guess what the teacher wants this time" variety. There is no support for punitive grades or grades used as a way of coercing students into studying material that is too difficult or irrelevant. Moreover, there *is* support for the processes of evaluation and assessment described in this book: involving students collaboratively in the response and assessment; using carefully articulated criteria; rewarding growth and effort as well as perceived absolute quality; including large amounts of response to student writing; seeking real-world audiences; and focusing writing as a whole on issues, topics, and concerns that are important to the writer. Thus, a reading of this book will, we hope, help the teacher who uses conventional grading to make that approach potentially and pedagogically more useful.

Still, the NCTE Committee on Alternatives to Grading Student Writing finds that both teacher experience and educational research argue powerfully for the abolition of letter grades on individual student papers. *We prefer and promote alternatives to grading student writing.*

I Background and Theory

1 It's Broken–Fix It!

Liesel K. O'Hagan
Billingurst Middle School, Reno, Nevada

Liesel K. O'Hagan teaches English to seventh and eighth graders at Billingurst Middle School, Reno, Nevada.

Winning points may be the final goal of classroom work as it is in the sports endeavor, but the grade, like the final score of the game, never taught anyone how to win again, or why they lost.

—Lucas, "Writing Portfolios" 2

Would a company like IBM keep producing a computer model if research demonstrated that their machine made the consumer's work harder and ruined all confidence in the process? Would consumers continue to keep these obsolete and impractical machines in their homes and at their businesses? The answer is, of course, no. No major corporation would refuse to make decisions for change and continue to market an inferior product. Why, then, would the educational system continue to use such an obsolete machine as grading? Despite years and years and piles and piles of research showing that grading is not helpful and is, at times, harmful, educators and institutions continue to sum up students' knowledge and abilities by assigning a number or letter grade. So why do they continue to use these grade markers on student writing? One of the answers lies in tradition.

Grading: No New Process, No New Complaints

The educational practice of grading emerged relatively recently, approximately 1850, and it was challenged almost as soon as it became widely used. Grading became part of the system in the late nineteenth century as the nation grew and legislators passed mandatory attendance laws that resulted in a larger and more diverse student body. In his detailed history of the grading system, Thomas Guskey explains that by the early 1900s, the original practice of writing down skills that students had mastered had given way to the use of percentages to certify accomplishments in particular subjects. Though elementary teachers continued to use written descriptions to document student learning, high school teachers found the number of students too large and instead moved to percentages. No one questioned the move to percentages because of the increasing demands on high school teachers.

Yet, studies as early as 1912 questioned the validity of grading, suggesting that in writing instruction, in particular, grades were far too subjective (Ellsworth and Willson 188). In a study done just twelve years after the introduction of percentages to student work, Starch and Elliot suggested that grades were not a reliable measure of student achievement (Guskey 18). They studied papers written in 142 different first-year high school English classes. The teachers assigned a wide range of scores to two essays, with one being scored on the basis of neatness, spelling, and punctuation and the other being scored on the basis of how well the paper communicated its message. Using a 0–100 percent grading scale, 15 percent of teachers gave one of the papers a failing mark while 12 percent gave the same paper a score of 90 or above. The other paper received scores ranging from 50 to 97 (Guskey 18).

In 1913, critics of Starch and Elliot's study suggested that writing is naturally subjective—therefore the initial study was flawed. Attempting to find a more objective topic, Starch and Elliot repeated their study by using geometry papers and found an even larger discrepancy, with scores on one paper ranging from 28 to 95 percent. Some teachers based their scores only on right and wrong answers, while others considered neatness, form, and spelling. Both studies raised questions about the subjectivity of grading (Guskey 18).

Several other changes in grading took place in the years following Starch and Elliot's challenge to percentage grades. In 1918, the current practice of using five categories—excellent, good, average, poor, and failing, with corresponding letters of A, B, C, D, and F—first appeared. Grading on the curve became popular in the 1930s, as educators attempted to make grades less subjective. With this practice, the most common grade was C, with grades being distributed along a normal probability curve. Some teachers even went so far as to decide in advance just how many of each grade would be awarded.

Between 1925 and 1938, at the height of the progressive education movement and in response to the controversy over grading and reporting, some schools abolished grading completely and returned to verbal descriptions of student achievement. Others adopted pass/fail systems, and still others attempted a mastery approach similar to the practices of earlier assessment. But most schools continued the traditional system of percentages in grading.

There have also been periodic attempts to defend grading. For example, in 1958, Ellis Page conducted a study which showed that students who received a score with individualized comments did better on their next assignment, while students who received only a score and grade did not. The study suggested that grades could have a beneficial effect when paired with individualized comments (Guskey 18).

Yet, from the early part of the century, researchers and educators have questioned the validity of grading, and it is clear that the challenge will continue into the twenty-first century. Despite extensive research, educators are no more successful at grading in the current system of education than they were a century and a half ago (Guskey 14–19).

Schools Teaching Failure

William Glasser claims that no child becomes a failure until he or she reaches school. In *Schools without Failure*, his classic statement of this thesis, Glasser explains how failure works against the process of education:

> The preschool-age child lives in an environment largely devoid of labels, scoring categories, or other classification systems, allowing him to develop according to standards set by himself. In such an environment there is no such thing as a "failure." Everyday life experiences have no structures for pinning labels on individuals, they have no set standards to be met, [and] they do not prescribe particular forms of thinking or select arbitrarily what is to be "learned" or committed to memory. (xiv)

Once a student is identified as a "failure," the continuing experience with failure lowers motivation. All school activities, from memorizing facts to critical thinking, seem irrelevant, especially once it is obvious that the chances for success are slim. School becomes irrelevant, since the child views it as a hostile environment. Even a passing score that is less than an A implies a degree of failure. This process of labeling a child a failure begins and ends with grades, and, as Glasser observes, it begins very early in a child's educational career.

Glasser argues for a nongraded elementary school. There have been schools of this sort in the past, and some elementary schools today are essentially nongraded. Despite fears that without grades students will not be motivated to work and parents will not know how their child is performing, research has shown that in a nongraded atmosphere, students are motivated without grades, and at the same time, their self-esteem is preserved. In this environment, fewer children are retained, and it appears beneficial for African Americans, boys, underachievers, and high-risk groups. These children do not have the chance to learn failure as do students in a graded school (Pavan 334).

What the Research Shows about Grades

In my ERIC search of over 1,500 journal articles on grading published since 1963, I found only a handful that attempted to defend the use of traditional grading practices. In "Boxed In by Grades," Howard Kirschenbaum summarizes the major criticisms of grades. Current and past research supports his observations; therefore, I will use his statements to serve as the skeleton for the survey of what research says to the teacher about grading, especially of writing.

Scientific Invalidity

"Grades are unscientific, subjective, and seldom related to clearly stated educational objectives" (Kirschenbaum 46). A grade, especially on a piece of student writing, suggests that there are very specific and precise criteria on which the student has been graded. This grade, especially if it is rendered in the form of points or a percentage, suggests that there is a measurable difference between the given grade or the one below or above: 98 or 96 percent, C+ or C-. The grade implies that all papers in any classroom that receive a particular grade are of equal quality. In *Response and Analysis: Teaching Literature in Junior and Senior High School*, Robert Probst suggests that

> a grade indicates a precision of evaluation that may not be possible. A grade may conceal other evaluative information that might be more useful to students and parents and trains them to accept an alphabetic or numerical symbol instead of useful information about literacy processes. (318)

In a 1977 study, Randolph Ellsworth and Don Willson questioned whether grades were highly related to student aptitude. The study examined correlations between eight grade-aptitude scores of students and the school grades obtained a year later. They found that the *higher* the average aptitude score for the classes, the *lower* the average grade point for the class and vice versa. They concluded by puzzling over this inverse relationship, adding: "Thus, a few more persons are wondering how much longer education can continue to place so much interest, value, and faith in letter grades. But then we all know what a grade of C means, do we not?" (Ellsworth and Willson 188–89).

As we have seen, studies from the early 1900s to the present have shown that any given composition can receive a range of scores from A through F. Teachers apply different criteria for grading writing, which means that an A can never have universal meaning. Canady and Hotchkiss point out that teachers have varying grading scales, and there are inconsistencies in application:

> A grade of 90 may have a totally different meaning in one place than in another. What constitutes failure in your school district may be totally different in mine. As teachers we may change our scale from day to day or from grading period to grading period. (Jongsma 318)

Guskey also discredits the notion that a grade is a scientific measure, addressing the fact that in a 100-point system, there are nine points of difference within a grade range. For instance, in order to earn a B, students must score between an 80 and an 89. Yet a student scoring a 79 earns a grade of C. The question is whether or not the teacher can point out the one-percent or even eleven-percent skill difference between the C and the B, a problem that the addition of pluses and minuses merely masks (Guskey 18).

By far the greatest problem with grades being unscientific is that they do not, therefore, provide a student with useful information. In 1995, Robert Lerner, Marsha Urban, and I conducted a survey on attitudes about grading, attempting to find out what role grading played in shaping students' views of themselves as writers. The survey was given to students ranging in age from thirteen to college level. In response to a question about understanding and learning from grades, one college student wrote:

> I don't even understand what the grade means on my paper. The top says something like a B and then all the comments say positive things and then there are all these errors marked. Then the person next to me wrote only half as much as I did and has even more errors marked and he got an A. It just doesn't make any sense to me.

If it doesn't make any sense to this obviously bright student, who is the grade for?

False Motivation

Another criticism of grades observed by Kirschenbaum is that "pupils learn to perform for the grade and as a result, show less initiative, independence, self-motivation, and creativity" (46). Teachers nation-wide hear the question "Is this for a grade?" when they give an assign-ment. This question implies that students might not do the assignment if not for the grade.

In his article "What Does Grading Mean, Anyway?" John Pres-ley explains how he worked to help his writing students realize the true motivation for getting an education by eliminating letter grades from their papers. He explained his low opinion of grades to a college composition class and informed them that he would not be putting let-ter grades on their writing. Students did not respond positively at first to this "wait and see" approach. Presley found that when the students got their papers back, instead of looking at the grade and tossing the paper aside, they actually read the comments and attempted to under-stand what would make their papers better. Throughout the semester, Presley refused to label the writing with a grade. Instead, he held con-ferences in which he asked his students to assign and defend a grade for the paper. He found that students' opinions of their work was usu-ally in line with his own and that instead of discussing the grade, "real information was being exchanged....The students did not see them-selves in a passive role before an arbitrary judge" (14). He repeatedly pointed out to his students that his class was just one composition class and that the students would continue to become better writers with every paper they wrote. He explained that his class was intended for learning and that a grade would not say whether they had taken anything from the experience. Presley says:

> I'm not allowing my students to use grades as a substitute for the reward of understanding. I think they are discovering that learning need not cease at graduation, the time those pesky little symbols finally disappear from their lives. (14)

Letter and number grading affects student writing by taking away a student's independence and creativity. According to Robert Meikle, grades affect the process of writing because students want to find out what is important to the teacher so that they can be rewarded with a good grade. Meikle explains:

> The huge danger in the psychological and motivational effects of evaluation is that it pulls the learner's cognitive focus away

from himself and aims it at some outside authority figure. The
learner engages with the authority and not with the intrinsic
issues. The writer is guided, not by realistic considerations of
meaning, structure, and audience, but by specific or assumed
stipulations from an extrinsic source. (25–26)

Meikle conducted an attitude survey which showed overwhelmingly
that the grade in a writing assignment was the prime source of students' interest in writing. Sixty-eight percent of students and 67 percent of the teachers surveyed felt that grades had become an essential
ingredient if the students were to be motivated at all to do their best
work. In a discussion of the value of grades, the comments Meikle
received all indicated grades as being the sole motivator for performance. Geoff, a student, said, "The mark kind of hurts you in some
ways, but in other ways it helps because it makes you do the essay."
Gary, another student, agreed: "If there's no mark, I really can't get
into doing it because, to me, why do something that's not worth anything?" (26–27).

Grades may motivate or scare students into doing all of their
work, but the research suggests that poor grades do little to encourage
students to do better. Researchers have found that many teachers use
grades for punishment, despite the fact that studies have found that
"failure or nonpromotion in school has negative effects on future academic achievement, self-concept, attitude toward school, behavior,
and attendance" (Johnson 12). Instead of motivating students toward a
better performance in the future, the failure suggests that what students are being asked to do cannot be done. Guskey supports the idea
that grades serve no purpose as negative motivators:

> Grades have some value as rewards, but no value as punish-
> ments. . . . Most students view high grades as positive recogni-
> tion of their success, and some work hard to avoid the conse-
> quences of low grades. At the same time, no studies support the
> use of low grades as punishments. Instead of prompting greater
> effort, low grades usually cause students to withdraw from
> learning. To protect their self-image, many students may blame
> themselves for the low mark, but feel helpless to improve. (16)

False Indicators of Worth

Kirschenbaum adds that although they "are misleading and focus on
only one aspect of the child, . . . pupils tend to develop feelings of self-
worth consistent with their grades" (47). Grades in any subject can

influence what a student believes about his or her capabilities—especially in writing, where a student must open up a very private side in order to share writing. With every word, a student leaves a piece of himself or herself on the page. In order to grade any piece of writing, a teacher must judge the student. That judging is exactly what students objected to in Meikle's survey of attitudes about writing. Meikle adds that students "perceive grades on written assignments as a personal judgment on their character, their drive, and their worth" (19).

This problem with being judged was strongly reinforced by the attitude survey Lerner, Urban, and I conducted. We found that virtually all of the 150 students surveyed included comments that reflected either positive or negative feelings of self-esteem. For instance, in response to the statement "Grading represents how well I write," one eighth grader responded: "It has made me realize that I am terrible at it and I hate it." Many students responded that they felt they were either good or bad writers on the basis of their past grades. One college student wrote: "I feel I'm an average writer. I base this on grades I've received in English throughout the years." These feelings were obviously generated by the grade values rather than students' genuine achievement or rhetorical success.

Superficial Learning

In the research literature, grades have also been criticized by Kirschenbaum for promoting "superficial, spurious, and insincere scholarship" (48). He suggests that "when 'wad-ja-get?' becomes more important than 'wad-ja-learn?'" students are "boxed in" by grades (46). He says that students work only for the grade and not for what can be learned through an assignment. He illustrates how early this problem develops with the story of his niece. After seeing her kindergarten connect-the-dot paper marked with "100%," he asked his sister if the kids were actually being graded. She told him that, yes, they were graded, and shared a story. During the previous week, his niece had brought home a paper with a "1," which represented the number of items wrong. After looking over the paper, Kirschenbaum's sister found one question that the teacher had failed to mark. When she tried to point this out, his sister found that her daughter insisted on pointing to the 1 at the top of the page, that there was only one mistake. Even at her young age, it was not the learning opportunity that mattered to Kirschenbaum's niece—it was the mark.

Student/Teacher Barriers

Kirschenbaum also maintains that grades "form a barrier between students and teachers" that is counterproductive in the writing classroom (47). In that classroom, there must be a feeling of mutual trust and respect. A student must not feel threatened by or unsure of a teacher. If he or she is, this will create a reluctance to share writing with that teacher. It is important for students to realize that, as Presley told his students, the grade "is the carefully rendered opinion of one fallible man with some experience in the field of writing" (13). Instead, grades perpetuate the myth that the teacher has all the answers, and it is the students' job to pick the right ones. Students believe that the teacher has the key to good writing and that they must match the ideas in the teacher's head to get the good grade. This myth is perpetuated because students sense the arbitrary nature of the grade: "Grading criteria may be regarded as . . . mysterious, a function of teacher taste rather than a representation of inherent and tangible standards" (Jongsma 318). When students do not understand the criteria for grades and comments, they must make up the meaning, decide that the teacher had a good reason, or assume that they just won't ever understand. There is also an idea of fairness involved. If a student feels a piece he or she has written is wonderful, yet it receives a poor grade, the student will cease to trust the teacher's opinion as a reader.

Limits on Teaching and Teachers

Finally, Kirschenbaum criticizes grading because it "leads to uncreative teaching" (46). In an effort to make more sense out of grading, many teachers reduce assignments to what is measurable. It is much simpler to grade a multiple-choice test than an essay exam. The teacher sticks to the knowledge level of Bloom's taxonomy, because there are right answers that are easily measured, rather than challenging students' critical-thinking skills. In writing, it is easier to evaluate usage, spelling, and punctuation, so grading is often reduced to these. Jongsma writes:

> While it may be easy to evaluate spelling and punctuation, these skills pale into insignificance beside the ability to create, to imagine, to relate one thought to another, to organize, to reason, or to catch the nuances of English prose. Inventing, reasoning, responding, and reflecting do not readily lend themselves to the testing or grading usually required by school districts and reported on most report cards. (318)

The activities that really allow students to have fun and to think are not easily measured or graded.

In short, piles upon piles of research suggest that grading definitely does not help students and, in many cases, may even hurt them. Grading is a practice that came under fire almost as soon as it was invented. Why, then, have we subjected students to this invalid practice for almost two hundred years? Will students continue to be subjected to it for the next two hundred years? Would IBM continue to market a product that did not perform its intended task? If it planned on succeeding, I think not.

> The grade is a hell of a weapon. It may not rest on your hip, potent and rigid like a cop's gun, but in the long run it's more powerful....(Tjarks 3)

Works Cited

Ellsworth, Randolph, and Don D. Willson. "Another Visit to the World of Grading." *Clearing House* 50 (1977): 188–89.

Glasser, William. *Schools without Failure*. New York: Harper, 1968.

Guskey, Thomas R. "Making the Grade: What Benefits Students?" *Educational Leadership* 52 (Oct. 1994): 14–20.

Johnson, Susan. "How Did You Do? The Myths and Facts about Grading." *Gifted Child Today* 18 (Mar./Apr. 1995): 10–13.

Jongsma, Kathleen Stumpf. "Rethinking Grading Practices." *Reading Teacher* 45 (Dec. 1991): 318–20.

Keepes, Bruce D. "A School without Failure: A Description of the Glasser Approach in the Palo Alto Unified School District." Paper presented at the Fifty-eighth Annual Meeting of the American Educational Research Association. 25 Feb.–1 Mar. 1973. New Orleans, LA. 32 pp.

Kirschenbaum, Howard. "Boxed In by Grades." *Teacher* 91.1 (Sep. 1973): 46–48.

Lerner, Robert, Marsha Urban, and Liesel O'Hagan. "Survey of Students' Attitudes about Graded Writing." Unpublished study. U of Nevada, Reno, 1995.

Lucas, Catharine. "Introduction: Writing Portfolios—Changes and Challenges." *Portfolios in the Writing Classroom: An Introduction.* Ed. Kathleen Blake Yancey. Urbana: NCTE, 1992. 1–11.

Meikle, Robert J. "Traditional Grade-Based Writing Evaluation and the Process Approach: Systems in Conflict." ED 229761. [Indexed in *Resources in Education* (Oct. 1983).] 29 pp.

Pavan, Barbara Nelson. "Good News: Research on the Nongraded Elementary School." *Elementary School Journal* 73 (Mar. 1973): 333–42.

Pemberton, W. A. "The Grade-Point Average: Snark or Boojum?" ED 047009. [Indexed in *Resources in Education* (May 1971).] 42 pp.

Presley, John C. "What Does Grading Mean, Anyway?" Paper presented at the Tenth Annual Meeting of the Southeastern Conference on English in the Two-Year College. 19–21 Feb. 1981. Biloxi, MS. 15 pp.

Probst, Robert E. *Response and Analysis: Teaching Literature in Junior and Senior High School.* Portsmouth: Boynton/Cook, 1988.

Tjarks, Larry D. "Grading as a Sadomasochistic Activity or an Erotic Benevolent Activity." Paper presented at the Conference on College Composition and Communication. 4–6 Apr. 1974. Anaheim, CA.

Interlude

The entire educational establishment is a house of straw built upon the grading system. If mommies and daddies didn't give children quarters for A's in elementary school, if secondary teachers didn't issue threats about bad grades and a dim future to their students, if colleges and universities didn't scare the hell out of everybody with their GPAs, then the entire institution would collapse in a tangle of arms, legs, minds, and educational chaff.

> — Herb Deetenforbes
> Salem High School
> Connecticut

2 Growth-Biased Assessing of Writers–A More Democratic Choice

Marie Wilson Nelson
National-Louis University

*Marie Wilson Nelson, associate professor at National-Louis University, is the
author of* At the Point of Need: Teaching Basic and ESL Writers, *a
synthesis of findings from forty teacher-researchers, which served as the text
for the yearlong online seminar offered at CUNY's FIPSE-sponsored
TESLFF-L e-mail discussion list. She has also lectured in Japan, where she
gave workshops on the teaching of writing, teacher action research, and
professional writing engagingly done.*

Like most citizens, teachers typically fall into one of two camps—those who see democracy as a finished product and those who see it as still evolving, as still in progress. I belong to the latter group, for soon after I started teaching, I realized that the "democracy" practiced in schools could use some work. Schools denied students and teachers rights protected for most citizens. Not only were teachers restricted to campus, even when not teaching, but our personal lives were also scrutinized carefully. Freedom of speech and freedom of the press were widely curtailed, with textbooks and student publications censored extensively, and teachers were fired for letting students read books that had not been approved. Teachers controlled students in the same way that administrators controlled the teachers. Students had almost no freedom of movement while at school, being required to sit still without speaking except during four-minute breaks, at which time they had to get supplies and tend to physical needs in addition to making their way from one building to another. Students could not even go to the bathroom without a signed pass or bury themselves in a book when a lecture was uninteresting. To make matters worse, they were punished for any expression of discontent with their loss of physical and intellectual freedom, often by being denied further access to school. It was an all-or-nothing proposition. My school—love it or leave it—so to speak.

As a sixth-, seventh-, and eleventh-grade English teacher, I grew increasingly frustrated over the years. Traditional schooling stripped school writing (and reading) of the rewards for which writers and readers write (and read) outside of school, thus undermining students' desire to write well and siphoning off their willingness to work hard. The result was that, regardless of ability, students who wrote well on leaving my class were typically those who had already written well when they entered it. For the most part, their families spoke standard English, and many of them were confident of attending college. I had little impact on the lives of others, whose continued poor writing would limit them to entry-level jobs. When that realization dawned, near the end of my first year of teaching, I set a goal that has shaped the rest of my career—making instruction work for every learner I teach.

Obviously, I've not pursued this goal in isolation. The work of dozens of others influenced my attempts. Change has swept writing instruction for almost three decades (Hairston), promising to democratize educational hierarchies in which the affluent are most likely to succeed. An alternative mind-set about schooling has attracted advocates for well over a century (Applebee; Dewey; Hearn; Mearns), but only recently have research-tested applications been described with enough clarity and detail to offer teachers at all levels a clear philosophical choice between traditional teaching—which co-occurs with widespread failure—and approaches that, skillfully used, offer success to all (Atwell; Calkins; Murray; Nelson, *At the Point*; Shaughnessy). In recent years, as connections between assessment and failure have become clearer, I've come to understand that my choice of approach for assessment functions as a vote either for or against democracy.

In traditional assessment, testing follows teaching, with teaching adapting itself to the kind of testing used. In this model, teaching and testing are discrete, but both focus on what students can't do or don't yet understand well. Deficiency-focused testing leads to teaching that is reductive, preventive/corrective, lockstep, and structured to cover content for everyone at the same time, at the same speed. It is also exclusionary, pitting students against each other in such a way that all but a few will eventually lose, and it sorts them into tracks that limit access to advanced study for all but a few. By contrast, in fully realized whole language classrooms and writing workshops, assessment is integrated into learning and teaching, making reciprocal influence possible. In addition to written products, teachers assess attitudes, the behaviors (and avoidances) those attitudes produce, and how their own teaching enhances or inhibits growth. This holistic kind of assessing—which rarely takes the form of tests—molds itself to the shape of learners' development, in turn shaping whatever practice further growth requires and focusing teaching/learning/assessing at the point of need. These integrated approaches are interactive and incidental; terms like *emergent, growth-shaped*, and *growth-biased* refer to them.

Growth-shaped assessing follows a positive principle, emphasizing what students are working on or can already do well, rather than zeroing in on errors and deficiencies. Informed by teacher observation and learner introspection, growth-shaped assessing is formative as well as summative. Its skillful meldings of teaching/learning/assessing rely on teachers and learners to map progress together so that writers' goals can individualize activities.

Characteristics of Growth-Biased Teaching/Learning/Assessing

The negative assessments that I did early on in my career gave me biased data about learners' abilities. Because those "objective" data convinced me that most students can't write well, I did not see how the grades I assigned forced capable learners to fail. Never having been exposed to another way of thinking, I had no idea how unfair the grades I gave students were. Nor did I spot the undemocratic assumptions on which they were based. After researching classroom practice for twenty years, however, I now opt for more democratic teaching/learning/assessing that allows anyone willing to work hard to succeed and that is remarkably good at getting all students to try hard. Figure 1 summarizes the features of a growth-related approach.

Growth-shaped teaching/assessing is *openly and positively biased*. It looks at the data analyzed by traditional thinkers—spelling, transition, grammar, clarity, organization, style—but it emphasizes strengths rather than weaknesses and reaches different conclusions about the meaning of the data used. Growth-biased assessing looks at other data too—writing attitudes and behavior, to take one example, not to mention *improvements* in writing and *changes* in attitude. Instead of subtracting points from a perfect score or measuring deviations from a "norm," growth-focused judgments are *additive* and *individualized*. Teachers begin by assessing the impact of prior instruction, document everything they can find that writers are doing well, and then inform learners so that they can build confidently upon these

Openly biased	Focused on whatever factors may be affecting development
Positively biased	Integrated and indivisible
Additive	Individualized
Balanced	Incorporates multiple perspectives, including peer review and learner self-assessment
Objective	Honest
Sequenced	Shaped by learners' perceptions of needs
Nonjudgmental	Rewards problem-solving activity, even when it fails
Emergent	Comprehensive
Emotionally supportive	Biased toward the formative
Advocacy oriented	Relies on rewards inherent in the activity learned
Asks rather than tells	Incorporates a shifting scale of concerns
Relies on measured response	Developmental
At the point of need	Improvement-based
Developmental	Has responsible self-assessment as the ultimate goal
Predicated on trust	

Figure 1. Traits distinctive to growth-biased assessment.

strengths. They look at effort, quality of writing, and progress made, and they offer suggestions for improvement at the point of need.

Growth-biased assessments are more *balanced*—and therefore more objective—than the negative (subtractive) deficiency-focused approaches for which "objective" claims have traditionally been made. Growth-biased assessors offer *sequenced response* in *nonjudgmental* ways. They define errors, and they view weaknesses as being no worse than strengths; together, in fact, the strengths and weaknesses learners become aware of structure an *emerging, individualized curriculum.* But writers arrive in growth classrooms scared and bleeding from past assessments, so teachers and peers begin each term by pointing out only strengths, leaving writers to deduce weaknesses through comparison with what they read and the work of their peers. They start by noting grammatically and mechanically correct passages— even ones that express, in clichés, superficial or boring ideas. They exclaim over passionate commitment to topics, ideas, or causes— whether or not early drafts are neat and well organized. They turn the spotlight on powerful images and honest feelings, even when early drafts lack audience awareness or precise vocabulary.

Growth-biased instructors teach writers to tell classmates, friends, and family members exactly what kinds of responses they need next on their work, encouraging them to comment first on strengths (to build confidence), to ask nonjudgmental questions after that (to learn where to add information or to clarify unclear parts), and finally, near the end of the discussion, to offer one or two specific suggestions for improvement, framing their comments *constructively* and trusting the writer herself to decide which suggestions to use and which to ignore. Trusting developing writers to make decisions is crucial, for feedback they can understand, use, and retain will never be more than a subset of the improvements most pieces need. (If it were, these writers would not be "developing.") The problems writers can solve and remember how to solve are the problems they can spot on their own or recognize once they've been pointed out. These self-delineated areas of weakness, clustered around the expanding edges of competence, serve a function that is critical to writers' growth. They indicate the areas where focused instruction will "take." In fact, in growth classrooms, both teachers and peers quickly learn to "follow the kid" (Nelson, "Bridging"), to ask what a writer is attempting in a piece (Murray, *Learning*), to offer help at what the Britton research team called "the point of need" and Krashen referred to as "the ideal instructional level." In other words, teachers and peers focus instruction within Vygotsky's "zone of proximal development." Unlike preventive/corrective teaching and assessment, which identify what an entire age group should know and then "cover" all of it whether or not students retain it, *need-focused* assessing makes teaching and learning efficient by offering instruction where there's somewhere for it to "stick"—around the edges of existing competence.

Giving *balanced and sequenced* responses helps teachers stay in the advocacy role by adopting a consistently *supportive* stance. So does *asking* (rather than telling) learners what help they need. Asking helps teachers discover what learners are able and willing to learn. Unlike deficit models that measure distance from adult standards (see Tchudi and Mitchell), *advocacy-focused* assessing adopts a different goal—the facilitation of individual growth. It avoids comparing students with one another, the only comparisons being with writers' own past performances. While assessing is *comprehensive*, response is *measured*, and only a few errors get attention at any one time. And so as not to undermine budding confidence, learners select these themselves, thus taking charge of their own growth. Doing so requires them to become skillful at *self-assessing*, which of course develops critical-thinking skills and is dependent upon high *mutual trust* in the classroom community.

Growth-biased teaching/assessing is *integrated and indivisible* and relies on a shifting scale of concerns, one successful writers use to cope with writing's complex demands. From fluency, to global issues like clarity, organization, and voice, to the fine-tuning done by poets and copyeditors, growth-biased teachers are constantly *upping the ante*, bringing writers along as far as they can come and encouraging them so that they can go even farther. Unlike traditional grading, which achieves "objectivity" by isolating traits, holding them constant, and assessing all the same way, growth-biased approaches *individualize*, broadening the scope of attention from finished products to include any factor affecting development—like attitudes, life experiences, current strengths, prior instruction, effort expended, and the degrees of responsibility writers take. Teachers observe the risks writers take when revealing weaknesses and study differences across writing processes, *integrating* assessing into the rhythms of learning and into individual patterns of development.

Growth on a Shifting Scale

Figure 2 shows the shifting scale of concerns that emerges when one abandons a preventive/corrective mind-set to examine all factors affecting growth. To determine what kinds of help individual writers require, so as to offer instruction at the point of need, teachers (and peers) gradually shift attention over time. As fluency, quantity, trust, effort, risk taking, and other early emphases become established, teachers up the ante, expecting more as the term progresses. They look for quality, aesthetic features, improvement, surface-level control, and other qualities that develop with experience. From fluency-building activities early in the term to more global, control-focused revising, to the honing and polishing of surface-level features that move to center stage as publishing deadlines draw near, growth-oriented teachers shift the teaching/assessing focus to whatever problems the writers they teach are struggling with, adopting the *shifting scale of concerns* on which professional writers rely (Cowley; Plimpton).

Several things contribute to the knowledge and know-how writers pick up naturally at the point of need in classrooms that use fully realized workshop approaches. One is the *honest response* which all writers need for improving. Well-meaning teachers and students rightly proceed with caution out of concern for others' self-esteem, but

1. Developing Sanctuary and Fluency

Getting to know each other
Learning not to undermine others' self-esteem
Working to build trust in the class
Working together to help each other improve
Learning to give positively phrased criticism
Writing a lot
Experimenting with topics to see which ones motivate more writing
Abandoning false starts in search of these better topics
Experimenting with different genres
Learning to keep learning logs
Getting comfortable with word processing
Sharing folders with writing partners
Meeting in permanent (or long-term) groups
Listening thoughtfully
Taking risks with writing

2. Giving and Getting Advice

Reading writing in class
Asking for needed help
Giving honest but kindly advice
Using process logs to direct your own growth
Working productively in small groups
Helping to solve any problems that arise in group
Writing more than you ever have before
Caring about your writing
Revising over and over again
Learning to find and correct your worst errors
Letting others know when you're having trouble so we can help

3. Revising and Editing

Breaking the revision barrier
Taking one or two pieces through several drafts each
Learning to judge whether your revisions are working
Noticing how other writers get their effects
Experimenting to find out what works for you
Asking others for help when you run into problems
Editing many times
Editing for one kind of error at a time
Developing an essay about ideas you care about
Letting group members know what kind of advice you need
Keeping your tutor posted on your progress and that of the group

4. Getting the Writing to an Audience

Choosing the pieces you want to publish
Working with others to design and print the class book
Copyediting your piece(s) for publication
Securing copyrights
Submitting favorite piece(s) for publication
Organizing your portfolio to reveal progress you've made
Celebrating getting your work into print
Anything else that affects the progress you or others make

Figure 2. A shifting scale of concerns for teachers of writing.

data suggest that honest response is also essential to improvement. Weighing and balancing feedback from *different perspectives* informs self-assessment—which must also be assessed along *a shifting scale*— by meeting each writer wherever she is and by focusing more on whatever goals she's identified and whether she's honest, takes risks, and works hard, rather than whether she's at the same place as others (Nelson, *At the Point*).

For groups to take the risks significant learning requires, each member must experience (and contribute to) sanctuary. When teachers require (and demonstrate) caring but honest responses, disallowing hurtful comments and body language—name-calling, prejudice, put-downs, eye rolling, exasperated sighs—writers learn the positive inter-active skills necessary for collaboration to succeed. In my classes there's only one rule, but I take it seriously: Each of us must protect the sanctuary everyone needs in order to take risks. Noncompetitive behavior and attitudes are also *best assessed developmentally.* Continuing improvement is the goal.

Integrated teaching/assessing offers a framework within which all growth-focused learning traits fit. In the growth philosophy, *comprehensive assessing* focuses on factors that play out inside writers' heads, factors that are seen in small- or large-group interactions, and factors that show up in written drafts. Another characteristic is a de-emphasis on grades, along with an increase in *formative assessing*—assessing that helps individuals improve in specific ways. A *formative bias* helps teachers *individualize* teaching/learning/assessing, thus increasing reliance on writing's inherent rewards. All of these are features writers must learn to assess for themselves, and as the ability to self-assess grows with practice, it too must be assessed developmentally, over time, in terms of progress from multiple starting gates, rather than in terms of the distance from a single finishing line.

Responsible self-assessing is, of course, the goal, but getting there is a process that takes time. When first asked to assess their efforts, most students act paralyzed. They must motivate themselves. They must also learn to trust others enough to take risks—to trust that revealing weaknesses (and claiming strengths) need not lead to punishment or censure from teachers or peers. Self-assessing means setting one's own standards. It requires meeting the rising expectations one develops when exposed to the rapidly improving work of hard-working peers. It also involves unlearning error-avoidance strategies and entails looking honestly at where one has not worked as hard as one might have.

One Teacher's Application of Growth-Biased Principles

Growth-biased assessing takes many shapes, but its truly distinctive features have no external form. They consist of philosophical beliefs capable of reshaping writing behaviors and attitudes. Because growth-bias is a mind-set, not a method, it plays itself out differently in every classroom, adapting with seemingly endless flexibility to teaching personalities and contextual constraints. In my efforts to enact it in three universities and, somewhat earlier, in small colleges, I've been helped most by the examples of mentors—Dan Kirby and Ken Kantor, then at the University of Georgia; Bernie and Martha Schein at Atlanta's Paideia Middle School; Sandra Worsham at Baldwin High in Milledgeville, Georgia; and Chris Thaiss, my colleague at George Mason University. These teachers helped me dislodge the default model's dominance in my mind, allowing me to look at my work in new ways. With further help from over one hundred colleagues in teacher research, I've been adapting the strategies I learned from these mentors for years, and though no end to the evolution of my practice is in sight, I hold a fairly clear vision of what I'm working toward.

My alternative to grading individual pieces of writing is one chosen by many writers and artists who teach. (Other approaches, shaped by a similar mind-set, can be found in the final section of this book.) I give only the grades I'm required to give—one grade per writer per term, and from day one I assess writers' growth. I tell them they'll succeed if they attend to the Truthfulness, Thoughtfulness, Thoroughness, Timeliness, and Supportiveness of all aspects of their participation in the course. (Thanks to Dan Kirby for the first three of the four T's.) I give more extensive response early in the term, when writers accustomed to using regular deadlines and grades to force themselves to write need to know that the teacher reads all of their work carefully. I focus first on writing processes, pointing out signs of growth in their folders and also doing so publicly, and look for symptoms of intellectual and creative abuse—like negative criticism or an early emphasis on structure. Responding weekly to drafts and process logs, I highlight strengths, underlining what I find interesting, powerful, funny, well crafted, or thought provoking. I respond mostly to content, asking dozens of questions, offering opinions and memories of my own.

Once writers relax and write with less anxiety, I start suggesting strategies they might try—lopping off stiff introductions to bring dramatic lines to the fore, or adding dialogue, narrative, feeling, and detail. I invite writers to relax and write more freely, circling spelling and mechanical uncertainties as they go so that they can find them easily should they decide to revise or to work on that error for an individualized assignment. If the writing bores me, I assume they're bored too and ask if they care passionately about the subject, reminding them that should they ditch this piece for a more heartfelt topic, they should save every scrap they've done for their portfolios so that they can see how much they've improved at the end of the term. My comments individualize, offering support and critique at the point of need, and serve as nonnumerical records of development, providing data for a quick, end-of-term review by me. Later, paging through comprehensive portfolios, I refresh my memory about effort and improvement, skimming in sequence my responses (and their "process logs"), looking for signs of growth.

The "lesson plans" I use for growth-shaped teaching/learning/ assessing are jot lists of authors and titles made while responding each week. I focus the first half of the following week's three-hour class on any strengths that emerged in writers' work the week before. Back in class, list in hand, I invite those who did something well to read excerpts aloud to the class from think writes, drafts, or process logs. On occasion, I encourage writers to read whole pieces, but I never offer praise to build self-esteem. That undermines expectations for quality, and growth in self-esteem *relies* on expanding quality. I therefore let unmotivated writers struggle without interference, knowing that my stepping in postpones their taking charge of decisions about their work. Hoping they'll work through instruction-induced writing blocks on their own, I wait until midterm to suggest that they might improve. My research with forty other teacher-researchers (Nelson, *At the Point*) taught me that writers more than make up for lost time once they break through because self-sponsored breakthroughs to writing resistance are more powerful. Students do not struggle in isolation, however, for I spotlight breakthrough writers, inviting them to share prebreakthrough anxieties and the rewards they experienced after taking the breakthrough risk. I foreground improvements in partner, small-group, or whole-class work and focus regularly on breakthroughs in attitude that pave the way for breakthroughs in the structure of writers' work, kicking off upward spirals of motivation and success. Confident of a "the bigger they are, the harder they fall" pattern that five research teams and I documented repeatedly, I ignore weak writing—and writing that never gets done—even while leading brainstorming discussions in class to solve whatever problems writers are willing to discuss.

For that rare writer who doesn't catch on fire by midterm despite being put in charge of decisions about her work, I address the issue in her folder, revising a short note repeatedly until any temptation toward a guilt trip, to coerce, or to cajole has passed and until I'm certain I have stayed in an advocacy role. Writer's block is a problem even professional writers face. Because, for beginners, its source is so often counterproductive instruction, I'm very nonjudgmental in my response, even when students have done almost nothing for the first half of the term. Leaving each writer at choice about her work, I express my concern that she may not be meeting her goals and affirm that "weak" and "strong" writers alike are entirely capable of A work:

> Jane, I'm getting worried about your work. You're capable of writing wonderfully and working hard, and under normal conditions I'd expect A work out of you, but you've done almost nothing and it's already midterm. I'd hate to see you not get credit for this course.
>
> Has some circumstance I don't know about kept you from writing this term? Or have you been struggling with writer's block (something even professional writers struggle with)?
>
> There's still time for you to earn an A if you start at once and work like crazy until the end of the term. Is there some way I can help you accomplish your goals for this course?

I keep a photocopy in case I'm challenged about a grade, but I never have been. Learners who practice self-assessing grow realistic. In the twenty years since I started developing this approach, I can count on one hand the writers who did not respond and ended up getting less than a quality grade. Nor do I hesitate to give "Incompletes," which puts responsibility back in the writers' hands. The week of exams I tell students, "I only give A's and B's and Incompletes. If you'd rather have a lower grade than an Incomplete, put that in writing to me and sign your name." I don't think I've ever given more than two Incompletes per term, and the time I save averaging grades more than makes up for the inconvenience they cause later. Since I stopped using grades to control them, most of my students work harder than a very few did before.

Because students learn as much from each other as they do from me, I invite them to share in the large group the best advice they've had from peers, newfound strategies for self-discipline, and pieces they're struggling with. I brag on those who write a lot, inviting them to explain how they motivate themselves. Once they've seen a few breakthroughs, I ask if anyone had a breakthrough during the past week. I structure class so that *they* compare their writing and work habits with those of others, but I never make comparisons part of the grade they get from me. I also hold a "disaster" workshop near midterm. I don't remember the name of the writer from whom I stole this idea, but students always share pieces they care about but can't make work. Buried by insecurity, these so-called "disasters" often lead to breakthroughs, the term "disaster" apparently making vulnerable writers feel safe enough in sharing to take the breakthrough risk.

After four or five weeks' practice giving and getting supportive response, the second half of each three-hour class is devoted to small-group work, the expectations for participation being determined by classmates in a repeat of a first-night-of-class activity. We do a think-write/read-around in which everybody describes the kind of atmosphere they want their group or class to maintain so that they can learn more in this course than they've ever learned before. And this part is critical—they enjoy doing it. Around midterm, when fluency and self-discipline have expanded and the time I spend responding has increased, I begin responding in writing only on alternate weeks. Increasingly skillful at giving and getting effective response, writers trade folders with writing partners the rest of the time.

From the start, writers guide my responses by including in their folders weekly notes describing the kinds of response they want from me, and by midterm, most are quite astute about what they need. I respond as requested and note every improvement I see. I comment on growing engagement and seriousness, congratulate the growing control of usage and mechanics that comes naturally when preventive/corrective pressures subside, and compliment all whose participation has somehow improved. The hardest part for me is to remember to leave them at choice about whether to use suggestions. I try, but don't always remember, to use noncontrolling expressions like "Have you thought about trying *X*?" or "If this were my paper, I might do *Y.*"

If they haven't all given themselves "individual assignments" by midterm, I suggest one or two based on patterns in their work—from contributing more in the large group (if they are shy) to speaking less and drawing out others (if they are not); from working with a list of words they misspell to paying special attention to strong verb forms; from weeding out double negatives from their prose to checking out and practicing semicolon rules. For students who've never experienced intense involvement with learning, finding topics they care about may, even this late in the game, be the most important thing for them to work on. Since those who care passionately revise draft after draft and enjoy working on their papers, caring is one of "the new basics" we need to teach. After a few weeks, I start referring classmates to each other for help. "Why don't you check with Amy about quotations," I write on Keith's short story. "She's the resident expert on punctuating dialogue." Writers work on these projects independently and in small groups, the goal being not to master every rule in the book, but to develop confidence that with the help of friends, they can teach themselves whatever it is they need to learn.

At the end of the term, writers turn in organized portfolios that include every scrap they've written so that I can quickly assess the total amount they've written and scan evidence of progress rapidly. They place all drafts together, latest on top, in clearly marked sections reflecting the diversity of their work: process logs, poems, memoirs, essays, songs, comic strips, stories, false starts, think-writes, letters to editors, cathartic free-writes (sometimes stapled shut for privacy), individual assignments, artwork, at least one camera-ready piece for the class book, other finished products (three in all), final self-assessments, and the like.

In addition to the quality of the three finished products, we assess their overall output (practice makes perfect, you know) at how many throwaway efforts they produced, at how many drafts they wrote on the topics they cared most about, at risk taking, at genres attempted, at amount of—and care with—revising and editing, and at improvement in attitudes, behavior, or successive drafts. I skim my past responses, looking over process logs to refresh my memory about participation, group and partner work, sensitivity to others' needs, applications of others' advice, and increasing commitment and confidence. Feedback to others shows up in their comments on partners' portfolios. I also consider how much unlearning refugees from competitive classrooms have had to do before motivation and self-discipline could kick in.

Writing notes here and there to remind me of specific circumstances, writers bring these portfolios to the last class along with a "final experience think-write" on eight or ten questions. We do a read-around with these to celebrate each other's growth. Following are typical final experience questions:

> What were you like as a writer when you came into this class?
>
> What are you like now?

What was the most helpful aspect of this course?

What was the least helpful?

What are you most proud of in your work?

What are you least proud of?

What are you working on in your writing currently?

What would you do differently if you could to it again?

What advice could you offer me?

What advice would you give my next class?

Is there anything else you'd like to say to me?

In recent years, the balance has shifted even further from assessing others to assessing my teaching.

Another self-assessment piece follows the read-around. Students go quickly down a one-page, two-column list of attitude, behavior, and writing traits discussed in this essay, giving themselves a check, minus, or plus on each one (for "Appropriate," "Less Than I'm Capable of" or "My Very Best Work"). They summarize, using the same check system with the following:

Truthfulness	Participation
Thoughtfulness	Effort
Thoroughness	Improvement
Timeliness	Overall Quality

Because first impressions are more accurate, I allot only five minutes for this activity. They then put the grade they deserve and their phone number (or e-mail address) at the top. After skimming portfolios, focusing on my responses and their process logs, listening to the read-around, and examining their checklists, if I disagree with the grade they've given, I schedule a conference, but I long ago learned deficiencies are more often in their documentation and not in their work. The final "exam" is a "reading" (planned by a committee) to celebrate the publication of their class book (produced by another group). This photocopied collection is one of two texts writers purchase, the other being a well-known writer's discussion of the writing process.

Hardwired for Failure: The Schooling Hierarchy

This new paradigm in writing instruction is nonhierarchical in that it allows all who work to succeed and, just as important, creates classroom conditions under which motivation to work hard is widespread. Unfortunately, however, hierarchy structures education and most other modern institutions—church, family, government, industry, sports, and military. As a result, our choices are not as clear-cut as they first appear. Pyramid-structured hierarchies—like schools and colleges—which have fewer and fewer positions as one approaches the top, must eliminate contenders at each level if they are to perpetuate themselves. Whether or not the people who work there hold elitist views, hierarchies operate economies of scarcity: At every level there are more applicants than jobs. That is why, unless teachers intervene consistently, evaluation and testing acquire a negative charge. Grades are curved, for example, when too many succeed, or points are subtracted from a hundred, a so-called "perfect score" that bears little relation to the sum of what may be learned.

Hierarchy's structural imperative, in other words, is to eliminate contenders for slots at every level, restricting access to power and resources to those at the top and keeping control in the hands of a select few. To mask the elitist nature of the enterprise, those in control have defined negative bias as "objective" in a verbal slight of hand that seems reasonable—until we unearth the discriminatory assumptions on which it is based.

The structural competition on which hierarchy relies tends to limit assessment to what can be measured numerically, even when such measurements isolate and distort, for hierarchies value reliability more than validity, or, in everyday language, consistency more than accuracy. Such assessment privileges those in power, who rarely seek feedback on the process from those assessed. After all, the goal is not to help everyone succeed; in the hierarchical mind-set, assessment must sort and rank those whom it tests. When we accept traditional guidelines for what data to examine, for how to interpret them, or for which standards to uphold, our classroom procedures hold inequities in place. For this reason, growth-biased teaching can attract disapproval from above.

But threats to growth-biased teaching come not only from the top. Hierarchies place all people in competition with each other, undermining their ability to trust, so threats to such teaching come from grade-addicted students, from peers insecure about change, from parents who want their children to "win" the race to the top—in other words, from throughout the hierarchy of nested hierarchies that structure postindustrial society. Politicians who play on public nostalgia and fear also put teaching and learning in jeopardy. But if they mean what they say about raising standards in schools, about reducing dropout rates, about keeping kids off the streets and developing a more sophisticated workforce, growth-biased teachers' professional judgments need greater acceptance—from students, colleagues, parents, supervisors, and public servants, and especially from those unfamiliar with the field.

Because hierarchy permeates society, even in caring classrooms students learn negative lessons unless teachers take deliberate steps to neutralize them. In school, many students learn to fear grades, develop low self-esteem, dislike learning, and resist authority. As the brains of the system, however, teachers are at choice. We can continue teaching lessons in hierarchy, or, with student cooperation, we can start to neutralize them. I suggest we put our money where our collective mouth is and shift part of our teaching/learning/assessing buck away from credit for basic skills and finished products and toward the behaviors and attitudes successful writing requires. We now have teaching approaches with which all learners can succeed. If that's what our society really wants, schools need to shift from ability-based to *work-based* economies.

By shifting the basis for grading from "ability" to effort and improvement, growth-biased assessing holds "gifted" writers responsible—for working hard, cooperating, and improving—rather than letting them jump up and down on what they already know. Growth-bias offers "basic" writers equal grades for equal work—whether or not they end up being the best writers in class. And it liberates learners whose "deficiency" is anger—at an elitist, hypocritical, power-driven system which punishes the honesty writing well requires. Growth-biased teaching rechannels the energy of resistance into writers' own and their peers' development (Nelson, *At the Point*).

I view the future with growing optimism. A holistic mind-set is transforming education. The theoretical foundations, backed by research, have been laid. Democratic practice and theory are converging, and field-tested principles we can trust have emerged independently across fields—psychology, linguistics, education, management. If we reject the hierarchical goal of progressive elimination, opting instead for a growth goal—to help all learners succeed—we have a new criterion for assessing assessment (and its objectivity)—the degree to which it facilitates every learner's growth. My own and others' research suggests that this is realistic. I still struggle, but the struggle is one I believe in now, the struggle to keep both feet—teaching and assessing—firmly planted in the growth paradigm.

Works Cited

Applebee, Arthur N. *Tradition and Reform in the Teaching of English: A History.* Urbana: NCTE, 1974.

Atwell, Nancie. *In the Middle: Writing, Reading, and Learning with Adolescents.* Portsmouth: Boynton/Cook, 1987.

Britton, James, Tony Burgess, Nancy Martin, Alex McLeod, and Harold Rosen. *The Development of Writing Abilities (11–18).* London: Macmillan Education, 1975.

Calkins, Lucy McCormick. *The Art of Teaching Writing.* Portsmouth: Heinemann, 1986.

———. *Lessons from a Child: On the Teaching and Learning of Writing.* Exeter: Heinemann, 1983.

Cowley, Malcolm, ed. *Writers at Work: The Paris Review Interviews.* New York: Viking, 1958.

Dewey, John. *The School and Society* and *The Child and the Curriculum.* Chicago: U of Chicago P, 1990.

Hairston, Maxine. "The Winds of Change: Thomas Kuhn and the Revolution in the Teaching of Writing." *College Composition and Communication* 33.1 (Feb. 1982): 76–88.

Hearn, Lafcadio. *Talks to Writers.* Ed. John Erskine. New York: Dodd, 1920.

Krashen, Stephen D. *Principles and Practice in Second Language Acquisition.* New York: Pergamon, 1982.

Mearns, Hughes. *Creative Power: The Education of Youth in the Creative Arts.* New York: Doubleday, 1929.

———. *Creative Youth: How a School Environment Set Free the Creative Spirit.* New York: Doubleday, 1925.

Murray, Donald. M. *Learning by Teaching: Selected Articles on Writing and Teaching.* Upper Montclair: Boynton/Cook, 1982.

———. *A Writer Teaches Writing: A Practical Method of Teaching Composition.* Boston: Houghton, 1968.

Nelson, Marie Wilson. *At the Point of Need: Teaching Basic and ESL Writers.* Portsmouth: Boynton/Cook, 1991.

———. "Bridging the Paradigm Gap—Adopting an Expert-Practitioner Stance." *English Record* 34.4 (1983): 22–28.

Plimpton, George, ed. *Writers at Work: The Paris Review Interviews.* 2nd ser. New York: Viking, 1963.

———. *Writers at Work: The Paris Review Interviews.* 3rd ser. New York: Viking, 1967.

———. *Writers at Work: The Paris Review Interviews.* 4th ser. New York: Viking, 1977.

Shaughnessy, Mina P. *Errors and Expectations: A Guide for the Teacher of Basic Writing.* New York: Oxford UP, 1977.

Tchudi, Stephen, and Diana Mitchell. *Explorations in the Teaching of English.* 3rd ed. New York: HarperCollins, 1989.

Vygotsky, L. S. *Mind in Society: The Development of Higher Psychological Processes.* Ed. Michael Cole, Vera John-Steiner, Sylvia Scribner, and Ellen Souberman. Cambridge: Harvard UP, 1978.

II Responding to Student Writing

3 Writing Students Need Coaches, Not Judges

Lynn Holaday
Prescott College

Lynn Holaday left the practice of law and began teaching writing several years ago, and she has not regretted it for a moment. She is currently a writing instructor in the undergraduate and master's programs at Prescott College in Prescott, Arizona, and is working on a doctorate in writing and conflict resolution at the Union Institute. She recently published a children's book, Harry Harrison Wigglesworth the Sixteenth and the Freedom Strain.

I teach a beginning-level writing course in college. My students range from the reasonably competent to the hopelessly inept, but almost all of them hate and fear writing, a phenomenon that has been duly noted by many writing teachers. Shaughnessy, for example, points to their "confusion and lack of confidence" (10) and their "attitude of mistrust and pessimism" (Tate 180). My students, like hers, are generally negative about their abilities, fearful of exposing their clumsiness, and often emotionally distraught about having to perform. If these attitudes showed themselves in other settings (social life, family life), they would be regarded as evidence of major neuroses; and that, in fact, is what they are—neuroses born of traumatic experience. Every time these students sit down to write, their past miseries resurface as avoidance, depression, anger, rebelliousness, or grief. I don't regard myself as a psychologist and have no desire to act like one; like Macrorie, I say at the beginning of the term, "No psychiatrist works in this room" (272). However, I cannot ignore the very real impediment to writing that these strongly held negative attitudes pose. In fact, I see changing them as the only really effective means of improving my students' writing, and I see my most effective tool as minimizing judgment, otherwise known as grading.

Most teachers of writing would agree, I think, that the way to become a better writer is to write (Britton et al. 3). One can talk forever about style and word choice and syntax and flow, but improvement does not come until a student actually works with these abstractions in a paper he or she has constructed. Musicians do not talk about phrasing, rhythm, and dynamics; they practice using them until they are an effective part of their playing. Improvement comes through application of the mind and the body to the instrument. The same is true of writing.

But students who feel incompetent at writing avoid writing. They do not practice. They do not get better. The truly traumatized, and I estimate that about 20 percent of my classes are in this category, will do anything to avoid the torture they experience when they are required to put pen to paper or finger to key. They may struggle through a writing course, put out a few scraps they are not happy with, make the changes the teacher demands, accept a C or a D or whatever is enough to get them past the requirements, and then rush out at the end of a semester, breathe a huge sigh of relief that that is over, and vow never to write again. Their experiences in a writing class and the C or D they receive for their efforts reinforce their belief that they cannot write and increase their determination to find future courses, and later, a career, in which they will not have to write. And when they find that they do have to write again, because physicists and psychotherapists and business people and even leaders of wilderness outings all have to write, they repeat the ghastly process over and over.

It is well established that positive reinforcement brings about greater change than negative reinforcement. If every time a child set out to speak he or she were graded and criticized about the effort, most children would have a much harder time learning to express themselves. Fortunately, learning to speak is accomplished during the early years under the guidance (in most cases) of loving teachers who smile at errors, expect success, and vigorously reward even the most lame attempts at communication: "Da? Da? He said Da! He must mean 'Daddy.' That's right! Da. Yes! Yes! Look, John, he said it again!"

Learning to write, however, coincides with a child's entrance into school, a place where humor is rare, expectations are low, there is little or no reward for bumbling effort, and most horrifying of all, there are grades: A, B, C, D; 95%, 85%, 75%, 65%; stars, bluebirds, apples, bells; excellent, good, average, bad. Well, I don't know about everyone else, but if anything I do is seen as bad, I don't find much incentive to repeat it. Even "average" doesn't provide much motivation. And even if the grading is held off until later years, until age ten, or twelve, or fifteen, the same feelings will arise. Just because we're larger doesn't mean our egos are any less fragile. No matter when it occurs, negative feedback is demoralizing and demotivating. Low grades are negative feedback.

I first discovered I couldn't sing when I was eighteen and so told by a college choral instructor. I instantly quit singing. Only on long trips in the car with my family did I utter a note, and even then I prefaced every warble with self-deprecatory comment. Recently, to my utter surprise, my seventeen-year-old daughter volunteered casually, not knowing the amazement her words would generate, "You have a pretty voice, Mom."

Me? A pretty voice? Well, maybe I knew the words to that last bit. But that's not singing. What about my scratchiness, my lack of tone color, my inability to breathe right, my screeching on the high notes? No, she was just being nice. But because somewhere we all want to believe that flattery is true, I asked my husband.

"You sound fine," he said. "When you stay in tune."

I did? Fine? Well, was staying in tune something I could learn? I tried. Tentatively, at first. Yes. Actually, when I put some attention toward the problem, it was possible. And when I stopped being afraid, the tension went out of my throat, the cracking in my voice stopped, and something resembling a song emerged. I wasn't all that bad. When I believed that I might be able to sing, suddenly I was able to forget my self-consciousness enough to think about where the tune was going. When I allowed myself to feel the music, I experienced something akin to pleasure. I'm not looking toward a career in opera, but singing in the bathroom has suddenly became an uplifting experience again.

That is the kind of experience I want my writing students to have. I want to give students reasons to believe that they can do well. I want to reward them for trying. I want to flatter them a little. I want to abolish the twin ogres of judgment and comparison from the classroom, ogres that are symbolized by our grading process.

Ah, but what about healthy competition as a goad to success? What about being honest with students about how they are doing? What about being fair? Shouldn't the best students be rewarded for their effort? What about providing measurement tools for colleges and employers? What about standards?

In my opinion, none of the reasons that are advanced in favor of grading are sufficient to justify continuing the process. Grades do not convey truly accurate information either to the students or to those who use the marks to reward or punish them. Grades do not motivate the vast majority of students to succeed. Instead, grades serve primarily to maintain a caste system in which the smart get smarter (and later richer) and the dumb get dumber (and later poorer). Instead of giving out grades, we need to give real information, and we need to offer help that does not humiliate.

Grades are a poor way to convey information to or about a student. How many students learn anything about their performance from a grade? If they know any more than that the particular piece of work is excellent, good, fair, or poor, it's due to the fact that the teacher has conveyed, either in writing or orally, some more information. So why not convey the useful details and leave off the overall judgment? It is more difficult, of course. Writing a B at the top of a paper is easier than commenting on the nice way a student introduced the topic in the first paragraph, mentioning the sentence fragments in the second, or suggesting that examples would help to get a particular idea across. But what can students learn from a B? They don't know what it is that they have done well or what it is that has kept them from getting an A. To be truthful, often the teacher doesn't really know either. I have wished on many occasions that I could just stick a grade on a paper that sums up my gut sense about it. But to expect my gut reaction to be accurately translated into usable information by the student is unreasonable.

Having to come up with a grade (and a rationale for one) puts the focus on the measurable aspects of writing—grammar, length, topic sentences—and often forces a teacher into an overly simplistic evaluation scheme. "That which is measurable drives out that which is important," says Edward White (*Developing* 111). And what do we measure? What do we emphasize? Counting the spelling errors may let students know how they spell, but it won't tell them how they convey meaning. Giving points for originality says nothing about how well those original ideas are organized. Giving points at all is an arbitrary process if one is evaluating anything that does not have right or wrong answers. While one may be able to assign a 78% to a math exam, a 78% on a composition is next to meaningless. Can we compare syntax, originality, flow, and quality of evidence? Should we have multiple scales with multiple grades? If not, how do we rank the different aspects of writing? How do we assign them a percentage? Small wonder that theorists on writing assessment suggest more holistic methods.

Grading is also not the best way to convey information about students. If colleges, employers, and administrators need methods of assessing student performance and ways to rank them, why not let those authorities design them? Actually, we have a plethora of these tools. We have placement exams, we have SAT's, we have GRE's, and we have LSAT's. If we have national standards, we will have national exams. These all tell us, or will tell us, how students are doing and how schools are doing. Using classroom teachers' grades for these purposes is likely to confuse rather than enhance the evaluation process. A grade may be influenced or contaminated by everything from flattery to a teacher's personal preferences, to a desire to warn, to a fear of causing psychological harm, to a need to reward good behavior, to a need to meet institutional distribution requirements. Yet, despite this, once given, grades are treated as scientific, immutable, factual.

Frequently, there is little correspondence across schools or regions or even among individual teachers within a school system. An A from one teacher may be the same as a C from another. Colleges and employers know this and try to take it into account, but how much better it would be if they didn't have to do that at all. While narrative evaluations, spoken evaluations, or even a stray comment may be useful, a letter grade and nothing else is more apt to mislead than inform. White points out that assessment is favored by those in power (colleges and employers and administrators) but not by the teachers and students who are most directly affected by it (*Developing* 89). Why do we allow ourselves to be pushed around in this way? We have managed to keep football talent scouts away from our elementary school gym classes and the marketplace out of our textbooks, so why can't we keep the grademongers out of our classrooms?

A better alternative in my opinion is to let students know when they do well and to tell them specifically what it is they do well. We do not need an overall hierarchy of excellence. Teachers can praise good work wherever it is found.

Assigning an A+ to a good paper says it's good. It also says it can't get better. I have never received a paper that could not get better. I have never written anything that could not have gotten better. So how does the A+ help the student to learn? A grade of D says a paper isn't good, but it also doesn't say how it could be improved. It doesn't tell the student the one thing he or she needs to know: how to become a competent writer.

So let's point out the good parts of everyone's work. Let's offer suggestions for improvement to everyone. If one student writes much better than others, that fact very quickly becomes known. Students know if they're stars or apples. Isn't that reward enough? Do we have to publicly compare our students, make them heroes and failures in the most visible of ways? Grades promote destructive comparisons among students and do not motivate the vast majority of students to succeed.

Students usually rated as A students have met a certain externally established standard or are perceived as being somehow "better" than B, C, and D students. I believe in standards. I think our standards are abysmally low. I am appalled at the quality of most writing I see, student and professional. I think we expect too little of our children and our adults. I think everyone should write grammatically, concisely, clearly, thoughtfully. But what do grades have to do with standards?

If students have mastered the material, why give an A? Why not tell them that they have mastered the material? And if students have not mastered the material, why give them F's, which will, with almost absolute certainty, turn them off learning it and probably off learning anything else. Why not tell them what they have mastered, praise them for what they have done, and thus keep them interested in learning more?

And even if we feel it is necessary to record achievement with a letter grade, why publicize these grades to other students who have not so achieved? Why bring such an instrument of comparison into the classroom? Do we fear that students will do nothing unless they have the carrot of an A or the club of an F? Why then do students learn to jump rope? Why do they investigate insects on their own? Why are they fascinated by dinosaurs? Why do they ask *why?* My answer is that they do these things because learning is natural to human beings. Maybe the problem is not that we need to motivate students, but that we need to stop demotivating them.

I personally come down on the side that says cooperation is better than competition, that healthy competition is an oxymoron, but I know some people who love competition and thrive on it. So, fine, let's not do away with competition entirely. But let's not make it the centerpiece of the school experience. For those who want them, there are contests everywhere: sports events, essay contests, spelling bees, recitals. Let our competitive students go for them. Let's add some more if we want to. But let's keep competition out of the classroom. Let's reward children for learning, not for being "better" than someone else. For every child who says, "I lost, so I'll work harder next time," there are fifty who say, "I lost, so it's not worth trying."

Teachers are not in the classroom to judge; they are there to help children meet the standards of the outside world. As Albert Shanker says in support of his campaign to establish national standards and a national curriculum:

> It's like the Olympics. There's an external standard that students need to meet, and the teacher is there to help the student make it. The existence of an external standard entirely changes the relationship of teachers and youngsters. . . . (18)

It changes the relationship from judges and defendants to coaches and team players. We don't need our teachers to be judges. We have more than enough judges in this world. Coaches, however, are something we don't have enough of. Coaches are on your side; judges are not. Coaches are friendly; judges are aloof. Coaches want you to do well; judges don't care. Coaches believe you can do well and show you how; judges lecture you on what you should be and are not. Coaches offer encouragement; judges offer—*judgment*. (Some teachers are even prosecutors.)

Coaches know what the game requires, what the standards and goals are. A good coach can encourage a student to practice by making him or her believe it is possible to reach the goal. Grading does not tell most students that it is possible. An A or a B says it is possible, a C says maybe but not so likely, a D or an F says it is impossible. So why, I ask, do we hand out C's and D's and F's to students who already feel there is no hope? Teachers should be in the business of offering hope.

A comment about a vivid phrase says its possible. Asking a student to tell you more about his or her ideas because you think they are original and interesting says it is possible. Pointing out how students might help others in areas where they have competence says it is possible. And all students are good at something—at humor, at rhythm, at metaphor, at word choice. I have never received a paper that could not be praised in some respect.

I believe in rewarding effort. If students request a grade in my class, I give them one. I evaluate their finished products, but I give most of the emphasis to their effort. A student who writes at a D level and goes to a B level (whatever that represents) can get an A in my class. You'd be surprised at how they all sit up and start paying attention when I announce that at the beginning of the term. It is as if they have suddenly been given a way out of their hopelessness. Not surprisingly, too, those who put in the effort also tend to make great strides in their competence. Often, they produce products that might in themselves merit an A. However, I doubt they would have done so well had they believed that they had to produce an "A" product to succeed.

But what will happen to our standards, people wail, if we give A's to people who write worse than those to whom we give C's? Just because I may give high grades to students who may not be all that competent as writers doesn't mean I don't expect a lot from my students. I think all students should strive to write competently, and I think all of them should put effort toward their writing. But not all students start from the same place. If one writes a 95 essay on the first day of class, and another writes a 65 essay, and then at the end of the term the 95 goes to a 94 and the 65 goes to a 79, isn't it the 79 who is most likely to have overcome emotional blocks, to have made the greatest strides in skill development, and to have really learned something?

We need to recognize and reward such effort. As teachers, we are not looking for perfection—we are looking for improvement. How can we expect any more or any less? School is a place where we should value learning over status and encourage development over performance.

We have to accept, of course, that not all our students will opt to try to improve. And that is their choice. But I think we do have to do all we can to make sure that the decision not to try is something other than a hopeless acknowledgment of defeat, and we need to make improvement seem possible and desirable for those who do want to try.

We need to reward growth, both intellectual and moral. In his now famous analysis of college freshmen, William Perry discovered that most freshmen have trouble moving from the idea that there is a right and wrong answer—an absolute truth that the teacher knows and should impart, a stage of cognitive development that he calls dualistic—to the understanding that there are multiple ways of looking at an issue. Grading, however, fosters dualistic thought. Grades say there is a good and a bad, a right and a wrong. Particularly in assessing writing, this kind of black and white thinking is not helpful. I can think of many essays I have read on teaching, for example, which, because of the different approaches they took, could not realistically be compared. If we want to move students from dualistic to multiplistic thinking, we need to avoid grades.

Grades also encourage superficial learning and even unethical behavior. Most A students can tell you that they weren't in it for the learning. Their particular skill was to scope out the rules of the game and play by them. This makes teachers happy. It makes parents happy. The students may or may not be happy. Some learning obviously occurs, but probably much less than would have occurred if it had been learning rather than a grade that the students had sought. Worse, however, are the attitudes that this kind of game playing fosters: winning is everything, I'll do just enough to get the grade, form is more important than substance, and the means justify the ends. At a time when we are decrying the lack of ethics in our world, surely we need to promote through our teaching those values that we want our students to demonstrate.

Grading leads to comparisons among students, another form of unethical behavior. If we are grading students to compare them, what motivation we elicit will be due to a desire to be better than someone else (or not to be worse). But to motivate through fear is bad psychology, as is to cultivate envy. As many have pointed out, there is only one at the top. For everyone else, grading is degrading.

In my experience, the people who push for grades are those who got good ones themselves or who want the vicarious triumph of having their children get them. "If I did it, so can they," they say, ignoring the fact that literature on environmental influences, different intelligences, cognitive development, and cultural impediments all tells us that not all others can. "Grades encouraged me to work harder," they say, or, "My son worked hard for that A. He should be rewarded." But the B and C students may have worked just as hard, or they may have been subtly discouraged from working hard by being told that they are not capable. And in most cases, the teacher is not grading the effort anyway—he or she is grading the product.

And what kind of a product can come from one whose native language is not English, who has had inadequate schooling, and who lives in a family that does not value verbal communication? How can this child's product be compared with the product of a child who has been surrounded by books since infancy, who has helped to name and describe and compare and generalize, and who has been told subtly from the day he or she was born that he or she will do well in school? If a college student comes to class unable to write a grammatical paragraph, how can we compare his or her initial products with a Zinsser essay or even with the best student in the class? And if he or she were to produce such a superior product, how much effort would that take, and how should it be rewarded?

As one of those who took the A's as my due and preened myself over my superiority, I would like to say right now that I apologize. I am ashamed, for myself and for all those teachers who held me up as an example, who singled me out, who praised me, not for really putting in effort and striving to get better, but for being better, for doing something that came easily, for being lucky enough to be someone who was read to as a child, who came from a home where books held center stage and where my every intellectual move was noticed with approval. Often, issuing grades is like giving an award at a beauty contest. Most of the time the spoils go to those who had it in the first place and just learned to embellish it a little. "It's only fair to reward those who do better" really means it's right to keep rewarding those who are already at the top; but it's not fair at all:

> There is no difference between the child who learns slowly and the one who learns quickly except their rate of absorption and someone's judgment. The judgment is that one is better than the other. But such assessments have devastating effects. For the so-called slow or average learner, it is a commentary on his self-worth and does more to keep him where he is . . . first, because of the teacher's expectation that he had limited capabilities (which is subtly communicated to him and which he begins to believe about himself), and second, because of his own anxiety and fears of continued disapproval. Even the fast learner or honor student does not escape the pressures. He must continually maintain his "exceptionality" or otherwise face the repercussions of failing (getting a B instead of an A). In that game, he too is distracted by the anxiety of having continually to perform in order to be accepted and applauded. (Kaufman 77)

Of course, eventually the world will publicly compare our students. It will give A's and F's and stars and bells in the form of money and status. That is why children need teachers. They need teachers to help them be as strong as they can be when they finally have to face these tests. They need teachers to explain what the standards are and what will be expected of them. They need teachers to model the type of competence that will be required. They need teachers to tell them that they can make it—that all of them can make it. They don't need grades—they need information, and they need encouragement. They need coaching, not judging.

Works Cited

Britton, James, Tony Burgess, Nancy Martin, Alex McLeod, Harold Rosen. *The Development of Writing Abilities (11–18)*. London: Macmillan Education, 1975.

Kaufman, Barry Neil. *To Love Is to Be Happy with: The First Book of the Option Process.* New York: Fawcett Crest, 1977.

Macrorie, Ken. *Writing to Be Read.* Portsmouth: Heinemann, 1984.

Perry, William G., Jr. *Intellectual and Ethical Development in the College Years: A Scheme.* New York: Holt, 1970.

Shanker, Albert. "Making Standards Count." *American Educator* 18.3 (Fall 1994): 14, 16–19.

Shaughnessy, Mina P. *Errors and Expectations: A Guide for the Teacher of Basic Writing.* New York: Oxford UP, 1977.

Tate, Gary, ed. *Teaching Composition: Twelve Bibliographic Essays.* Rev. ed. Fort Worth: Texas Christian UP, 1987.

Tate, Gary, and Edward P.J. Corbett, eds. *The Writing Teacher's Sourcebook.* 2nd ed. New York: Oxford UP, 1988.

White, Edward M. *Developing Successful College Writing Programs.* San Francisco: Jossey-Bass, 1989.

———. *Teaching and Assessing Writing: Recent Advances in Understanding, Evaluating, and Improving Student Performance.* San Francisco: Jossey-Bass, 1985.

Interlude

Writing should not be graded; it should be praised. Oh, don't get me wrong—I have to give a grade. I base grades on the student's self-evaluation. If there is a conflict in what I think is fair and what a student thinks is fair, we conference. (There is seldom a conflict because the kids set higher goals for themselves than I do.) In the conferences we look at use of the writing process, published pieces, etc. The students almost always get the grades they feel are fair. We do portfolios, but these are primarily used in our evaluation process and to show parents how we have progressed. Each writer comes to me with a different level of education, confidence, and talent. At the end of our year together, each kid knows how to write and feels confident that she or he can handle any writing assignment. I couldn't get them to that point if I graded their writing instead of their effort.

—James F. Williams
  Ridgewood Middle School
  Shreveport, Louisiana

4 Response: A Promising Beginning for Learning to Grade Student Writing

Carole Beeghly Bencich
Indiana University of Pennsylvania

Carole Beeghly Bencich is director of English education at Indiana University of Pennsylvania and co-director of the Southcentral Pennsylvania Writing Project. She has published articles on tracking and critical thinking, and she maintains an active research interest in literacy autobiographies written by people of all ages. She has found that, quite often, grades play a determining part in the way individuals construct their identities as readers and writers.

Teaching in an undergraduate English education program carries a double responsibility with regard to grading. Not only must I assign a course-ending grade for each student, but I must plan instruction and model my practice in such a way as to help students understand the purposes and possibilities of the grading system. There's no point in "teaching" future teachers that student writing should be evaluated in ways that promote the growth of writers if I don't follow that advice myself. They, as students since the beginning of all time, will learn what I *do*, not what I say. If I want student teachers to experiment with alternatives to grading their students' writing, I need to ensure that they have experienced some of these alternatives in their own undergraduate classes.

Since the very beginning of my career, I have always known that I hated grading student papers, but that I loved reading them. It was fun and not particularly time-consuming to read through a set of papers. In a sixty-second deskside conference, I could read and respond to a typical eighth grader's paper. For a long time though, I accepted that it was my responsibility to grade each and every one of those papers. So I struggled with the normal mix of students: those who wrote grammatically correct but voiceless papers; those whose work bubbled over with voice and style but lacked mechanical polish; those who cared mostly about grades and those who weren't motivated at all by grades; those whose writing was uneven and sporadic;

and those who wouldn't do all of my writing assignments but were brilliant when they did.

Theory and many years of experience have given me no evidence that the grading—which I still hate to do—has helped my students become better writers. However, I have frequent evidence that responding—which I love to do—has encouraged and motivated my student writers and has also helped them improve their writing. Discovering one day that the words *response* and *responsibility* share the same etymology—*spondere,* to promise—gave me a new way to think about the response techniques I had been *using* in writing workshops and not *teaching* to English education majors. I had assigned readings on ways to respond to student writing. I had given nongraded narrative responses to their writings. We discussed response in class and brainstormed ways to respond without premature judgment, ways to respond instead of grading papers. I realized, however, that my English education students had never experienced what it was like to respond nonjudgmentally; what's more, they very seldom received that kind of response to their own writing.

Accordingly, I decided to rethink the emphasis in my methods courses. Instead of stressing the many ways to grade student writing and practicing with sample student papers, I decided it was more important to involve future teachers in response activities that were focused on one another's writings. I reasoned that suspending judgment on a paper initially would not only focus attention on the complex processes of writing, but it would also acquaint students with all the affective and rhetorical factors involved in making a summative evaluation. If I could help them learn to respond fully to writing, I wouldn't be worried about their ability to assign grades when the time came. That perceived need to *correct* another's writing, which often obscures any impulse to *respond* to it, can be examined and modified when teachers learn to respond and experience response to their own writing.

Learning the Difference between Evaluation and Grading

Undergraduates preparing to teach English are nervous about their ability to grade student writing—an uneasiness which reflects their perception of the role of evaluation in the classroom. Juniors in my EN 324: "Teaching and Evaluating Writing" course usually feel confident about their ability to teach writing. After all, textbooks like Kirby, Liner, and Vinz's *Inside Out* and Zemelman and Daniels's *A Commu-*

nity of Writers and resources like NCTE's *Ideas Plus* present more than enough ideas for designing writing lessons. Thinking of writing instruction only in terms of assignments is typical of preservice teachers, and it does carry a built-in security. Fill a notebook with surefire writing activities, and you're set for life, or so they think.

Learning to grade student papers is another matter, however, one tied to their own development as writers and their uneven experiences with academic evaluation systems. As often as not, grades have at some point generated tension and divisive feelings among students and created barriers between students and teachers, as well as between students and their own writing. Just as Peter Elbow notes, grades provide too much encouragement to successful students and too little to unsuccessful students ("Ranking" 190).

English education undergraduates tell of high school and college papers returned with sarcastic remarks or with a grade and no marks or comments, good papers given low grades and average papers given A's, plagiarized papers undetected, and papers turned in twice receiving different grades from different teachers. As a community, they have experienced the full range of teacher subjectivity, with all its variance in standards, methods, and outcomes. While some English education students even look forward to the transition from grade getter to grade giver, most are troubled by the complexities and responsibilities of the grading system. They've heard about the competitive pressures from parents and students, and they've read newspaper articles about the grade inflation that is eroding standards of evaluation. They worry about their ability to weigh effort and achievement in an individual student's work and to encourage writing as well as to reflect performance. Most of all, they wonder how they can be fair to all their students and still stem the tide of incorrectness they've read about in the popular press. They seldom doubt that every bit of student writing must be graded by the teacher, and they enter EN 324 expecting me to teach them, in no uncertain terms, the mysterious rites of paper grading. The title of the course, "Teaching and Evaluating Writing," does seem to promise just that, for at the beginning of the semester they believe grading and evaluating mean the same thing.

After an initial exploration of attitudes at the beginning of the course, I introduced the active writing and responding strand which is the heart of the course. Adapting the National Writing Project's principle that in order to teach writing well, one has to be a practicing writer, I reasoned that in order to respond to the writing of others, one would have to have experienced response to one's own writing. I wanted my students to learn to give nonjudgmental response, and I knew that that learning had to involve them both as readers and as writers. I wanted these future teachers to experience response that "dramatized the presence of a reader" (Sommers 148) and thereby helped them to become questioning readers themselves. Ultimately, of course, it is this active responsive reading that will help them to understand evaluation standards for their own and others' written work. As Scholes writes in *Textual Power:* "Reading and writing are complementary acts that remain unfinished until completed by their reciprocals" (20).

Similarly, Robert Probst reminds us that transactional theory has helped teachers change their reading habits with regard to student texts. In classrooms where both teacher and students are engaged in the pursuit of meaning, response to student writing is just as important as response to published literature. The teacher becomes the "manager of a small interpretive community" instead of the "judge and executioner" (70).

Louise Wetherbee Phelps (1989) describes how teachers' response practices evolve, in tandem with theory development, from closed-text evaluative readings to contextual readings that consider the language and socially constructed circumstances of student authors. Teaching response procedures in English education classes can jump-start the growth processes that are necessary in order for teachers to understand and practice effective ongoing evaluation, rather than ineffective short-term grading.

Peter Elbow defines the differences between ranking and evaluating and creates an important third category that he calls "liking." Ranking, he says, "is the act of summing up one's judgment of a performance or person into a single, holistic number or score. Ranking implies a single scale or continuum or dimension along which all performances are hung" ("Ranking" 187). Elbow's definition makes ranking synonymous with grading, a word derived from *gradus,* a step, degree, or rank. When we grade, we classify hierarchically, according to quality, rank, and worth. We grade eggs and meat. We separate students by grade levels. When we graduate, we literally "make the grade."

Elbow defines evaluating as "the act of expressing one's judgment of a performance or person by pointing out the strengths and weaknesses of different features or dimensions....Evaluation implies the recognition of different criteria or dimensions—and by implication different contexts and audiences for the same performance" (188). Thus, evaluation points to the process of determining worth. Etymologically, it is linked to value, from *valere,* to be strong. Over the years, value has been associated with the idea of intrinsic worth. When we value something, we hold it in esteem. We do not necessarily rank it according to a formal rubric.

A grade is a product, expressed in a number or letter whose meaning is determined by its place in a hierarchy. Evaluation, on the other hand, is often expressed in a narrative which represents the standards and values of the evaluator. Evaluation need not result in a grade. It can be ongoing, with opportunities for revision built in to the process.

Elbow's third category of "liking" student writing reminds us that "only if we like what we write will we write again and again by choice—which is the only way we get better." More than that, he notes that "the way writers *learn* to like their writing is by the grace of having a reader or two who likes it—even though it's not good" (200). By creating private, nonevaluative zones for writing, a teacher gets to know students better, and they get to practice writing in a supportive context. "Let's do as little ranking and grading as we can," Elbow urges. "Let's use evaluation instead." And finally, "[L]et's learn to be better likers; liking our own and our students' writing, and realizing that liking need not get in the way of clear-eyed evaluation" (205).

Instead of giving English education students the "free fish" of a perfect grading system (which isn't mine to give anyway), I teach them to "fish for themselves" by creating a context for peer writing and responding that provides the opportunity to sharpen their awareness of how to read and value another writer's work.

Attitudes of English Education Students

Teacher education students are in a unique place, shaped by images of teaching and learning that they experienced during their formative years and at the same time developing within the influences of current pedagogical theory. Connors and Lunsford note that, from the 1880s onward, "the idea that the teacher's most important job was to rate rather than to respond rhetorically to themes seems to have been well-nigh universal" (201). Paul Diederich, in *Measuring Growth in English,* wrote that "my predominant impression has been that (writing classes) are fantastically over-evaluated. Students are graded on everything they do every time they turn around" (2).

Written remarks on student papers often do little more than justify or mitigate the teacher's ranking. These remarks combine generic praise ("Nice idea...," "Interesting thesis...," or "Clever treatment...") with a defining "but" clause ("...flawed by diction," "...lacks coherency," "...fails to develop"). A graduate student told me that, when faced with the assignment of "critically marking" a peer's paper for a class in critical theory, she imitated generic comments from her own undergraduate papers. She wanted to sound professional, but had no idea where to begin and no basis from which to respond to the paper.

Early in the semester, I asked students in EN 324 to complete Nancie Atwell's "writing survey" (270), which probes attitudes, habits, and beliefs about writing. In response to the question "How does your teacher decide which pieces of writing are the good ones?" students wrote comments that revealed the confusing messages from their own experiences:

> I've found the majority of teachers I've had put on a letter grade without any response or commentary.... (Sally)

> Usually the teacher makes a pile ranking them according to other students in the class. (Jane)

> Through preset categories of writing factors such as clarity, development, mechanics, etc. (Rob)

> I still haven't figured that out. I can hand in the identical essay and get an A in one class and a C in the other. There are no hard, fast rules for writing. (Bob)

> Possibly by personal reactions to it.... (Chuck)

> Perhaps originality? (Arlene)

Their scanty experience in either giving or getting responsive feedback to writing causes them to confound response with judgment, criticism, and, even, proofreading. In their established belief that *ranking* or grading is what ultimately matters, all their responses tend toward a simplistic formula: Say something nice to the writer and then find every mistake or weakness so it can be fixed in time to generate an appropriate grade.

Students are not the only ones lacking confidence in this area. In 1982, Nancy Sommers commented on the general lack of understanding for "what constitutes thoughtful commentary or what effect, if any, our comments have on helping our students become more effective writers" (148). Chris Anson, in his introduction to *Writing and Response*, acknowledges that "response to writing is often difficult and tense. For the teacher, it is the schizophrenia of roles—now the helpful facilitator, hovering next to the writer to lend guidance and support, and now the authority, passing critical judgment on the writer's work…" (2).

Response procedures are seldom taught formally, even when the pedagogy involves peer writing groups. Usually, at most, a checklist may be provided to guide students' feedback to one another. In *Sharing Writing*, Karen Spear gives examples of three such guides, one of which features a list of forty-two specific rhetorical and mechanical features (48). Students who merely answer yes or no to each dichotomous item on such a list may quickly complete the task without understanding the rhetorical terms involved and without experiencing the meaning of the paper in question.

When they enter their first teaching experience, then, students quite naturally mimic the response and evaluation procedures which they have directly experienced. As a supervisor, I have observed student teachers using effective classroom methods to evoke interest and growth in writing, only to undermine the process by premature and overzealous grading of papers. *Everything* had to be graded, they assured me. Otherwise, "the kids just won't do the work." Or, "I have to have two grades a week for each student. It's a school rule." Commonly, student teachers talk about the many, many hours they spend in grading papers and in adding or averaging summative grades. Although they "love" reading students' work, they "hate" assigning a grade to it. They often report with amazement that grades of B, C, or D, with careful comments, do not lead to improved writing, and they agonize over their students who want higher grades than the ones they're receiving as well as the students who seem totally unmotivated by grades.

My problem in EN 324 has been to find a way to fit the ambiguities and demands of evaluation into the context of learning. Rather than letting the need to grade drive both curriculum and pedagogy, I believe student teachers should assert what they know about learning and human development. I want them to plan meaningful evaluation that will provide insights into their students' thinking and learning habits, promote the development of writing abilities, and involve their students in developing standards for evaluating their own work.

Learning to Respond

The textbooks for EN 324 included Kirby, Liner, and Vinz's *Inside Out*, Zemelman and Daniels's *A Community of Writers*, Dunning and

Stafford's *Getting the Knack,* and Spear's *Sharing Writing.* The syllabus asked students "to establish a schedule of regular personal writing":

> Most of the texts for this class include writing activities which sound great. Guided imagery, memory writing, people photos, mad/soft talking, wordshaking…the list is endless. Make these activities come alive by doing them yourself. For instance, choose one of the Kirby/Liner/Vinz activities, or one of Dunning/Stafford's poem starters. Begin by writing the name, brief description, and source of the activity (e.g., "What *color* do you feel like today? Talk about why you picked that color," from p. 46, Kirby/Liner/Vinz). Then spend about 20 minutes writing the activity yourself. Conclude with a five-minute evaluation of the activity. What was it like for you? Did you generate writing which you would like to continue working on? Can you imagine what it would be like for students? Can you think of specific ways in which you might use this writing activity in the classroom? Etc.

Students were to do one of these writings in their journal for each Tuesday meeting. Modeling the philosophy of teacher as co-learner, I would write every week too. In class, we exchanged journals and wrote responses to one another's work. My instruction in responding was brief, using three favorite prompts appropriated from a Stephen Dunning workshop years ago: "I notice…," for making global observations about the writing's impact, mood, and effect; "I wonder…," for asking questions about information not included in the writing; and "What if…?" for making suggestions regarding the form or content of the writing. The real instruction took place when I modeled response and in the metacognitive discussions I initiated after responding sessions. Throughout the semester, I described additional ways of responding, such as those given by Peter Elbow in *Writing with Power* and by Elbow and Belanoff in *Sharing and Responding.* Finally, I requested that all writers choose a different response partner each Tuesday, so that we could experience a full spectrum of individual responding styles.

The second stage of the process took place in Thursday's journal, when each writer was to reflect on the response process from the point of view of both a writer and a responder. I asked students to consider their own responding techniques and also their reactions to the responses they received from others. "What did the responder do, and how did it work?" were the guiding questions. More specifically, "How did you respond to ＿＿＿'s work?" and "What was your reaction to ＿＿＿'s response to your work?"

Students began the semester in confusion, not quite sure of what was expected of them. "I must admit that I find it difficult to *evaluate* other people's writing," Sarah wrote, despite my stress on response as opposed to evaluation. During week four, Jack wrote: "I am still confused as to what I am doing as the responder. Is my response purely affective? Am I suggesting structural changes? Specific word changes? Asking for clarifications or expansions?" After each Tuesday's journal exchange, we identified responding techniques and talked about how they worked. Some of the methods which students liked best were

- circling or underlining strong word choices or vivid phrases, with a note in the margin;
- asking questions about the content;
- relating personal associations or connections to the content;
- noticing a theme or mood which informed the writing, often without the author's awareness; and
- comments which treated the author as a writer, and the writing as a work-in-progress.

"Each time a teacher or fellow student reads and reacts to a student's paper, the social and interpersonal dimensions of the classroom come fully into play," write Anson and his colleagues (34). Hidden insecurities and tensions emerge. Sensitive feelings are tapped. Although rich, helpful responses greatly outnumbered the weak or generic responses, nearly everyone did receive a response which disappointed in some way. On the other hand, nearly everyone *wrote* a response which disappointed someone else. Feedback was immediate. If two writers miscommunicated in their responses on Tuesday, they had a chance to discuss it on Thursday, with the implicit realization that both reading and writing were active meaning-making processes. Very quickly, several truths were established: Every writer wants response, and every writer resents the generic "nice work" kind of comment that substitutes teacherly judgment for honest specificity. Comments in the Thursday journals reveal the spectrum of reactions:

> I had my feelings hurt a bit today. Okay, I know I am not strong in poetry, but I really did like my poems about Buddy & Zippy a great deal....My feelings were hurt on the line, "Now that you practiced a few, do you think you could do better?" Somewhere in that statement is an unstated, "This really isn't that good." (Helen)

> I liked the way Alan summed up my story of child abuse by calling it a story of the killing of creativity. I enjoy someone

being able to make an analogy of a story I told. It makes me feel as though my message got through. (Arlene)

One thing that she wrote to me was the word "Nice." I guess with that response I felt like I was being patronized because she just agreed with me. It was just kind of a non-response. (Arlene, about Sally's response)

Rita's response showed me that I was able to achieve my desired effect. Specifically, Rita pointed out a word choice which I was unsure of—her comments showed me that this is the correct word, that it does work....I have noticed from responses I've received images, moods, word choices that I had not thought to be especially effective are pointed out by the responder as being effective. (Jack)

She wrote her response in the margins and would draw lines around the parts that she commented on. I can't help but wish that she had been more specific. Did she like the word choice? The omitted punctuation? (Sally, about Tammy's response)

Here's my reaction to what is on the left. Either he's too busy to write this reaction, he's under the impression that he has to spew out "writing knowledge" to the teacher or me, or he just didn't get my objective. (John, about Chuck's response)

Response from others makes me focus more on "Am I getting this across? Am I saying what I mean?" A lot of times I feel I'm saying what's in my thoughts but I'm not! Also, response has encouraged me to write more—I've gotten positive response about the images I can doodle with words....It makes me feel good. (Lee Ann)

I know that two times I have been a little disappointed because I didn't feel a connection being made to my writing. Therefore, I feel that part of my writing purpose is lost. (Karen)

Students experienced a rich spectrum of response, but it did not come quickly. Always, they had to separate out their habits as responders and their expectations as recipients of response. When they received what they viewed as poor response from a classmate, they would take a closer look at their *own* responding habits. Likewise, when they received a helpful response, they would attempt to pass this on by imitating the techniques of the helpful responder. As writers, they had to consider whether a response showed them anything new about their work. They could evaluate their work on the basis of the response it evoked in a given reader.

At least six weeks passed before I felt that honest response had replaced judging or hypercritical suggestions for improvement as a primary reaction to a classmate's writing. For one thing, the weekly writing, mostly expressive, sparked community interest. Instead of talking about teaching and evaluating writing, we were all writing and talking about our writing.

When Lee Ann tried the Kirby/Liner/Vinz "life map" visual (54) one week, the response went beyond her partner that Tuesday. Karen wrote: "Pardon me, but this is just the damn coolest thing!! Everyone was eyeing this up as I brought it over to begin looking at. Your doodles are great." In following weeks, three other writers tried the same prewriting activity. Throughout the semester, there was active imitation of both writing and responding styles. Although writers only shared work once a week in class, they shared informally outside of class.

A "golden rule" of responding emerged. "Respond unto others as you would have them respond unto you" was echoed in these comments in the fourth-week journals:

> With responses that I am not comfortable with—such as psychoanalysis—I can see that I do not want to respond in this way because it may turn writers away from writing. (Helen)

> The responses which I find most useful are those which encourage through specific comments about what was good in my writing and challenge me to do more through questions and suggestions. So I try to respond in a like manner....(Jack)

> I wanted my responses to make the writer think more about their entry and expand on it. I feel that I am getting better at responding. When I respond I try to respond in the same ways that other people have responded to my log entries that really made me reflect on what I wrote. (Lisa)

Audience awareness grew alongside metalinguistic awareness of reading and writing habits. Because writers had a different response partner every week, they experienced a variety of writing styles and a variety of responding styles. When I asked them to describe "a good responder," the following characterizations emerged:

> Alan responded well....I liked how he commented as if my writings were literature, like "Good imagery!" It made me feel like a real writer. (Lee Ann)

> I also like to know the feelings that are generated by my responder, instead of just they like it or don't like it. Helen...is a good responder. (Rita)

With Sally's response techniques, I like the way she underlined words—this made me more aware of my own statements and the effects that these statements had on her....Sarah is so personal when she responds—I really like this. She asks me questions and makes observations which show me that she really is interested in what I am doing. For example, her comment, "I suspect there are many stories to be told about St. John's Church. . . ." There are! (Helen)

I was pleased to find that Karen at least pondered over the things I did: Were they intentional or not? They were, and although she really didn't know what they were for, neither did I, I guess. The point is that she didn't hold back. She wasn't sure of what was going on in all cases. So she wrote what she knew and she asked about what she didn't. That is very important—to not be fake, but sincere (really sincere) in your responses. I think I was happiest when she said she wanted more, wanted to know what came next (I wasn't finished). (John)

Students worked at improving their responding habits. The assigned textbook chapters on conferencing and peer writing groups took on an immediate relevance because they could be directly applied. For instance, Arlene noted that Sarah's response questions "reminded me of the responses given on pages 148 and 149 in the Spear book." Sarah's use of Spear's "challenging feedback questions" and Arlene's notice of it added relevance to an otherwise routine reading assignment. Overall, the initiative and energy which students applied to responding reminded me again of that etymological connection between *response* and *responsibility*.

EN 324 also included a teaching component, where students were to involve classmates in a ten-minute mini-lesson. This activity began in the fourth week of the semester, and students were asked to write a response to each presenter. Naturally enough, they used the same techniques they had been developing in journals, discovering that honest, specific feedback applies equally well to oral or written products.

As a full participant in the writing and responding, I not only had an unusual window into my students' growth, but I learned a great deal about my own habits and about the symbiotic relationship between responding and writing processes. Ruth's reaction to the experience of exchanging journals with her professor was fairly typical:

As for last Tuesday when you and I traded, I was a little nervous about that. I wanted to be as good a responder as I want

> responded *to*. (I always do.) But how was *I* supposed to respond
> to *your* writing. So I finally decided to just respond like I would
> to anybody else's writing—as a *reader* who is also a writer. And I
> enjoyed reading and responding to your writing. (By the way, I
> was driving in today and I was thinking about your description
> of the "little man" Mexican boy. Have you considered turning
> that one little vignette into a poem?)

What I treasure in that note is the fact that Ruth thought, and talked to
me, about my writing (a narrative about an incident in Mexico) two
days after she read and responded to it. Like any writer, I appreciate
genuine interest in my work. Her suggestion that I consider condens-
ing my story into a poem was a valuable writer-based response. I saw
evidence of that kind of personal connection among all twenty-two of
the students in the course. They were observing and thinking about
one another as practicing writers, giving and acting upon one
another's advice, and constructing their own standards for writing
and responding. And it went beyond the minimum requirements for
coursework. Not for whimsy alone did they name the final publication
of their writing, "We're All in This Together."

Practicing What I Teach

One of my goals for EN 324 was for students to learn to like their writing. I planned to achieve this goal through a program of regular nongraded writing which received active and nonjudgmental peer
response. I hoped that, by learning to like their own writing, they
might be able to see their students' writing as more than a deficient
text in need of improvement. I hoped that they would want to replicate our class's experience with community-developed standards in
their own classrooms. I knew that I would undermine all these hopes
and efforts if my own evaluation system failed to reconcile my pedagogical theory with the institutional demands for a semester grade.

In the syllabus, I published a description of my 100-point grading scale. The dialogic writing journal, which I consider responsible
for most of the learning in this course, counted for 25 percent of the
final grade. A writing portfolio counted for an additional 50 percent, a
demonstration lesson for 15 percent, and overall oral participation for
10 percent. In order to minimize the risk and also to demonstrate my
belief that not all writing need be graded or even revised, I offered an
automatic full credit of twenty-five points for each completed writing
journal. Although I did read and respond to these journals, not ranking them saved me time and anxious decisions. Students contributed

their favorite work from the journal to a class anthology that we published at the end of the term. In addition to the dialogic journal, students compiled a portfolio that included a writer's autobiography, an article on teaching or learning to write, and a teaching unit. For the preface to this portfolio, they described the writing, peer feedback, and revision processes they had employed in each piece, and they discussed their own strengths and problems as writers.

At the end of the term, each student wrote a self-evaluation, complete with suggested points for each category of evaluation, and brought it to an individual conference with me. At this conference, the student and I compared our point estimates, discussed rationales for the estimates, and negotiated a final grade.

I never did teach my students how to grade papers, but I think I *showed* them some valuable alternatives. My hope is that the responding voice which they developed in EN 324 will enable them to see student papers as individual texts in process rather than products to be judged, and to understand evaluation itself as a complex process rather than a formulaic product. After all, awareness of their own reading and writing processes and how those processes function in the valuing of student texts is a worthy preparation for learning how to grade papers.

Works Cited

Anson, Chris M., ed. *Writing and Response: Theory, Practice, and Research.* Urbana: NCTE, 1989.

Anson, Chris M., Joan Graham, David A. Jolliffe, Nancy S. Shapiro, and Carolyn H. Smith. *Scenarios for Teaching Writing: Contexts for Discussion and Reflective Practice.* Urbana: NCTE, 1993.

Atwell, Nancie. *In the Middle: Writing, Reading, and Learning with Adolescents.* Portsmouth: Boynton/Cook, 1987.

Connors, Robert, and Andrea Lunsford. "Teachers' Rhetorical Comments on Student Papers." *College Composition and Communication* 44 (1993): 201–23.

Diederich, Paul B. *Measuring Growth in English.* Urbana: NCTE, 1974.

Dunning, Stephen, and William Stafford. *Getting the Knack: 20 Poetry Writing Exercises.* Urbana: NCTE, 1992.

Elbow, Peter. "Ranking, Evaluating, and Liking." *College English* 55 (1993): 187–205.

———. *Writing with Power: Techniques for Mastering the Writing Process.* New York: Oxford UP, 1981.

Elbow, Peter, and Pat Belanoff. *Sharing and Responding.* New York: Random, 1989.

Ideas Plus. Urbana: NCTE, 1984+ . [In twelve volumes thus far.]

Kirby, Dan, Tom Liner, and Ruth Vinz. *Inside Out: Developing Strategies for Teaching Writing.* Portsmouth: Boynton/Cook, 1988.

Phelps, Louise Wetherbee. "Images of Student Writing: The Deep Structure of Teacher Response." *Writing and Response: Theory, Practice, and Research.* Ed. Chris M. Anson. Urbana: NCTE, 1989. 37–67.

Probst, Robert. "Transactional Theory and Response to Student Writing." *Writing and Response: Theory, Practice, and Research.* Ed. Chris M. Anson. Urbana: NCTE, 1989. 68–79.

Scholes, Robert. *Textual Power: Literary Theory and the Teaching of English.* New Haven: Yale UP, 1985.

Sommers, Nancy. "Responding to Student Writing." *College Composition and Communication* 33 (1982): 148–56.

Spear, Karen. *Sharing Writing: Peer-Response Groups in English Classes.* Portsmouth: Boynton/Cook, 1987.

Zemelman, Steven, and Harvey Daniels. *A Community of Writers: Teaching Writing in Junior and Senior High School.* Portsmouth: Heinemann, 1988.

Interlude

Has anyone read Alfie Kohn's _Punished by Rewards: The Trouble with Gold Stars, Incentive Plans, A's, Praise, and Other Bribes_? Kohn raises some crucial questions about how and why rewards stifle intrinsic motivation and often encourage tedious, routine class work, whereby students are constantly being led to get something (external reward) if they do something. "Do this and you will get this." That's the constant refrain in the classroom. So rather than hearing students say *what* they learned, we more often than not hear them say what they *got*. They are taught to lose sight of the learning and to focus on the outside carrot or stick. And so many times, whatever they do, what they receive is never good enough—thus they receive the punishment of not being good enough.

> —Bajaru Chavanu
> Florin High School
> Sacramento, California

5 Can You Be Black and Write and Right?

Elaine B. Richardson
University of Minnesota

Elaine B. Richardson recently received her Ph.D. from Michigan State University in the African American Language and Literacy program. Her dissertation project, "An African-Centered Approach to Composition" for AAVE speaking freshmen, focused on AAVE culture and language and the African American literary theme of "freedom through literacy" as the bases of acquiring critical literacy skills and academic discourse. She has recently joined the faculty of the University of Minnesota.

This essay and experiment is a contribution to the developing interest in the exploration and analysis of the use of African American Vernacular English (AAVE) discourse style and rhetorical patterns and how this type of language use is received in writing classes. I would like to define myself for you in conjunction with AAVE. Then, I would like to share some student texts that display use of AAVE rhetorical patterns. One of the main goals of this essay is to discuss alternative assessment of AAVE patterns in student texts and to offer suggestions about how we might break the cycle of the violence of standard literacy practices.

Who Am I?/What Is AAVE Rhetoric and Discourse Style?

I am a product of the AAVE oral tradition. I grew up in Cleveland, Ohio. I attended Cleveland Public Schools. My parents were working-class people. Some of my neighbors, in fact, most of them, were under-working class, meaning that they may have been on welfare or did what ever kind of hustle they could do to survive and keep their families together. I tell you this because I want you to know that I am representing these kinds of students in your classrooms. I don't want to front like I was better educated or of another class, and therefore did not speak and live the vernacular life. I did, and in many ways, I still do. I like to define myself in the tradition of the language and the black experience because, as I hope you will see, the two are one.

I think it is important for you to see me as a student of the vernacular culture, and I think it is important for people to know that the
vernacular culture is more than systemic grammar, syntax, and a particular way of expressing ideas. It is a way of being in the world. People usually overlook this major aspect of language. Language and culture are inseparable. AAVE is a direct result of African-European
contact on the shores of West Africa and in what became the United
States of America. The result of African-European contact, an experience of subordination and dominance, has implanted double consciousness into the very core of African American being. Historically
speaking, Africans had to become proficient in English just to survive.
They had to prove that they had more use than just to be and to
remain "ignorant niggers," the creation of slavers. Smitherman (*Talkin'
and Testifyin'*) says that

> The push-pull momentum is evidenced in the historical devel-
> opment of Black English in the push toward Americanization of
> Black English counterbalanced by the pull of retaining its Afri-
> canization. . . . White America has insisted upon White English
> as the price of admission into its economic and social main-
> stream. (11–12)

By the same token, whether or not AAVE students have had the
same experiences as white middle-class students (the norming group
for the American educational model), they must come to the institutions speaking or writing right (or writing white). So we can see then
that the game still has not changed. In our nation's beginning, cultural
difference was used to justify inhumane treatment, and nowadays it is
used to justify inequality; it is at the very core of the politics of education and literacy. The fact of the matter is that African Americans have
retained much of their Africanness in spite of slavery. The African
worldview, which is a part of African American culture, is opposite to
the dominant European worldview in fundamental ways.

One of the major differences can be seen in the ways African
peoples view ideas and phenomena holistically, while European and
Euramerican peoples view ideas or phenomena analytically and hierarchically (Smitherman, in progress). This list of fundamentally different aspects of worldview encompasses other facets of reality, such as
orientation to time, nature, family life, spirituality, and more. But I
want to focus on the relationship between language use and reality.
Marcyliena Morgan has described AAVE as a "counterlanguage." She
says that Black English began as a "conscious attempt on the part of
[enslaved Africans] and their descendants to represent an alternative

reality through a communication system based on ambiguity, irony, and satire" (Morgan 424). Hence, Africanized English reflects the black experience. In its most sophisticated uses, Africanized English resists white ways of knowing and being and speaking about those ways of knowing and being. This language that I am referring to is spoken by at least 80 percent of African Americans (Dillard) in their homes and sometimes at school! It carries the beliefs, values, and ideology of its speakers.

Features under Consideration

Black language creates meaning differently because of the ideology embedded in the language and the way that the discourse may be structured. Smitherman (*Talkin' and Testifyin'*) has explained the ways in which much of African American verbal style is acquired from the folk traditions learned in the black church. There is a growing body of research which investigates the degree to which AAVE oral tradition features influence the black discursive and rhetorical patterns that may arise in AAVE-oriented students' texts (Noonan-Wagner; Ball; Redd; Balester; Richardson, "Paradigms and Pedagogy"; Campbell; Smitherman, "Blacker the Berry"). Most of these scholars find that features such as "narrative sequencing," "repetition," "topic association" (as opposed to the development of one point in speech or writing), "field dependency/lack of distance from events," and others are associated with the black church, black culture, and the traditional African worldview.

Three aspects of the AAVE oral tradition that I want to look at are "signification," "narrative sequencing," and "testifying" in some students' texts. These texts were gleaned from a freshman composition course at Cleveland State University which I taught as part of my training as a teacher of composition. I obtained my idea for the "diagnostic" assignment in a course in which I was enrolled for composition teaching assistants. Below is the "diagnostic" essay assignment I used for the freshman English course. It was common practice that students be required to take the writing lab in conjunction with the freshman course if their performance on the "diagnostic" assignment did not signal their familiarity with received rhetorical approaches. (All of the students dreaded such a fate because they—correctly—perceived that they were stigmatized by writing lab placement.)

Reading/Evaluation

Following is a "diagnostic" essay assignment for a freshman English course:

Diagnostic Essay—Freshman English

For this essay, the knowledge of essay writing you have acquired in previous writing classes or high school will be of most help to you. Please feel free to freewrite, use outlines, or use any other prewriting or organizational technique which will help you achieve a well-thought-out, conscientiously devised piece of writing.

Construct an essay of at least two pages using the following quote:

"Where there is much desire to learn, there of necessity will be much arguing, much writing, many opinions; for opinion in good men is but knowledge in the making."

—John Milton

The papers were to be evaluated following criteria like that of the evaluation sheet in Figure 1. The evaluation sheet is a variation of the rubric used by the National Assessment of Educational Progress (NAEP) called the primary-trait scale (see Smitherman, "Blacker the Berry" 88). Although the evaluation sheet in Figure 1 is not the exact one that I used in the Cleveland State course, I use it here because it is the same one I used in a study of instructor evaluation of AAVE discourse patterns, entitled "Paradigms and Pedagogy." The findings of that study are reported here to inform my estimation of conventional rating practices. I invite the reader to evaluate the papers and ponder your reasons for assigning the score that you give.

Paper I

The quote by John Milton reminds me of a theory of cognitive development. In cognitive development, before a person can learn something, interest must be developed and an idea must be recognized as something that is either similar or different. In other words, a person analyzes an idea to find out what it is made of. Uniformed opinions are not knowledge. After a person makes sense of an idea or has had a chance to look at it from all possible angles, then it becomes a part of the person's knowledge base. Usually a person has an opinion about something before exploring an idea or a topic. After arguing and writing or analyzing, a person usually has a better opinion because it is more well thought out.

Evaluation Sheet

Score

4   Elaborated. Students providing elaborated responses went beyond the essential, reflecting a higher level of coherence and providing more detail to support the points made.

3   Adequate. Students providing adequate responses included the information and ideas necessary to accomplish the underlying task and were considered likely to be effective in achieving the desired purpose.

2   Minimal. Students writing at the minimal level recognized some or all of the elements needed to complete the task but did not manage these elements well enough to ensure that the purpose of the task would be achieved.

1   Unsatisfactory. Students who wrote papers judged as unsatisfactory provided very abbreviated, circular, or disjointed responses that did not even begin to address the writing task.

Figure 1. Evaluation criteria.

In order to understand an idea a person must analyze it. This corresponds to Milton's arguing. Arguing means looking at all the parts that make up an idea. When arguing, it is good to write down all of the parts of an idea. In this way, a person can visualize an idea more clearly and see how it fits in with what is already known. It is like all of the parts of an idea are sitting there in view in order to figure out how they fit together or do not fit together. But if a person only looks at one part of an idea or topic, the information is limited.

If we have interest and an opinion we must argue and write or analyze to see what the idea is made of. Therefore, like Milton said: "opinion in good men, is but knowledge in the making."

A Conventional Evaluation and Assessment of Paper I

The introduction sets up the audience for an analogy between the student's interpretation of the Milton quote and cognitive development. We can understand why the writer moves to an explanation of "analysis" and "arguing" in the first body paragraph. We get the feeling that the student author is going to move through each aspect of cognitive development and compare it with the author's interpretation of the ideas in Milton's quote; however, although the writer's discourse evidences an interesting condensed version of the analogy between cognitive development and the writer's interpretation of the Milton quote, the writer seems to have abandoned the analogy, leaving the audience to fend for itself. The author, rather, moves to a summarizing concluding paragraph. The paper is reminiscent of Labov's example of standard loquaciousness, in which a speaker (or writer) substitutes verbosity for depth and content.

Given an "Evaluation Sheet" like the one above and those that many of us have to work with, our training as writing instructors, and the fact that the writer did employ a fresh approach to the topic, conventional standards bind most instructors to score Paper I somewhere between 4 and 3, especially because the writer adheres to the language of wider communication (LWC) grammar and academic prose style, and there are no glaring departures from academic style. Seven out of nine college writing instructors scored the paper 3 or 4 in the AAVE discourse-patterns study (Richardson, "Where Did That Come From?").

Paper II

Milton's quote reminds me of the writing process. In the writing process, a person writes every possible issue on a topic down in order to learn about it. In the writing process this is called arguing or exploring an issue. In the beginning of the process, the writer has an opinion. After finding out all of the information on a topic, the writer has a better opinion because it contains truth not just a personal belief.

It takes lots of practice to become an efficient writer. Through practicing writing and thinking about issues one can effectively communicate one's ideas. Good writing persuades someone to believe what you are saying is true. The writing process involves changing opinions and looking at an argument from another point of view.

A writer does this so that readers will believe that the writing is well thought out. Opinions are like birthdays everybody's got one. As Milton said, "opinion in good men is but knowledge in the making."

A Conventional Evaluation and Assessment of Paper II

The introduction sets up the reader for a discussion of the similarities between the writing process and the elements of the Milton quote. The writer discusses methods that efficient/good writers use—practicing writing and thinking and looking at ideas from alternate viewpoints. The concluding paragraph tells the reader why writers must use these methods. The paper moves to closure with a colloquial aphorism— "Opinions are like birthdays everybody's got one." Finally, the paper ends with a quote from Milton which approximates to: Good men don't view opinions as fact, but as a step toward discovery of fact. Upon first reading Paper II, an instructor may be inclined to suggest that the writer should have referred to Milton more throughout the discussion to reinforce the similarity between the writing process and the Milton quote. Further, there is one run-on sentence located within the colloquial aphorism.

What score does the "Evaluation Sheet" allow you to assign to Paper II? Conventional standards dictate somewhere between a 3 and a 2, especially because of the colloquialism, which signals a shift in tone from formal objective prose to informal conversational tone. In the AAVE discourse-patterns study, nine instructors were split evenly between 3's and 2's, with one instructor giving the paper a 1.

Even though Paper II receives lower evaluation, the lower evaluation may be due to unfamiliarity with integral AAVE rhetorical features. Paper II evinces *signifying*. Let me explain. Gates's definition of signifying helps us to understand how the student is using language. Gates says that African Americans distinguish themselves from other speakers of the English language by *signifying*. In the AAVE oral tradition of signifying,

> The very meaning of meaning is being questioned by a literal critique of white meaning. (Gates 46)

When words are used in this way, they can have at least two levels of meaning. This AAVE way of using language is not just restricted to the term or the speech act of "signifying." The speech act of signifying, as described by Smitherman (*Talkin' and Testifyin'*) refers to speakers putting each other down (or up) for fun, or making indirect points as behavior correctives. What I am calling signifying here is the use of indirection to make a point in which a familiar AAVE maxim is invoked by a writer (speaker) to express a commonly held belief (mother wit/experiential knowledge), although the maxim applies only metaphorically to the situation at hand. The writer applies the maxim to a rhetorical situation in which the readers do not share the same background of the writer and thus miss the connection that the writer is trying to make. As we can see, the student author is striving for objective academic prose: the use of "one's," the hypercorrect use of an apostrophe where none is needed, etc. However, the student shifts to a personal point of view in the statement: "opinions are like birthdays everybody's got one." This usage is not usually readily comprehensible to non-AAVE-oriented speakers. In the AAVE communities, phrases similar to this are used when a speaker is talking about a subject about which she does not have straight all of the information or facts. As the writer has pointed out, "writing is supposed to hold one's interest, entertain, or persuade someone to believe what you are saying is true." In AAVE contexts, a speaker may be questioned by a listener for talking about a subject without having all the facts; he may be told to keep his opinions to himself. Hence, "opinions are like _____ holes, everybody's got one." We see, in the text, the student shifting between AAVE and academic styles. The student is hoping that the audience will infer the connection between this contextual formula in the AAVE community and the present writing situation. The student knows that the absence of fact and uninteresting use of language or ideas in writing results in uniformed opinions or uninteresting writing, but demonstrates this indirectly. She applies an AAVE form of *signifying* to a rhetorical context in which it is not expected, giving her AAVE-oriented perspective.

Paper III

Like John Milton said, "much arguing and much writing" lead to learning. But opinion is not good unless it is held by a good man.

I agree with Milton because if a man is not willing to argue and write about something he believes in, then he obviously does not know enough about it. Or, if he does know about it, his argument is so weak or evil that no one will be persuaded to his beliefs.

A good man will take the time to explain his beliefs; but a bad man will try to rush through explanations so he can trick someone. It's just like one time a Jehovah's Witness came to our house. This lady was trying to gather her following by putting other religions down. My mother told her what our family believed in and was trying to show her in the Bible the reasons for our beliefs. Instead of the Jehovah's Witness lady doing the same as my mother, she was talking fast like a travelling sales man. She never took the time to write down or explain their beliefs carefully. As far as I'm concerned, if you can't show me something in black and white, you can keep it!

A Conventional Evaluation and Assessment of Paper III

The introductory statement gives us an idea of the writer's stance: good men hold good opinions. In the second paragraph, the student is still in the objective/academic mode, even though there is the use of "I." The final paragraph concretizes the writer's abstraction, "a good man will take time to explain…"; "a bad man will try to rush…" with the story. This final paragraph tells the story about the family's encounter with the Jehovah's Witness and ends with an aphorism. The last sentence serves as commentary on the story about the Jehovah's Witness and on the writer's understanding of the Milton quote.

If one follows typical composition text criteria, this paper would be generally graded somewhere between 3 and 1, especially because the writer's tone is informal, although the writing adheres to grammatical conventions of LWC. In my AAVE discourse study, this paper received two 3's, three 2's, and four 1's.

The AAVE discourse paradigm shows that Paper III employs *narrative sequencing* and *testifying*. Smitherman's definition of narrative sequencing appears helpful here:

> The story element is so strong in black communicative dynamics that it pervades general everyday conversation. An ordinary inquiry is likely to elicit an extended narrative response where the abstract point or general message will be couched in concrete story form. . . . The Black English speaker thus simultaneously conveys the facts and his or her personal sociopsychological perspective on the facts. (*Talkin' and Testifyin'* 161)

In this particular student's interpretation of the Milton quote, there is a shift to narrative to carry the main point. The narrative occurs in the student author's discursive reenactment of the family's encounter with the Jehovah's Witness. Also, the student's interpretation is filtered through values of black culture. So, we can see this narrative as a form of *testifying*. Again, we must turn to Smitherman:

> To testify is to tell the truth through "story." In the sacred context, the subject of testifying includes such matters as visions, prophetic experiences, the experience of being saved, and testimony to the power and goodness of God. (*Talkin' and Testifyin'* 150)

In this case, the testifying is sacred because the writer refers to religious training. In other words, the writer anticipates that the reader has a reverence for pious writers. As readers, we should (from the writer's perspective) respect the fact that the writer uses a religious story which demonstrates the writer's Biblical literacy and reliance on *The Word*.

According to traditional standards, Paper I earns the highest grade because it adheres more to standard rhetorical paradigms. The paper begins with the idea of relating the quote to cognitive development and then pursues that idea (although in a shallow way) throughout the text. After all, isn't that what an essay is supposed to do? One meaning of the term "essay" as defined in the compact *OED* is

> A composition of moderate length on any particular subject; originally implying want of finish, "an irregular undigested piece" (J), but now said of a composition more or less elaborate in style, though limited in range. (Burchfield 896)

The earlier part of this definition was adapted from Samuel Johnson's dictionary. It appears that Johnson was ahead of his time in that his definition more aptly describes the writing of students whose language use conflicts with the form now known as the academic essay. As the latter part of the definition notes, the academic essay is more "limited in range," as is Paper I. Jean Sanborn's definition of the academic essay describes that range:

> The academic essay is not a vehicle for exploring ideas and making knowledge; it is a vehicle for presenting formed ideas, a didactic, authoritative model rather than an interactive form. (143)

Recent studies in sociolinguistics and composition point to the constraints that the academic essay places on AAVE-speaking students (Troutman-Robinson; Redd; Richardson, "Where Did That Come From?"; Ball).

This is not meant to say that AAVE students are not capable of constructing a piece of writing that contains introduction, identifiable thesis, body paragraphs, and conclusion; rather, AAVE students may use language in ways that are not acknowledged by writing instructors as valid ways of demonstrating knowledge. More often than not, both the students and the teachers are unaware of AAVE rhetorical patterns in the writing. Usually, when such devices are used, essays are referred to as unconventional at best, or worse. The rhetorical patterns and ideological stances these patterns express in terms of their employment in AAVE-oriented students' texts deserve fuller exploration.

Throughout kindergarten through college schooling, students are increasingly evaluated by their adherence to academic discourse. They are expected to know the conventions, and if they don't, they are treated as remedial students, as though something is wrong with them (Rose). That just simply is not a good place to start. In fact, Smitherman says, in her retrospective on "Students' Right to Their Own Language," that

> In spite of recently reported gains in Black student writing,
> chronicled by the NAEP and higher scores on the SAT, the rate
> of functional illiteracy and drop-outs among America's under-
> class is moving faster than the Concorde. A genuine recognition
> of [AAVE] students' culture and language is desperately needed
> if we as a profession are to play some part in stemming this
> national trend. (25)

Writing teachers, of African American or any other descent, may
not realize that students are operating within the realm of the AAVE
oral tradition. Elsewhere, following Bakhtin, I have argued for the
need to recognize form and content as one, because discourse is a living social phenomenon that is shaped by the context from which it
occurs (Richardson, "Where Did That Come From?"). Unfamiliarity
with the social aspect of language perpetuates narrowly informed
interpretation and assessment of AAVE-oriented writing that comes
off as flat.

We must develop ways of incorporating the students' cultural
literacy experiences with those needed to enhance their futures and to
succeed in a society where only one kind of literacy is valued. Composition experts are beginning to work out transcultural (Gilyard), multicultural (Miller), and Afrocentric/multicultural (Evans) writing classrooms.

Grading should not be used punitively against AAVE writers.
Clearly, the papers presented here which reveal the AAVE perspective
evince substance and ideas that the students related to their interpretation of Milton. Yet, when the ideas and the experience that those ideas
represent are unfamiliar or not within the instructors' experiential
base, they are not well received.

One way in which to bridge this cultural gap may be to describe
the ways in which students are using language in their texts. What I
believe we should do is to allow students to explore and experiment
with the AAVE oral tradition to expand the student's repertoire of
available styles. I am now experimenting with AAVE discourse and
rhetoric in my course. One example of what we are doing is analyzing
writings published in magazines written for the African American hip
hop audience. We talk about the shared assumptions and backgrounds
that these writers expect of their hip hop-age audience. Students are
writing letters to these magazines and then rewriting the letters to the
local newspapers and other publishing outlets. The course is based in
theories of bidialectalism. We talk about the power of expressing ideas
in black language, and we experiment with ways of trying to retain the

black voice and make our prose accessible to non-AAVE members. Instructors must come to recognize and acknowledge the AAVE styles as extensions of students' cultural orientation, if in fact such is the case. Exploration of diverse linguistic orientations and how these influence textual creation provides an additional method of scaffolding students to academic styles in a way that does not lock us into evaluating (AAVE) students' cultures. Curricula must be conceived in such a way that students are trained to discern, appreciate, and master diverse styles. Students can be black and write, and black and right. Thinking along these lines may enable us to halt the perpetuation of the violence of standard literacy practices.

Works Cited

Balester, Valerie M. *Cultural Divide: A Study of African-American College-Level Writers.* Portsmouth: Boynton/Cook, 1993.

Ball, Arnetha. "Cultural Preference and the Expository Writing of African-American Adolescents." *Written Communication* 9.4 (Oct. 1992): 501–32.

Burchfield, R. W., ed. *The Compact Edition of the Oxford English Dictionary.* Clarendon: Oxford UP, 1987.

Campbell, Kermit. *The Rhetoric of Black English Vernacular: A Study of the Oral and Written Discourse Practices of African American Male College Students.* Diss. Ohio State U, 1993.

Dillard, J. L. *Black English: Its History and Usage in the United States.* New York: Random, 1972.

Evans, Henry. "An Afrocentric Multicultural Writing Project." *Writing in Multicultural Settings.* Ed. C. Severino, J. Guerra, and J. Butler. New York: MLA, forthcoming.

Gates, Henry Louis, Jr. *The Signifying Monkey.* New York: Oxford UP, 1988.

Gilyard, Keith. "Cross-talk: Toward Transcultural Writing Classrooms." *Writing in Multicultural Settings.* Ed. C. Severino, J. Guerra, and J. Butler. New York: MLA, forthcoming.

Labov, William. *Language in the Inner City: Studies in the Black English Vernacular.* Philadelphia: U of Pennsylvania P, 1972.

Miller, Carol. "What Students of Color Can Tell Us about the Multicultural Composition Classroom." *Writing in Multicultural Settings.* Ed. C. Severino, J. Guerra, and J. Butler. New York: MLA, forthcoming.

Morgan, Marcyliena. "The Africanness of Counterlanguage among Afro-Americans." *Africanisms in Afro-American Language Varieties.* Ed. Salikoko S. Mufwene and Nancy Condon. Athens: U of Georgia P, 1993. 423–35.

Noonan Wagner, Delsey. *Possible Effects of Cultural Differences on the Rhetoric of Black Basic Skills Writers.* Thesis. U of Houston, 1981.

Redd, Teresa. "Untapped Resources: 'Styling' in Black Students' Writing for Black Audiences." *Composing Social Identity in Written Language.* Ed. Donald L. Rubin. Hillsdale: Erlbaum, 1995. 221–40.

Richardson, Elaine. "Paradigms and Pedagogy: Reading AAVE-Oriented Student Texts." Unpublished paper, 1993a.

———. "Where Did That Come From? Black Talk for Black Student Talking Texts." Thesis. Cleveland State U, 1993b.

Rose, Mike. *Lives on the Boundary: The Struggles and Achievements of America's Underprepared.* New York: Free Press, 1989.

Sanborn, Jean. "The Academic Essay and Voice." *Gender Issues in the Teaching of English.* Ed. Nancy Mellin McCracken and Bruce C. Appleby. Portsmouth: Boynton/Cook, 1992. 142–60.

Smitherman, Geneva. "'The Blacker the Berry, the Sweeter the Juice': African American Student Writers." *The Need for Story: Cultural Diversity in Classroom and Community.* Ed. Anne Haas Dyson and Cecelia Genishi. Urbana: NCTE, 1994. 80–101.

———. "Students' Right to Their Own Language: A Retrospective." *English Journal* 84.1 (Jan. 1995): 21–28.

———. *Talkin' and Testifyin': The Language of Black America.* Detroit: Wayne State UP, 1977.

———. Work-in-progress.

Troutman-Robinson, Denise. "Whose Voice Is It Anyway? Marked Features in the Writing of Speakers of Black English." *Writing in Multicultural Settings.* Ed. C. Severino, J. Guerra, and J. Butler. New York: MLA, forthcoming.

Visor, Julia. *The Impact of American Black English Oral Tradition Features on Decontextualization Skills in College Writing.* Diss. Illinois State U, 1987.

Interlude

It will take decades to break the back of our eigh-
teenth-century method of "marking papers." I was an
English chair for quite a while and was not very successful convincing anyone to stop using the terms
"grading and correcting and marking"—words loaded with
anything but positive connotations. Administrators
were suspicious, but frequently acquiesced and said to
use anything I wished, provided it could somehow be
wonderfully translated into the conventional rubric of
the moment for report cards. I simply tried to use the
phrase "reading essays," but students yearned for traditional numbers or letters since getting into the college of their choice used them and those colleges of
choice seemed to dictate what was done in high school.
It seemed we were always marking and grading for someone else: parents, administration, final GPA, college
admission. I tried in vain to convince even the best
students that the reward for writing was being read and
being taken seriously. They still wanted to know,
"Yeah, but what did I get?" I relied heavily on revision and rewriting. Once a piece of writing reaches the
point where nothing else can be changed, there is no
point to a grade or a mark.

—Harry Anderson
Long Island High School
New York

6 Alternative Assessment of Second-Language Writing: A Developmental Model

Janis Massa
Lehman College, CUNY

Janis Massa is a faculty member in the English department at Lehman College, City University of New York. She is an educational researcher and practitioner whose professional interests focus on second-language academic literacy development of Spanish speakers. Her research has been most influenced by Vygotskyan psycholinguistic theory and Freirian social theory, which view language development as socially situated. She is currently completing a book-length publication, Beyond Language: Teaching and Learning in an Urban Setting.

Introduction

The nationwide advent of open admissions in colleges has sparked new directions in composition research for skilled and unskilled speakers of English (see Bruner; Heath; Mayher; Perl; and Vygotsky, for the work of some of the most prominent theorists and practitioners who have succeeded in uncovering the multitudes of factors that influence the development of writing). Innovative research has extended to the writing development of nonnative English speakers as a result of the growing population of culturally and linguistically diverse learners in institutions of higher education, especially in large, urban centers such as New York City, Boston, and Los Angeles (see Cazden; Dulay, Burt, and Krashen; Edelsky; and Nelson, *At the Point of Need*, for some of the most pioneering work by second-language researchers).

Second-language writing assessment is undergoing rapid change as well. Standardized evaluation procedures that rely on rote recall or decontextualized multiple-choice items designed to measure recognition of lexical items have expanded to encompass assessment of rhetorical components of writing, including topic at hand, clear sequencing of ideas, appropriate paragraphing, and consistent point of view (Cohen; Conners). One of two widely used assessment tools is the "six-point scale" designed to evaluate the writer's control over language and organization. Essays that contain evidence of a pattern of development and a command of syntax are awarded the maximum six points. A score of five is allotted to essays written in clear language contained in grammatically correct sentences. Essays that show evidence of basic logical structure with only occasional digression in sentences containing correct grammatical inflection are given a score of four on the six-point scale. A score of three is assigned to essays that show no overall pattern of organization, written in language that reveals recurring grammatical problems. Two points are assigned to essays in which the response to the test prompt is not developed and in which conversational language is used, with errors in grammar, punctuation, and spelling. And essays that are incoherent and unorganized and contain sentences with lapses in punctuation, spelling, and grammar receive one point for effort (City University of New York, *CUNY Writing Skills Assessment Test*).

The second widely used assessment tool designed to diverge from evaluation of rote recall is the more detailed "composition profile," which dissects the essay into five categories: content, organization, vocabulary, language use, and mechanics. Such guides, created to assess impromptu essays written on teacher-chosen themes, are used by more than 70 percent of colleges (see Sandra Murphy et al. in White, "An Apologia"). The six-point scale and the composition profile provide a breakthrough in the assessment of first- and second-language writing by establishing guidelines that look beyond factual recall. An advantage of these assessment tools is their effectiveness in broad screening decisions.

Such evaluation scales, however, are not without their limitations. One drawback is that they obscure variability among learners. Essays written by two different learners, each with his or her own distinct abilities and needs, may receive the same grade due to the arbitrary nature and broad range of the criteria, which are open to interpretation by individual readers from paper to paper (Nelson, "Reading Classrooms as a Text"). A score of three on a six-point scale may be assigned to essays on the basis of any one of a number of lexical, syntactic, or rhetorical criteria. Peter Elbow has concluded that such scores do little more than provide "agreement about a faint, smudged, and distorted picture of the student's writing ability" (see White, "An Apologia" 30). A second drawback is that product evaluation, which is based on the categories outlined in the scales mentioned above, ignores the cognitive and linguistic development made by learners as they devise strategies to complete the writing task.

Fortunately, the foci of writing assessment are beginning to expand. I will present a developmental model that redefines writing assessment by targeting the strengths students develop as they struggle to reach their potential as academic writers. In the approach I use, tasks are designed to provide opportunities for learning, not solely for displaying knowledge. Teacher feedback is designed to encourage, not punish. The purpose of this essay is to present an alternative model-in-progress for developmental writing assessment.

I will describe an assignment given to low-intermediate ESL students enrolled in a public college in the Bronx, New York, and present a detailed assessment of the strategies devised by a second-language learner as she struggles to make meaning of a poem and respond to it in writing. Classroom instruction will be linked to outcomes of the developmental assessment.

Meaningful Assessment Tasks

The developmental writing assessment model described here is grounded in two underlying premises drawn from the work of Vygotsky (*Mind in Society*) and Bruner (*Acts of Meaning*). First, writing ability develops in response to the productive use of language, not "fill in the blank" recognition tasks. Short-answer questions related to reading passages result in truncated responses that obscure strategies used by the learner. The number of right answers is quantified, and the final score is presumed to be an indicator of achievement. In contrast, developmental writing assessment tasks, such as the one described here, elicit interpretation of ideas and analysis of information, intrinsic to academic composing, reasoning, and learning (Langer). According to the model, it is the strategies devised to carry out a task—not the quantifiable components in the evaluation scales listed above—that indicate academic achievement. The second underlying premise argues that cognitive and linguistic development are linked to the self-confidence needed to formulate interpretations, make statements, and derive conclusions. Developmental assessment tasks are designed to be carried out in an environment in which student writers gain the needed confidence, along with a feeling of safety from ridicule due to academic "deficits."

A Significant Classroom Event

At the center of the lesson focused on here is a poem written by Julia de Burgos, the renowned Puerto Rican poet, who recounts her rise from her denigrated role in society. The poem, like subsequent materials used during the semester, is selected on the basis of the opportunity it provides for students to interpret and express their ideas in writing. I distribute a copy of the poet's most famous work, "A Julia de Burgos" ["To Julia de Burgos"], and ask for a volunteer to read the poem in the original Spanish, using clear pronunciation. Reading the poem in Spanish serves a number of purposes. One is to bring the knowledge base, background, skills, and strengths of the learners into the higher education classroom, a setting in which some Caribbean-born, Spanish-speaking incoming freshmen feel alienated. Next, readers are more likely to comprehend the nuances of poetry written in their native language than in translation. The Spanish language provides a familiar link to the genre and to references contained in the poem, both of which are new to some of the students. Alternative assessment tasks are grounded in such links. I encourage non-Spanish speakers to listen to the "music" of the poem read in the original, a concept appreciated by all learners who function in two languages.

A student eagerly walks to the front of the room and reads the poem in Spanish. When he is finished reading, the class applauds vigorously. I ask for a volunteer to read the English translation; once again I remind the class of the importance of clear pronunciation and clear writing in order to communicate ideas in English. Reading and hearing the work read a second time reinforces comprehension. Hearing the poem in the original Spanish, followed by the English translation, turns the ESL classroom into a place in which the native language is merged in the target language setting. This is a unique experience for the majority of the students, who live, work, and socialize in communities in which Spanish, their native language, is spoken exclusively.

A second student, Elena,[1] volunteers to read the English translation. Somewhat reluctant to stand in front of the room, she stands up next to her chair and reads, dramatically, the English translation. The integrity of de Burgos's decision to discard her outer, social self in order to preserve her inner, private self is reflected in Elena's voice. When she completes her recitation, the class applauds.

I ask the students to reflect on their impressions of the poem in writing. The task serves dual purposes. First, it requires the learners to explore and formulate their ideas. Second, reading and then responding to the poem introduces the concept of expressing the thought process in writing. The assignment is the first of its kind for many students whose voices have been harnessed into the limited spaces of worksheets that contain no space for original thought.

A Developmental Assessment of a Written Response

Sandra writes the following in response to the poem:

> This poem was not common to my senses because I have never read one like this before. Also, when I started reading it I thought somebody was reciting a poem to this lady.
>
> I must not be using the right words, but I think this is a poem which have a lot of religion involved. She talked to her negative part: or ego, then expressed her essence or conscience feeling and finally made a contrast of the two different parts.
>
> In Conclusion this poem was an instruction that shows us the good & bad parts of our insides.

The appearance of Sandra's paper is deceiving (see the original, Figure 1). Becker warns against the dangers of graphocentrism—our preconceived notions of what the paper should look like, adhered to while holding on to our paradigms of modes of analysis or our preconceived notions of what it should read like—when evaluating our students' work. Using simplistic words and inconsistent penmanship, the learner's response to the assignment reflects an initial state of confusion, resulting from her lack of exposure to the genre, to interpreting literature, and to expressing her opinion. When asked about her prior experience, Sandra does not recall ever having written an essay or having read an entire book, from the time she arrived in the U.S. and entered junior high school, followed by enrollment in high school in the Bronx. She remembers filling in handouts designed to test recognition of grammatical structures and learning how to format business letters in her language arts classes.

Sandra's response represents a contrast from her earlier work in the ESL class. What appears to be a breakdown in the control of language is actually an indication of the student risking courageously a break with the five-paragraph essay form from which she has not been able to deviate up to this point—an important advancement. Walsh observes that "teachers who do not know these meanings usually find the response of the pupil baffling, annoying and exasperating" (81).

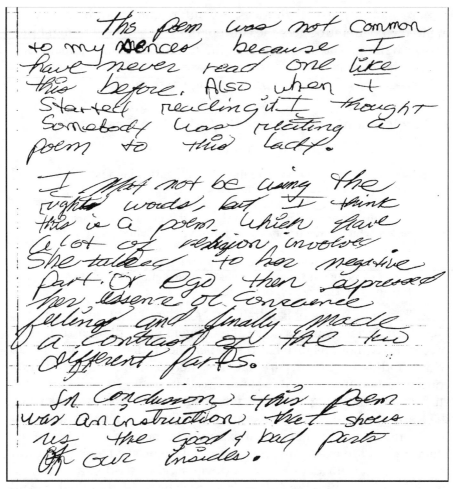

Figure 1. Sandra's response to the poem "To Julia de Burgos."

The opening sentence—"This poem was not common to my senses because I have never read one like this before"—reveals the learner's lack of familiarity with the genre and with the process of interpreting literature. Sandra's struggle for clarity and control over her initial state of confusion continues into the next sentence: "Also, when I started reading it I thought somebody was reciting a poem to this lady." Such states of confusion provide optimal moments for inexperienced writers to develop language skills and achieve intellectual growth (Mayher). Cognitive development occurs as the writer moves from unfamiliar patterns of interpretive thought to new patterns that help her make sense of the task (Erickson). Both teacher and student need to recognize Sandra's successful attempts to devise a strategy to transform her sense of chaos into order. In the sentence that follows— "I must not be using the right words, but I think this is a poem which have a lot of religion involved"—the student anchors herself to a recognizable reference, i.e., religion, which appears at the end of the poem, while she continues to grope for meaning. The next sentence— "She talked to her negative part: or ego, then expressed her essence or conscience feeling and finally made a contrast of the two different parts"—is written with a greater sense of self-confidence. Sandra recognizes the conflict between two aspects of the self that appear in the poem: the unconscious, spontaneous inner self and the negative, and calculated, outer self.

A breakthrough occurs in the final sentence as the learner places herself in a position of equal footing with the "expert" poet and is able to synthesize the thoughts of the poet with her own. She writes: "In Conclusion this poem was an instruction that shows us the good & bad parts of our insides." This is a clear manifestation of Sandra's triumph over her sense of confusion and an indication of her ability to recognize and generalize the message contained in the poem. Sandra's final sentence indicates her control of the writing task.

Teacher Feedback

A grammatical or rhetorical assessment of Sandra's response paper which does not acknowledge the successful, albeit awkward, demonstration of beginning fluency in academic language and thought is an abortive assessment. Rather than elicit answers to informational questions about the poem, my role as teacher is to create a setting in which students feel confident to formulate their own views and state them in writing. Additionally, it is my role to acknowledge and reinforce indications of development that appear in the student's work. This is accomplished by writing comments in the margin and by reading the student's paper aloud to the class, while collectively pointing out its strengths. Mayher points to the advantages of reading students' papers aloud to the class, including the motivating effect on the writer and the other students.

I distribute a copy of Sandra's paper to each student. The class takes some time to read it. In order to place the focus on development rather than error hunting, I note the consistent movement from personal to abstract thought, an ability prized in higher education. I also point to the student's achievement as she pursues the tasks of interpreting and analyzing the poem, she having no prior experience at either. My goal is to dissect and, thus, demystify the task at hand, while at the same time discovering the strengths and needs of the learners in order to integrate both into the classroom curriculum (Nelson, *At the Point of Need*). I wish to convey the message that this and other such tasks are, indeed, within the reach of all, including those students, who, like Sandra, may never have encountered a literature-based writing task before. Sandra's facial expression reveals a sense of pride at having her work singled out and taken seriously, perhaps for the first time.

A Follow-up Assignment

Reflecting on literature provides an optimal moment for the students to pose and resolve relevant questions (see Henry Giroux's comments in Freire and Macedo 78–79; Rigg and Kasemek). A follow-up task asks the students to identify themes contained in the poem and to design corresponding questions to be used as essay prompts. The two follow-up tasks, along with the tasks of reading and responding in writing, form a continuum of poem-related activities and thus have no determined beginning or end that can be evaluated. The goal of the follow-up tasks is to encourage the students to discover universal issues found in the autobiographical poem that may apply to their lives as well.

I ask the class to break up into small groups. Some students lack confidence in their ability to abstract knowledge or contribute their insights to a small group. Both skills have been circumvented in their prior educational experience by informational questions requiring rote-recall transfer of facts onto worksheets. More important than intervening, my role at this point is to maintain a nonthreatening setting which the students can work in and eventually feel safe enough to contribute to. Some students listen silently as they carefully observe others model strategies used to respond to the academic task. Each group of students chooses one or two larger issues from their list. I write the suggestions on the board. The final list of student-generated themes elicited from the poem contains the following:

- hypocrisy/honesty
- materialism/spiritualism
- dependency/independence
- repression/liberation
- male/female roles

From the list on the chalkboard, the students vote for two sets of concerns that they find most pertinent. They choose "materialism/spiritualism" and "male/female roles." We then formulate the following questions to address in essay form:

1. Some people think that it is better to be rich in material things instead of rich in the love and concern for friends and family. Do you agree or disagree? Explain your answer.

2. Relationships, in which the male dominates and the female is passive, result in harmony since the roles of the man and the woman are clearly defined. Do you agree or disagree? Explain your answer.

After that, we pause for a moment to reflect on the significance of the work completed thus far. The ability to recognize universal themes and formulate questions that lend themselves to examining the human condition must not go unnoticed. Nor do I pass up the opportunity to demystify the wide variety of tasks accomplished by Sandra, which cannot be quantified but need to be acknowledged. I begin by pointing to the risk that Sandra took by moving from her concern with the formulaic five-paragraph essay to a concern with reflecting on her impressions of the poem in writing. She reorganized her initial insights while at the same time moving from personal to abstract thought. She ends by connecting the issues found in the literature to issues found in her personal life—and accomplishes all of this in English.

For their exam, the students choose one of the questions to write about in essay form. Creating their own examination provides an opportunity for them to contribute meaningfully to the curriculum. Additionally, student-created exams are intended to reverse the intimidating and sometimes punitive association with assessment. Finally, the assignment provides an initial opportunity for some students to identify and solve existential problems in writing.

The class is encouraged from the success of Sandra's essay and from the modeling by participants in the smaller groups. Sandra's paper, including imperfections, was read with seriousness and respect. It received positive feedback from the students and from me, which is important to other inexperienced students who are unsure of their ability to complete analytic reading/writing tasks. The students use the remaining hour to write an essay on one of the two questions. I wish them luck.

Alternative Assessment and Traditional Grading

Once the students have completed their essays, I assess those and all subsequent written work throughout the semester in the manner described on Sandra's response paper, above. I look for indications of movement from each student's starting point toward his or her potential, the area which Vygotsky terms

> the zone of proximal development, [or] the distance between the actual development level as determined by independent problem solving and the level of potential development as determined through problem solving under adult guidance or in collaboration with more capable peers. (*Mind in Society* 86)

Rather than artificially quantify development or reduce the multiple revisions of an essay to a single grade, I note indications of growth on the essay exam. Instead of pointing to specific grammatical errors, I place parentheses around segments of writing and label them "unclear." By doing so, the students are left to explore and discover their options as writers, independently, and to rewrite the segment clearly.

I compare each student's writing progress to prior final drafts of a limited number of essays written throughout the semester. My comments are instructional and related to the development apparent in the work submitted. Thus, I reinforce the concept of writing development as evolving. The students are given credit for completion of the assignment once the final draft is handed in. With no numerical or letter grade at risk, communication of ideas becomes the goal of the students, who are left to find their own ways of reaching clarity. Some students choose to work in collaboration with others in groups, some work in pairs, while others work alone on draft after draft and approach me or another student only when they reach an impasse.

The class is given a midterm and a final exam in the form of an essay question based on an article or the literature read. The midterm essay is assigned a "pass" or "no pass" grade by an outside teacher who reads the essay impressionistically for evidence of control of the language and a logical response to the question. A second grade of "pass" or "no pass" is assigned by me. The graded midterm is returned to the student and is treated like any other first draft of a work-in-progress to be revised, with the exception of the added outside input. The grades are intended to be instructional and to be used as a benchmark for informing the student of the progress made up to the midpoint of the semester. Equally, the grades inform me of students' needs to be addressed in the curriculum. A revised draft of the midterm exam is handed in to me for credit, consistent with all prior assignments. The final exam is given during the last class, with no opportunity for revision. The final essay culminates the development made throughout the semester. The letter grade for the course is determined by the student's ability to answer the essay question thoroughly, using clearly written English.

Implications for Classroom Instruction

There is a need to redefine the objectives of writing assessment, moving it from a punitive, gatekeeping tool that measures deficits, to a facilitative tool that informs novice academic writers of the characteristics of clear expression of thought, informs teachers of students' potential, and informs the classroom curriculum. The definition of writing development needs to be extended from the indication of increasing proficiency in editing mechanical errors to the increasing ability to successfully complete a wide variety of tasks. An alternative assessment model transcends quantified evaluation. The ultimate goal of the developmental writing assessment model presented here is to prepare students to meet the rigors of academic language and thought. It is accomplished by designing tasks that foster written solutions to abstract problems.

The movement from personal to abstract levels of thought promoted in this assignment is seen in Sandra's response. She begins: "This poem was not common to my senses because I have never read one like this before. Also, when I started reading it I thought somebody was reciting a poem to this lady." A transformation occurs as the learner broadens, reorganizes, and finally assimilates her insights with those of the poet. Sandra ends her paper thus: "In Conclusion, this poem was an instruction that shows us the good & bad parts of our insides." She progresses from her own starting point, as an inexperienced writer, and uses writing to reflect on her impressions. The assignment requires students to devise strategies with which to understand the ideas in the poem, formulate their own opinions, and express their ideas in writing.

Writing assessment models that evaluate surface errors in response to teacher-chosen topics may provide useful information about mastery of lexical, syntactic, and rhetorical features of second-language writing. Such assessment procedures, however, conceal thought processes and patterns of development that may provide the teacher with a rich database for assessing educational progress, strengths, and needs. The ability of Sandra and her classmates to control the initial writing task signals the next phase of instruction—in this case, the complex follow-up tasks of identifying universal themes and integrating them into a writing test prompt.

Subsequent classroom research in the form of longitudinal observation of language interaction is needed. Such observation will permit teacher-researchers to document and assess how students develop from the abilities with which they enter the classroom to reaching their potential. The model presented in this essay is a more reliable indicator of the development of academic language and thought, while at the same time serving a facilitative function, not a gatekeeping one.

Note

1. All names included in this essay are pseudonyms.

Works Cited

Becker, Alton L. "Literacy and Cultural Change: Some Experiences." *Literacy for Life: The Demand for Reading and Writing.* Ed. Richard W. Bailey and Robin Melanie Foshiem. New York: MLA, 1983. 45–51.

Bruner, Jerome S. *Acts of Meaning.* Cambridge: Harvard UP, 1990.

———. *Actual Minds, Possible Worlds.* Cambridge: Harvard UP, 1986.

Burgos, Julia de. "To Julia de Burgos." Trans. Carmen D. Lucca. Trans. of "A Julia de Burgos." *Rosas en el Espejo [Roses in the Mirror].* Ed. Carmen D. Lucca. San Juan: Ediciones Mairena, 1992. 23–24.

Cazden, Courtney B. "Language, Cognition, and ESL Literacy: Vygotsky and Literacy Teaching." *TESOL Quarterly* 28 (1994): 172–81.

City University of New York, Freshman Skills Assessment Program. *The CUNY Writing Skills Assessment Test: Student Essays Evaluated and Annotated By the CUNY Task Force on Writing.* 2nd ed. New York: CUNY, 1983.

Cohen, Andrew. "Reformulating Compositions." *TESOL Newsletter* 17 (Dec. 1983): 4–5.

Connors, Robert J. "Mechanical Correctness as a Focus in Composition Instruction." *College Composition and Communication* 36 (1985): 61–72.

Dulay, Heidi, Marina Burt, and Stephen Krashen. *Language Two.* New York: Oxford UP, 1992.

Edelsky, Carole. *Writing in a Bilingual Program: Había Una Vez.* Norwood: Ablex, 1986.

Erickson, Frederick. "Transformation and School Success: The Politics and Culture of Educational Achievement." *Anthropology and Education Quarterly* 18 (1987): 335–56.

Freire, Paulo, and Donaldo Macedo. *Literacy: Reading the Word and the World.* South Hadley: Bergin & Garvey, 1987.

Heath, Shirley Brice. *Ways with Words: Language, Life, and Work in Communities and Classrooms.* New York: Cambridge UP, 1983.

Langer, Suzanne. "Facilitating Text Processing: The Elaboration of Prior Knowledge." *Reading Research Quarterly* 4 (1984): 149–62.

Mayher, John S. *Uncommon Sense: Theoretical Practice in Language Education.* Portsmouth: Boynton/Cook, 1990.

Nelson, Jenny. "Reading Classrooms as a Text: Exploring Student Writers' Interpretive Practices." *College Composition and Communication* 46 (1995): 411–29.

Nelson, Marie Wilson. *At the Point of Need: Teaching Basic and ESL Writers.* Portsmouth: Boynton/Cook, 1991.

Perl, Sondra. "The Composing Process of Unskilled College Writers." *Research in the Teaching of English* 13 (1979): 317–36.

———. "Composing Texts, Composing Lives." *Harvard Educational Review* 64 (1994): 427–49.

Rigg, Pat, and Francis E. Kasemek. "Adult Illiteracy in the USA: Problems and Solutions." *Convergence* 16 (1983): 24–30.

Vygotsky, L. S. *Mind in Society: The Development of Higher Psychological Processes.* Ed. Michael Cole, Vera John-Steiner, Sylvia Scribner, and Ellen Souberman. Cambridge: Harvard UP, 1978.

———. *Thought and Language.* Cambridge: MIT P, 1962.

Walsh, Catherine E. *Pedagogy and the Struggle for Voice: Issues of Language, Power, and Schooling for Puerto Ricans.* South Hadley: Bergin & Garvey, 1991.

White, Edward. "An Apologia for the Timed Impromptu Essay Test." *College Composition and Communication* 46 (1995): 30–45.

Interlude

In my freshman comp classes, I encourage a lot of expressive and nongraded writing. I also have my students write about literature in alternative—often "creative"—as well as analytical forms. In the hopes that it will encourage them to experiment with their writing, I don't put formal grades on anything they turn in. Instead, I comment in writing on their drafts, and I meet individually with every student at least once. My grades are based on a modified contract approach. When we're doing a sustained piece of writing (a unit essay), I run a process-centered workshop. If they show up to class prepared, participate in groups, and write with reasonable effort and skill, they can get no less than a 2.0–2.5 (in a 4.0 system) for the course. Just so they don't get too worried, I give them all a ballpark grade at the end of each unit. Most students who meet the minimum requirements of the contract have little trouble getting at least a 3.0. I reserve the right to give 3.5's and 4.0's on quality of effort, attitude, and initiative. Those who get the highest grades must show some genuine interest, potential, and skill.

> —Mike Steinberg
> Michigan State University

7 Scribliolink: Inviting Parents to Respond to Their Children's Writing

Joyce C. Fine
Florida International University

Joyce C. Fine is assistant professor at Florida International University, where she teaches reading, language arts, and children's literature.

Teachers traditionally give grades to tell parents about their children's academic progress. But in truth, little useful information is exchanged about the children's knowledge or performance capabilities. Assigning letter or numerical grades involves translating the context of the classroom into a solitary letter or number that, in the case of the developmental writing process, essentially fails to capture critical aspects of such a complex task. In this paper I will describe Scribliolink, a strategy that bring parents into the school to share in the writing process by freely responding to their children's written work. Parents become partners with schools in supporting children's growth academically and emotionally.

The idea of Scribliolink—to enhance the exchange of meaningful information between home and school—developed from my experiences as a tutor. When I shared students' written work with parents, the parents often gleaned more meaning from it than I could because they knew the related social situations. For instance, when I worked with a second grader who was having a great deal of difficulty learning to read, she wrote that only her "real" dad read. Her mother responded, "Joanna wrote that nobody in the family reads except her real dad because she's angry about having a new step dad." The mother's explanations added insight about family relationships, suggesting that Joanna's anger over her parents' divorce could be a factor in her "inability" to read. Because she could retell stories so well, I had suspected some intervening factor was influencing her poor reading performance. Without her mother's response, I would not have known that I needed to help Joanna change her self-concept from that of a helpless, dependent little girl, to someone who could read for herself. By reading stories such as *The Very Little Girl* by Phyllis Krasilovsky, which is about changes and growing up, and by allowing her to write her response, Joanna changed her self-concept. As she developed pride in being an independent reader and writer, she made substantial gains.

Situations such as Joanna's, in which a parent's remarks were critical for instructional decision making, occurred repeatedly. Each time, the collaboration gave insights that, although different, were nonetheless similar in that they guided problem solving which led to the student's academic growth. The process provided an effective link among students, parents, and teachers. Because of the pattern of these observations, I coined the term "Scribliolink."

As a teacher and educator, I worked with several schools, using Scribliolink's general procedures: (1) participants (parents and students) are informed about the process, and parents are invited to come to school at a later date for a conference; (2) teachers facilitate students' writing, using the developmental writing process in response to literature; and (3) parents, students, and teachers confer to support students.

In one private school, I worked with a population of sixth graders. Most of the students were bilingual, coming from Cuban and Nicaraguan backgrounds. The teacher had been in my undergraduate and graduate classes and welcomed me to come to her classroom to do the project.

We sent letters home requesting permission for students to participate and invited the parents to school. We explained the strategy to students, telling them that their parents were going to read and respond to their writing in a conference. The parents showed they were eager to participate. Many arranged to meet with us, even if it meant taking time off from work or finding a babysitter.

The developmental writing process was based on a personal response to literature. I read aloud *The Art Lesson* by Tomie dePaola, an autobiographical story about a strong character who knows he wants to be an artist from the time he is in elementary school. Students then responded by writing their own stories about their interests and goals. The stories were either futuristic biographies, stories about themselves from some future point in time, or about their career goals. I told the students to think about their interests and the related occupations they might pursue. The main point was that one's interests and experiences from early in life contribute to the occupation that person chooses as she or he grows and matures. What one did in the past, or does now, may have an influence on what that person later becomes. Most students pretended they were already working and expressed their experiences or interests that helped them select particular careers. An example from a child who wanted to be an entertainer focused on a local celebrity from a similar cultural background:

> This story is about a girl who wanted to become a singer ever since she was little. When she was little her inspiration was a very talented singer named Gloria Estefan.... Gloria Estefan is her idol because she is talented and was blessed with a very special gift and she is wise enough to use it.

A few had difficulty with the futuristic time frame and wrote from the present about their thoughts or concerns about particular careers. A typical career goal was to become an astronaut. This example shows the thinking of a student attempting to understand his own motivation in setting his future goal:

> When I grow up I would like to be an astronaut or an aerospace engineer. I would probably like to be an engineer because my parents are architects, and I like to draw with their rulers. As for being an astronaut I do not know why I would like to be that, it cannot be that I was watching a shuttle lift off because the first one I watched exploded.

The interview questions were open-ended, asking parents for their opinions, perspectives, concerns, feelings, and sources of support. The teacher recorded the parents' responses and discussed ideas or concerns that parents wished to comment on from the writing. She recorded responses both by hand and with a tape recorder, with the parents' permission. Writing responses by hand intentionally slowed the pace of recording and responding, allowing waiting time for parents to think through their thoughts (see Figure 1).

In typical conferences, the teacher gave suggestions for guiding parents. The parent of the Gloria Estefan fan said her daughter always liked to entertain and noted with pride the cultural tie. We decided it would be beneficial to supply books about other Hispanic leaders from a variety of careers. The parent of the student who wrote about the exploding space shuttle Challenger realized how images on television can affect children. I suggested that she try to get her sensitive son to talk with family members about his feelings after viewing television or movies.

Scribliolink

Interview the parent or guardian using the following questions:

1. What is your first reaction to the writing?
2. What do you see as the most important theme or idea?
3. Is this consistent with what you know about this child?
4. How would you rate the intensity of feeling in the writing from 1 to 5, with 1 being mild, to 5 being intense?
5. Can you read meaning into this to get any special message?
6. Are there any feelings expressed that give you concern?
7. (If yes) what suggestions do you have regarding this concern?
8. Where could you seek guidance?
9. Do you feel you talk openly with your child?
10. Do you feel there are others in the family with whom your child talks openly?
11. What action could you take at this point?
12. What other thoughts do you have?

Figure 1. Scribliolink parent questionnaire.

Generally, students wrote about situations from their own lives that had left impressions on them, such as the boy's haunting memory of the Challenger explosion. One student wrote about seeing an accident in which paramedics removed a pregnant lady from a car with the "jaws of life" wrecking equipment. Since witnessing the accident, the boy had decided to become a doctor.

Parents understood their own child's words with a unique perspective because they brought prior knowledge of their child, or the situations, to the text. The parent of the student mentioned above said how worried the child had been after witnessing the accident and how she had to call the hospital to see how the woman was. Her son had stopped being so concerned when he heard that the woman was fine and that she had delivered a healthy baby at the hospital. The parent also said she was not surprised that her child wanted to become a doctor: "I'm happy to know that he has the principal ideas of accomplishing these goals, getting good grades and scholarships to get into a science college."

Another child had written that he wanted to be president of the United States. His parent spoke emotionally of how, as a child, her family had been waiting a very long time in Cuba for permission to emigrate to the United States. She revealed that as an adult, she had an American flag hanging in her bedroom for her to see when she opened her eyes, in case she had a nightmare about her childhood. In their home, they often talked passionately about how grateful they were to be in the United States. Evidently, the child had a very strong sense of patriotism for his family's adopted country and wanted to become the highest elected official. In each interview, the parents' insights gave direction for making decisions about appropriate materials, methods, or the need for other support. This young man was eager to read American history and biographies of presidents, while the others engaged intently in reading about their current idols and heroes. Through writing and conducting the conferences, each student had examined his or her own values, goals, and self-concepts.

The school had a very traditional report card in which teachers gave letter grades. Instead of giving only a letter grade for writing, teachers assessed students on a rubric in three areas: meaning, structure, and language (see Table 1). They shared criteria with the students before the assessment and parent conferences. During the Scribliolink conference, the student and teacher explained each area to the parent. This gave the parent much more information about the child's performance. And yet, the 4 through 1 scale translated directly to A through D grades for report cards. Through the Scribliolink experience, students could verbalize what they needed to work on, an important metacognitive step in improving writing.

Table 1. Holistic Rubric for Student Writing

Score	Meaning (focus, support)	Structure (organization, flow)	Language (correct sentences, word choice)
4	The writing has one important idea or focus, with facts (details) to support it.	The ideas are clearly organized, with the ideas flowing.	The language is vivid, with correct sentences.
3	The writing has an important idea or focus, but gives few details to support it.	The writing is unclear in some parts, affecting the flow.	There are appropriate word choices and mostly correct sentences.
2	The writing has some ideas, but no clear focus and lacks details.	The writing is confused. The flow is not smooth.	Word choices are limited. There are many incorrect sentences.
1	The writing lacks a clear focus.	Ideas are unrelated and do not flow.	Word choices are inappropriate. There are errors in sentence structure.

Scribliolink was also introduced at an inner-city school in which all the students were either Hispanic or African American and qualified for free lunch. A group of ten students in one class participated. Three out of the ten parents came in for conferences. The teacher said this was one obstacle to the Scribliolink process which she overcame by letting the rest of the children take their papers home, along with the list of questions. All seven of the other parents wrote answers to the notes, responding to their children's writing. One mother's written responses were that "he believes in himself," that his writing "comes from his heart," and that his mother wants "him to be whatever he wants to be." The support was there for the student, and the parent still communicated with the school, though she could not come in for a conference. The teacher contacted each parent as a follow-up. She realized that the parents were "extremely interested in what their children wrote. The parents gained knowledge about their children on many aspects. The children also gained a sense of additional support from their parents." Even with this modification, Scribliolink provided a means for positive interaction and communication.

In another inner-city school that serves as a magnet school drawing from all socioeconomic backgrounds, one teacher used the response form for an open-house parent-teacher meeting. Parents read their child's work and responded to the attached questionnaires. Then they all participated in a group discussion of the grading rubrics. The teacher responded to the parents individually, maximizing the effect of their participation.

After working with a private school with a minority population, a public inner-city school with a minority population, and an inner-city magnet school, I realized that this alternative grading procedure changes and extends the teacher's role in the classroom. I believe that professionals need to experience processes themselves if they are going to be change agents. To this end, and to study Scribliolink further, I worked with graduate teachers at a predominately minority university who agreed to try the Scribliolink process themselves before working with their students. Using the process from the students' perspective helped teachers appreciate how difficult it may be for one to share his or her own writing with those who are close to us. The teachers listened to *Aunt Flossie's Hats (and Crab Cakes Later)* by Elizabeth Fitzgerald Howard and wrote stories about people who had influenced them to become literacy professionals. The teachers then had conferences with their own parents, their spouses, or a close friend. Their experiences with response to their own writing showed them the potential for this strategy. One student shared her deepened appreciation for her mother, who had been "an immigrant to a new country, getting adjusted to a new homeland, trying to make a living," and still finding time to read to her. She felt the process of Scribliolink allowed her to tell her mother "thank you" for all that she had done for her. Another teacher said that when her mother read what she had written, it sparked emotions she had never expected. Several of the teachers found that their spouses, siblings, or friends responded to what had been written as an effort to begin a dialogue on a topic. One teacher and her husband decided to take a more active role in getting their children interested in reading and writing. One of the teachers reflected, "Although there were no obvious expressed concerns or problems, the process allowed us to share and discuss things never mentioned before." This method, adding a step to the writing process, has much potential for opening avenues for writers and responders.

After seeing how Scribliolink worked in a variety of classroom settings with regular students and regular classroom teachers, I realized that some teachers might have reservations about using Scribliolink. For instance, some might fear that they would get into an area they weren't qualified to handle. Teachers might be working with children with complex, varying exceptionalities. To explore Scribliolink with this population, I worked with the school's family counselors. The variation one counselor used was to have each child write his or her story and make a book. The parents came to hear the children read their books at an "authors' tea." The children wrote books with titles such as "The Time I Felt Confused":

> I ran away from home because I got hit in the back by my mother for hurting people. I got hurt by my mother's boyfriend. He was a drinker. He beat my brother for the stupidest things. My brother didn't put his clothes away so he got beat and grounded.

Because the counselor also works with the students' families, she found that the parents were so impressed with the children's openness to their problems that the parents began to talk more openly about their situations. Several other school-affiliated family counselors who work with severely emotionally handicapped children found this technique a wonderful way for parents to interact positively with their children and their schools.

With regular education students, teachers' training in child development and in decision making is adequate. They may need to engage in problem solving to the point where the parent sees a course of action or to refer the parent to resources to further explore problems. Directing parents to places or people where the parent might seek guidance is well within the scope of a professional educator. If stories contain information about more serious situations, the writing should be shared with resource people in the school system.

Some teachers might say that the only parents who will come are those who already are caring and involved. Not coming to school does not mean that the parent doesn't care. The teacher may use some of the methods described above to modify the procedure, such as sending home the questionnaires. I found that some of the parents who had not responded to phone calls or invitations to come to school for other reasons did come in to discuss Scribliolink. When I first met one parent, I thought she had a problem speaking because of her lack of proficiency in English. However, when I offered her a translator, she said that that was not the problem. She had had a stroke and had not had the courage to speak with anyone except her immediate family or her doctors until that day. She said that since the teacher and I had been interested enough in her child to ask that she respond to her child's writing, she knew we would be patient enough to talk with her despite her handicap. Until Scribliolink was used, the school did not know about her stroke and did not know why she had not answered their phone calls or notes. Parents found out that coming to read their child's writing and having the individual attention of the teacher was not threatening. Indeed, it was very positive and showed a welcoming, accepting attitude.

Other teachers might feel that they have a special population for whom Scribliolink will not work. Perhaps their students are too young to write. However, Scribliolink still works with pictures and sentence dictation. Perhaps some teachers feel that their students' problems are too severe or complex for them to gain from this process. Sharing what students write is, at least, a beginning upon which to build. For many teachers, the problem of a different home language might interfere. Why not ask parents or teachers at the school who are proficient at translating if they will volunteer their services? We found this to be another positive aspect. This project is a way of connecting with those parents and helping them feel welcome.

Some teachers may feel that the time to do another project is just not available. The conference takes only about fifteen minutes and could be done once or twice a year. A form with the interview questions serves as the documentation from the parent session. Underlining or highlighting key words is all that a teacher needs to do to be able to refresh his or her memory about specifics from the conference.

Whatever reservations teachers have against adopting Scribliolink seem surmountable when considering the benefits to all those involved. The interactions Scribliolink provides give much more information to aid parents and teachers in making decisions about directing learning experiences in support of students' literacy development. Parents see and respond to their child's actual work (instead of getting just a meaningless grade), are introduced to the writing process, and enjoy being recognized by the school as a valued resource for their child. Students gain from the attention and support they receive from this combined audience, empowering them with a sense of ownership and an awareness of their writing voice. This alternative to grading is well worth the effort.

Scribliolink not only serves to communicate students' progress as an alternative to grading, the conference also serves to link the social context to directly enhance literacy growth.

As with ethnographic research, Scribliotherapy evolved from one-on-one tutoring observations. These observations suggested that a conferencing procedure which includes an open-ended survey be added to the writing process as an alternative to simply putting a letter grade or a happy face on children's work. The benefits of the process expand upon a theoretical perspective proposed by Grover Mathewson.

In "Model of Attitude Influence on Reading and Learning to Read," Grover Mathewson explains attitude as a major influence on one's intention to read. He calls the factors that influence attitude "cornerstone concepts": values, goals, and self-concepts. These are built over years, beginning in infancy during interaction with caregivers. The cornerstone concepts create attitudes which give rise to intentions to *read*.

Because reading is one aspect of literacy development and writing is the reciprocal process of reading, I theorize that these cornerstone concepts also impact students' intention to *write* and have therefore chosen to call the last box "literacy" in his graphic, rather than only reading (see Figure 2). I have also added a line for Scribliolink, running from the literacy box back to the cornerstone concepts, because it is a way to open dialogue on those concepts. After listening to parents responding to their children's thoughts and writing, teachers can facilitate meaningful exchanges. Involving parents in respond-

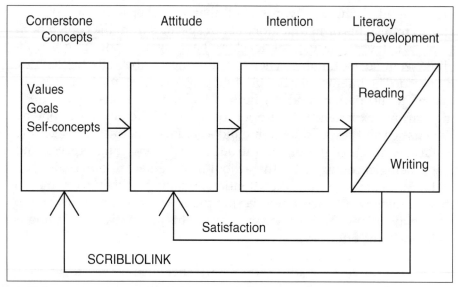

Figure 2. Model of attitude influence on literacy development showing the role of Scribliolink.

ing to their children's writing provides a critical link that influences students' literacy development.

Works Cited

dePaola, Tomie. *The Art Lesson*. New York: Trumpet Club, 1989.

Howard, Elizabeth Fitzgerald. *Aunt Flossie's Hats (and Crab Cakes Later)*. Illus. James Ransome. New York: Clarion, 1991.

Krasilovsky, Phyllis. *The Very Little Girl*. Illus. Karen Gundersheimer. New York: Scholastic, 1992.

Mathewson, Grover C. "Model of Attitude Influence on Reading and Learning to Read." *Theoretical Models and Processes of Reading*. Ed. Robert B. Ruddell, Margaret Rapp Ruddell, and Harry Singer. Newark: IRA, 1994. 1131–61.

III Classroom Strategies and Alternatives to Grading Student Writing

8 Student Attitudes toward Grades and Evaluation on Writing

Jean S. Ketter and Judith W. Hunter
Grinnell College

Jean S. Ketter was a high school English teacher for eleven years and is now assistant professor of education at Grinnell College. She has conducted research on portfolio assessment of writing and portfolio assessment in teacher education. She has published in English Education *and* Teaching Education.

   Judith W. Hunter was a high school teacher for five years and is a professional tutor in the Grinnell College Writing Lab. She consults with faculty about the teaching of writing and edits the Writing Forum, *the Grinnell College newsletter on the teaching of writing. She also serves on the Grinnell-Newburg Board of Education.*

The evaluations that I find most useful are those that are balanced: when a teacher points out the good along with the bad, it is much easier for me to work on improving my writing. Obviously, there may be times when a paper really does need major restructuring, but the task is made much easier when a little encouragement is given along the way.

> —Irene, a junior science major who has chosen to devote time to improving her writing

Those who teach don't always listen to students discuss how they feel about themselves as writers and how grades affect their view of themselves as such. When students at Grinnell College

We would like to thank the following students for filling out the questionnaire: Natalie Christensen, Alice Gates, Melissa Hess, Camille Johnson, Sonam Lama-Sherpa, Jennifer McCormick, Matt McKinney, Msawenkosi Nxumalo, Taimur Rahman, Amy Robinson, Sayaka Sawada, Helen Siefert, and Bryon Witzel. We would also like to thank the following students for filling out the questionnaire and for being interviewed: Eric Brue, Sarah Daney, Mike DeWaay, Masako Koyangi, Carmen Nunez, Rachel Phillips, and Sarah Slack. Additionally, we would like to thank Karin Connelly, Mathilda Liberman, Christopher Hunter, and Lisa Mulholland for their help with this project.

responded to a questionnaire asking them what kind of assessment they find useful, they indicated that they value discussion, revision, and collaboration with an evaluator:

> When the evaluator writes a little paragraph explaining why he/she did certain corrections and/or writes positive comments about the assignment. (Emily)

> Revision of papers. (Phil)

> Insights into why I did it one way and why it should be the other way. (Ned)

> I don't know. Maybe the best evaluation I have received is when someone goes through my writing and shows me their criticism. (Frank)

> When the teacher asks me questions to make me think about what I'm trying to say. (Tina)

> I really appreciate it when my instructor questions the ideas and problems sentence by sentence. This technique reveals a lot of assumptions I've made about the nature of the material I'm writing about, and also gets to the crux of the technical problems I have. (Georgia)

In these remarks, students show that they value the chance to revisit a paper and to talk with someone about their writing. None of these students mentioned grades as a useful tool for assessment.

As the authors of this essay, we define assessment as feedback intended to shape a student's performance to meet clearly established and expressed criteria. Thus we view assessment as communication, not as judgment, not as a method of sorting students. As does Nick Peim, we question the ethics of grading practices devised to sort students and to grant status to certain kinds of language on the basis of claims that universally understood criteria for good writing exist (188). As Grant Wiggins suggests in *Assessing Student Performance,* we believe that grades should result from clearly expressed criteria and standards which the student has knowledge of prior to writing; we believe that faculty should evaluate students according to how well they meet those criteria and standards on the basis of their abilities (168). Many teachers currently use grades to rank order students' writing performance in comparison with others'. We believe that teachers should consider whether grades are an effective means to encourage students' thinking or to communicate information students can use to improve their writing, that is, to alter it to meet better the evaluator's criteria. We assume that students, in order to improve, have to feel confident, have to feel as if they can succeed. Beginning with these assumptions and beliefs, we investigated how grades affected students' attitudes. The student voices we listened to reverberated with discouragement that resulted from evaluation that conveys only the presence of faults and the finality of judgment.

Our shared interests in how students learn to write spurred us to conduct research into the effects of grades. Jean's experience both as a high school English teacher and a college professor has convinced her that current grading practices are subjective, reifying, and ultimately unethical because they marginalize and sort students according to the too narrow parameters of performance. Judy's work in high school English and as a professional tutor in the Grinnell College Writing Lab has led her to believe that assigning a grade which compares one student with other students merely interferes with the individualized process of teaching students to write. Both researchers believe that eliminating grading altogether is a desirable goal, but one unlikely to be achieved.

We looked into student attitudes about writing and grades by administering a questionnaire to twenty-one students taking a one-credit course, "College Writing," in the college writing lab during the spring semester of 1995. From among those students, Jean interviewed seven volunteers, all of whom received comments on a number of papers, both from professional tutors in the college writing lab and from their professors; they were interviewed about their reactions to this feedback and to the grades they received from professors. By listening to the feelings they expressed in these interviews, we hoped to understand the complicated reactions students have toward assessment and grades.

The seven student volunteers agreed to two interviews with Jean, one in which they would bring a graded paper to discuss. They were a group likely to be interested in improving their writing because they were taking the nonrequired "College Writing" course. In their academic work at this very selective college, none of these students would be described as marginal or at-risk. However, their struggles with conquering the art of communicating in academic discourse marginalize them at our college and cause most of them to perceive themselves as unsuccessful writers. The group is highly diverse as to background, age, and experience with writing.

We do not claim that these students' perceptions give a complete picture of grading practices at Grinnell. Students' perceptions may be mistaken: Students may misinterpret what a professor says, or they may read into comments an attitude which the professor does not intend to communicate. Some of their views may be clouded by their negative reaction to the grade they received on the paper or may be influenced by the opportunity we offered in this study to speak out about the process of grading. Despite all of these possible difficulties with studying students' perceptions, we still maintain that it is important to look at them. We who teach need to know how our grading practices affect our students and how our students interpret the grades we give them.

At Grinnell College, the paper that students most often bring to the writing lab is what we will refer to as the "standard academic paper." Although writing assignments that differ from the standard academic essay are becoming more common at the college, the majority of assignments are still discipline-specific, thesis-driven articles. Evidence of the prevalence of the standard academic paper at Grinnell is found in an inventory of writing assignments taken during a recent semester. Such standard academic papers—including what individual professors refer to as analyses, synopses, grant proposals, term papers, and research papers—are by far the most common types assigned (Gross).

In this essay, we discuss student reactions to grades on the standard academic paper. We do not mean to communicate that this type of writing is more valuable than other modes of discourse or that it should be the dominant mode of writing assigned at college. We are aware of the current controversy among compositionists about the dominance of academic discourse. One view holds, like Bartholomae, that "academic writing is the real work of the academy" because "there is no better way to investigate the transmission of power, tradition, and authority than by asking students to do what academics do" (65–66). Another view asserts that in asking students on the margins to "mimic the discourse of the academy" while simultaneously critiquing it, we place these students in an untenable position (Hourigan 41). Judging from the preponderance of assignments at our college that call for academic writing, we conclude that our faculty believe that the structure of the standard academic paper can provide students with a useful tool for expressing sophisticated ideas. Although this belief may be problematic and in need of investigation, many at Grinnell currently hold this view. Perhaps faculty see themselves as responsible for preparing students to succeed in graduate school, since a high percentage of Grinnell students do go on to do graduate-level work. Whatever the reason, this emphasis on the academic paper at Grinnell has widespread effects. One effect is that the writing lab staff see it as their obligation to teach students how to write the academic essay because that is what the students are asking to learn and what they believe will bring them success at Grinnell. However, because many students (as the ones we interviewed demonstrate) are not familiar with the discourse community's tacit assumptions about appropriate style, because they are uncomfortable with the certainty that the structure and voice of the academic paper imply, and because they are unacquainted with the academic audience, they may find their expression restricted by the expectations of the discourse community.

Grades are one of the rewards that faculty use to reinforce the notion that the standard academic essay is not just different from, but better than, other kinds of writing. The students we talked to come to the writing lab, for the most part, because the grades drive them. Grades indicate to them that they haven't been successful with the type of discourse they believe is expected of them, the type that they believe means success at the college. Their comments reveal that they don't understand how to write the A paper that they believe meets the professor's expectations for the standard academic essay.

With the exception of Melissa, a confident sophomore with well-developed writing skills, the students we interviewed conceive the form of the academic paper as a rigid heuristic which limits them. They see the structure not as a flexible, manipulable organizing tool, but as a box into which their ideas have to fit. In the interviews, students gave the impression that they knew the right words to explain the structure of their paper, but when pressed to elaborate, they responded with formulaic explanations, almost as if they had been drilled on the components of a good essay and were reciting them by rote. For example, Tina, a junior transfer student who had attended a state university, explained the rigid structure she believes she must fit her ideas into: "You do your introduction, you do one side, you do the other side, and then you discuss which you think is better." Jenny, an active first-year student, told us that she has figured out that the best way to write a paper is to "find what citations I was going to use and make that into my outline...and then write around the citations." These students' restricted notions of the form for the standard academic paper do not allow them to take into account such possibilities as considering counterarguments or allowing for failures of their own argument, possibilities valued by most faculty.

Although one student, Melissa, saw the possibilities inherent in the structure of the standard academic essay, she still criticized it. Melissa was a sophisticated writer, interested as much in discussing composition theory and modes of discourse as in improving her own writing. She explained what she disliked about the expectations for writing at the college:

> I was really getting frustrated with just feeling that every one of my papers was the same, in a way. I just had to focus on all that we had been studying and choose some very small minute thing to focus on and to try to prove that everything we'd ever looked at fit into the theory or idea. Or to just be so selective in finding evidence and not [pause]—I prefer to look at things in a broader perspective, and usually that's not what we're expected to do here. We are supposed to make kind of half truths into truths in our papers.

Despite this critique, Melissa admitted that "it's a good skill to have, to be able to argue well, and I think that's what I'm learning from writing the types of papers that my teachers expect of me." She saw how the structure has the potential to help writers, but recognized that she does not feel at ease enough with that structure to use it well:

> I may not be a strong enough writer yet to be able to get past that with this framework. I think that if a prof who's a good writer were to take the same formula and structure that we're taught to use—the introduction, development and conclusion— if a prof were to take that and write a good expository piece on something, it would probably be a lot better at incorporating contradictions and incorporating ideas and the prof's own thoughts in a way that would still be a good example of that genre, but I feel that I'm not a strong enough writer to be able to take in those less [pause]—the more ambiguous elements into the paper and still be able to make it a good paper within the framework that we're supposed to work in.

Most of these students believe that there is some "code" for the A paper that they are missing. We discovered three main factors that contribute to their difficulty with breaking this "code." First, they struggle with the voice of the academic essay. Second, they are unacquainted with audience and with how audience expectations shift in different disciplines. Third, they are confused by the idiosyncratic and highly individualistic expectations for writing that teachers communicate through their grading and comments.

First, the problem with voice. These students were mystified and somewhat befuddled by the voice of the academic paper, what Elbow calls the "rubber-gloved quality to the voice and register of most academic discourse—not just author evacuated but showing a kind of reluctance to touch one's meanings with one's naked fingers" (145). Ned, a serious, thoughtful first-year student, described this sort of "author-evacuated" voice that he believed he was being expected to use in his writing: "I mean, this paper was definitely written by me and it's all my thoughts, but it doesn't really feel like it....[I]t feels like, sort of like VCR instructions; it doesn't feel really personal....I didn't get to write it the way I want to write it." Jenny explained that academic writing frustrated her because she is a "passionate person" who feels "strongly about ideas." However, she has been advised that the "idea you're passionate about isn't always the best idea...that I should maybe step back and like look at some other options before I just start writing." Jenny perceives the standard academic essay as robbing her of her own passionate voice. She may not know what kind of voice she is expected to use to replace it, although she does know that she needs to master another, more impersonal voice in order to get good grades.

Second, these students are inexperienced in writing for the academic audience. They struggle to envision the person to whom they are writing their papers and cannot make the subtle adjustments in audience that different disciplines require. Delores, a vivacious and voluble woman frustrated with her inability to understand what is expected of her in her writing, explained:

> It's really important for me to grasp that...a humanities paper would be different from an education paper or from a science write-up. I want to be able to, and I don't know that I ever will be, but to know the types of styles and what's appropriate and what's not....Each one has a different technique...and is approached in a different manner and I have to know and distinguish them.

Ned, who was working hard to improve his writing in his first year of college, described the process he believes takes place as he learns to adjust to the expectations of different professors and disciplines:

> These first two years you're coming away with all these different...little things that professors have...and that's basically when you need the writing lab, you need to figure out what's going on. And then once you, once you have...all these styles.... But, I think it [would help] a lot if...the professors would tell you before each paper what exactly [they wanted].

These students understand that in different assignments, they are speaking to different audiences, but they do not know how to address these audiences appropriately. One way teachers in the specific disciplines may help students learn about audience is by clarifying the spe-

cific audience stances they assume when they read each assignment—
to help students move away from a rather inchoate and intuitive
assumption about audience to one that is more particularized, developed, and clearly articulated. In doing so, teachers will help students
clear up what Charles Moran describes as the difficult "rhetorical situation of the student in 'academic writing'," one that is "extraordinarily
murky—writing-to-be-evaluated-by-someone-you-don't-know" (146).

Third, although students appear to believe that some "standard
academic essay" exists, they discover that each professor has a slightly
different notion of what that essay is. In addition, they find that, even
in the same class, professors sometimes have different expectations for
different papers. Mary Minock explains that students lack a

> metatheory that would allow [them] to interpret the differing
> expectations and make coherent the differing advice from dif-
> ferent teachers about the different writing they do and will
> do....[Therefore,] they often simply are left to figure out our
> prejudices. (166)

Ned revealed his inability to understand independently what the professor wants:

> I went in and talked [the paper] over with [a writing lab tutor]
> and she sort of interpreted it for me...and I got a feeling for
> what [the professor] wanted, got a feeling for what I should
> write and what I sort of did wrong.

Many of these students, needing more information about professors'
expectations, use the writing lab as a resource for discovering each
professor's prejudices and idiosyncrasies. Ned explained that he
learned about "points that certain professors—that really bug them,"
but he was not convinced that these same "points" would "apply to
other professors....It seems like every professor has this little stylish
niche that they've created." Frank, an intense, gentle, first-year student
who felt discouraged about his writing abilities, expressed his worries
about whether the professor who had just handed back an assignment
with what Frank considered to be a good grade would have different
expectations for the next assignment: "It kind of worries me
because...this turned out well, and so I'm worried that the next won't
turn out as well." Ned stated a desire for his professors to give clearer
statements of philosophy about writing:

> I think if all the professors would start giving a handout at the
> beginning of the semester saying what they are looking for—

what their philosophies are and all that—then you'd be learning yourself by following that."

Delores, clearly frustrated by a professor's marginal note on a paper she was sharing with us, gave a graphic description of the kinds of comments she cannot use or sometimes even understand:

> ...well, [reading a comment from her paper] "needs transi-
> tions." Well, if I didn't do it the first time, there's a reason why.
> There are some times when I consciously don't put transitions
> because I don't know how to find them. And when I get a pro-
> fessor, for instance, who says [adopting an arch tone and imitat-
> ing an imagined comment], "The thesis must not only incorpo-
> rate your analytical assessment of it all but also must answer the
> 'So what?' question," I think...so give me an example! You can
> read about how to hop and if someone doesn't show you how
> it's done, you can't do it.

Clearly, these students want the professors to show them how to hop: to explain what their "secret code" is and to provide models of essays that have "broken" the code successfully. If a professor wants students to write what he or she conceives of as a standard academic paper—one with an introduction that piques the reader's interest, with the thesis at the beginning, with topic sentences relating explicitly to that thesis at the beginning of each paragraph, with an orderly sequence of paragraphs culminating in a conclusion that explores the "so what" question—then the professor, understanding that other kinds of papers exist, ought to make that expectation clear. Faculty ought not to assume that everyone knows that formula, knows what it looks like or how to do it. Faculty ought to explain, to model, to make explicit their often tacit expectations for the papers they require.

By engaging in these practices, teachers will prepare students to better understand the assessment they receive. In this way, the assessment will better meet the criteria which Wiggins (26–27) says should guide it:

- In assessment, the interests of students should be paramount.
- Assessment should provide information which the student can use to identify strengths and to guide improvement.
- Assessment should motivate students positively.

Let us look at the first criterion: In assessment, the interests of students should be paramount. The students in this study were interested in improving their ability to write, to perform the tasks their professors want them to perform. And they regarded the grade as an accurate reflection of their ability to do so. It is in the student's interest that assessment should provide him or her with good information about how to learn better and do better. This goal is not met if a grade merely interrupts or ends the process of improvement, rather than encourages the student.

Often, the grade, instead of working in students' best interests, merely discourages them; indeed, they may write poorer papers because they are worried about the grade. Yasuko, an exchange student struggling to express complicated ideas in a second language she was trying to master, exemplifies how students' concern for the grade may cause them to say something other than what they mean or to eliminate ideas: "So sometimes I have to change what I want to say or give up something to write down—it's too confusing." Jenny, too, even though she did not have the problem of writing in an unfamiliar language, described her frustration with trying to improve her writing and the paralysis she felt as she saw her performance worsen: "The harder I tried, the worse [the papers] got. I don't understand, because the more revisions I do, the worse it is, so maybe I am just not seeing things." The discouragement caused by grading makes them so worried about meeting teachers' expectations that their writing becomes more unimaginative and stilted.

When we look at the second criterion—that assessment should provide information that the student can use to identify strengths and to guide improvement—we clearly need to question whether the grade does either of these. The grades these students received on their writing did communicate to them whether they were close to achieving the ideal essay their teachers have in mind when they make an assignment and which the rhetorical situation they invent for students demands. But the grade, even with comments, gave students little useful information about how they should alter their future work to meet the professor's standards for success. The students we talked to viewed grades and comments as not very informative about strengths and only generally so about weaknesses. Jenny said, "Comments on a paper are there and depending on the grade you're like, [pause]…you just don't read them because you're like, I deserve better than that." Ned explained that, because each teacher had his or her "little niches," he was not certain it was possible for him to use comments on future papers: "The comments point out what you did wrong. I think you get a general picture of what you write like, but nothing that will really help you improve your writing." Because the students saw the ending comments and the marginal notes as intensely contextualized, they did not perceive them as information that could be carried over or applied to new writing. Melissa, the confident writer, said, in describing marginal comments: "It's nothing you can take and use...'cause I think of that being entirely about the particular idea that you thought of. Like this, this [comment] here is about a connection between two ideas in a paragraph...and I could never use that again." Perhaps they have difficulty applying evaluative comments to future writings because each assignment demands that they adjust to slightly different rhetorical situations and slightly different audiences.

In all the cases we examined, the students were looking at papers that had received a final grade. From the students' remarks, we infer that it is terminal grading which is the problem, grading which stops revision. It seems questionable to argue that teachers can expect students to improve their writing by building on skills they develop during the semester if the students are given no opportunity to revise or rewrite each assignment. We realize that allowing students to revise or rewrite does not guarantee that their writing will improve. According to research on revision (Bridwell; Calkins), inexperienced writers struggle to improve texts effectively through revision because their strategies tend to be superficial and because such writers fail to look at writing holistically or globally. However, experienced writers tend to make more holistic or global revision and to view revision as a way of discovering incongruities and dissonances in their writing (Sommers). Whether students are inexperienced or experienced, some evidence exists that they can be taught to revise more effectively (Wallace and Hayes). In general, even with inexperienced writers, revision does seem to lead to improved writing (Wallace and Hayes). It seems obvious to us that, although allowing for revision does not guarantee improvement, not allowing for it certainly makes improvement even less likely. When students revise their papers after receiving feedback unaccompanied by a grade, they can grapple earnestly with real problems in communicating.

These students see the grading process not as a guide to improvement, but as a mysterious and inviolable process—something that is done to them by experts who almost magically uncover their inevitable mistakes and shortcomings. It is unsettling how meek and willing they are to allow themselves to be judged by a standard they neither understand nor feel capable of achieving were they able to understand it. They regard the grade as an immutable judgment. For example, although Melissa, a strong writer with sophisticated views on writing, agonized about the organization of one paper, she assured us that she would not go to the professor to try to change the grade:

> I could hit myself over the head....I think I want to go in and talk to him about it too, just, not to change the grade or anything, 'cause I mean, the way that I handed it in is, I can't change that, but...uhm, just to kind of see if he thought it would have been better if I hadn't done that.

Ned praised his professor for her teaching of writing, even though he couldn't understand her comments:

> Mrs. [name withheld] is, she's a really, she's really good when it comes to writing; I mean, she's a good critiquer of writing. ...And she knows what she's doing....But it's just, I can't really make sense of some of her comments.

If he can't "make sense" of them, how can he use them to improve?

Instead of viewing grades as communicating information useful to their future writing, these students view grades as indicating whether their ideas agreed with those of the professor, with those of the respected authority. Many of the students interviewed believe that earning a good grade requires saying what the professor wants to hear. Yasuko explained that "sometimes I know that maybe if I emphasize different things she likes, maybe I might get a better score because she likes it. So sometimes I do that." Yasuko's remarks exemplify the idea of many of these students that they are expected to construct their ideas to fit the views of the professor. Delores expressed her appreciation for an "objective reader" in the writing lab to counterbalance what she saw as the subjective grading of a professor:

> [A writing lab tutor] is so objective and I know that...she's going to be objective and she's going to tell me what's wrong with my work, but if...I get something back from my professor and he didn't feel quite the same way then I know...that it's just a matter of opinion and it's just a matter of what he expects and...that makes it easier for me not to get so upset with myself and not to get so upset with the professor because I know that...somebody did think that I did well and that's important to me.

Melissa explained, most eloquently, this influence of the professorial authority:

> Sometimes when you go to talk to a professor...they can't withhold their ideas or kind of their own image of what your paper is going to be like, and a lot of times I have been in to talk to a prof and come out with the prof's conception of how the paper

should be and have done it according to that because I know the prof will like it that way.

Ned expressed the notion that the purpose of the standard academic essay is to demonstrate that the student has the right answer; this purpose, in his view, precludes any chance of the student improving on a draft of an essay. Ned told us that some professors did not like students to come in to discuss papers before they were submitted for a grade because it would be "like cheating." He explained further that

> [I]t might get tricky when you start talking with the professors because, they're the ones that grade you on it, and they don't want to give everything away....[I]t's like, you're here to learn....[I]t's sort of like a little game....It's like, if you talk to a philosophy professor, he's not just going to sit down with you and tell you the meaning of life. You've got to figure it out for yourself.

According to this view, if students succeed in figuring out the right answer, the secret, they earn an A. Few of these students appear to believe that they might actually write about something the professor did not already know or did not agree with; instead, they appear to view the writing task as reporting back to the professor something he or she expected them to gather from the course—writing with no surprises, no discoveries, no mistakes.

The third criterion we consider—that assessment should motivate students positively—is particularly telling in relation to these students. The poor grades students had received on their writing at the college undermined their confidence. Jenny, who was advised by one professor that she "may not be small-liberal-arts-college material," recalled the trauma of trying to prove herself to that professor:

> There were times when I went in to talk with him and I had to fight off tears, just because I knew he was trying to help me...and I was trying to make him proud of me in a way....And I...just couldn't do that somehow. The harder I tried, the worse I did....One of the reasons why I wanted to please him so badly was to prove to him...that I did belong here.

If we hope to motivate our students to improve their writing by grading it harshly or by holding it to rigorous standards that have not been clearly communicated to all students, then these students' comments provide us with cautionary advice. They are eloquent in communicating the discouragement—and, in some cases, the paralysis—a low grade creates in them and the encouragement and confidence a simple comment like "good" brings them. Jenny, astutely, used a meta-phor of teacher as coach to explain the effect of criticism:

> The good coach is the one that will sit you down and say, "Now you did this wrong but you did this really well and you, you've got that part down, you just have to work on this other part." As opposed to a coach that will just, like, ream you out for the one thing you did wrong....[Y]ou could have won the game and you...could have thought you played really well, and he will just ream you out for this, like, one thing you did wrong....It makes you not...like that person because you did do something well and you deserve to be acknowledged for that. You shouldn't just be taken, ya know, taken off just because of the one thing you did wrong.

Similarly, Delores described her frustration with a paper for which she had earned what she perceived as a low grade: "It is really frustrating when you put everything you possibly could and sweat blood for this paper and get back a B-. And you think, 'This is the best I can do; it's my very best!'" Tina said, "I don't think I will ever get an A on any-thing I write here" and went on to explain: "I just feel continuously unconfident in my writing skills. I mean, when I try to make an effort, then sometimes I don't do well and when I blow it off and do it at the last minute, sometimes I do do well." Jenny described her experience when her grades for papers in a class

> went downhill....I kept trying harder and harder to write these papers for him and they just kept getting worse...actually worse. And so, that's another reason I took writing lab this semester. That class really undermined my confidence in my writing ability. I really, after that class, I really thought that I wrote like shit.

Frank explained the importance of self-confidence in writing:

> Probably one of the most valuable things that the writing lab helps me out with, when I bring my paper in really early, and the writing lab helps me out with just giving me confidence in writing....When you start out the writing process and you're, if you're writing with confidence, that's a huge advantage....

These comments indicate that grading, rather than motivating these students positively, merely discourages them.

These students tend to view grading as the only part of assess-ment that matters, a final score that terminates the possibility for improvement. In contrast, we believe that if grading must be a part of assessment, it should be a part of the learning process, a process that takes place in the public discourse of the classroom community: students should collaborate in establishing criteria; they should collaborate on revision; and teachers should delay grading and grade only what the student, through these collaborative activities, has selected as his or her best work.

One way in which the grade can become part of the learning process is for students to participate in the delineation of criteria for that grade. In "Myths of Assessment," Pat Belanoff, describing grading as that "dirty thing we do in the dark of our own offices," urges teachers to bring assessment and grading into the classroom community, where students and teacher collaborate on defining criteria clearly (57). Even if teachers do not involve students in developing criteria for grading, they are obligated to make clear their own criteria for judgment and to communicate, prior to grading, how students can meet them. For the students we listened to, the combination of a letter grade and comments does not communicate these criteria well enough, or communicates them only after the fact.

It seems to us that teachers would do well to model their assessment of writing on the collaboration that occurs in the writing lab at our college. In this writing lab, the tutor functions as the average, educated reader for the paper; although students maintain responsibility for their papers, they hear the way such a reader reads it, they hear the questions such a reader has, and they see where they may have made unwarranted assumptions about such a reader's knowledge or attitudes. Few professional writers would publish something without having a trusted reader give an opinion on it; coming to the writing lab affords students that same privilege. Even if the services of professional tutors are not available, students can benefit from the feedback of other readers, whether they be classmates, peers, or the teacher.

Obviously, teachers do not have the time to sit down with each student for a series of talks about each paper, but perhaps there are ways to get closer to that ideal. Some teachers at Grinnell have reading days in class or in special sessions; in these classes, students share early drafts with one another and get feedback from classmates and from the teacher. Some teachers read and comment on early drafts and allow revision of all or several papers. Many teachers encourage students to revise globally, not just to correct usage, by insisting on such holistic revision in rewrites. Some teachers delay grading as long as is practically possible and involve each student intimately in that final grading moment. Until that moment, some teachers keep collaboration open; students may continue to tinker with their writing, sharing it with many others, just as we do as professional writers. By providing feedback to students as they are writing—instead of after they have "completed" a performance—teachers make it possible for students to adjust and improve their performance.

A final way in which teachers can make grading a more useful part of the learning process is by avoiding practices that make writing seem to be a test, that is, a one-time performance that cannot be altered or revised. If writing is merely a test, students, hearing little praise and much criticism, may fail to understand what they are doing right and may believe that they are doing it all wrong. Students learn nothing positive from the double insult of first writing poorly and then learning that the teacher agrees with their estimate of their poor performance. One way to avoid grading papers that students perceive as failures is to use a portfolio for which students choose the pieces they wish to have evaluated. If students recognize that not all of their writing will be submitted for a grade, they might possibly come to see writing not only as a means of demonstrating what they know, but also as a means of discovering something new.

The students who spoke with us in these interviews about their attitudes toward grading are perhaps not typical of all college students, but their negative reactions to grades are predictable. No one likes to struggle to speak in a new language, about subjects one is unfamiliar with, in a form that seems rigid and unforgiving, to an audience that seems unfriendly, and with the firm prospect of receiving a grade that will symbolize failure. We assume that the goal of teaching writing is to improve students' writing skills; we find that the grades these students get, mainly on the standard academic paper, tend, instead, to convince them that they can't write.

Until students come to see the grade as merely a part of assessment and to see themselves as an essential participant in the development of the grade, the effects of grading will remain negative and counterproductive. Before students ever receive a grade, they should collaborate in the development of clear, specific criteria. The teacher and students should explore and articulate the particular idiosyncrasies of the discipline and the specific audience for each writing assignment. Students would also benefit from access to exemplary models to imitate and from support and encouragement as they work toward reaching the criteria. Short of abandoning grading of writing altogether—which we see as a desirable but unlikely goal—it seems to us that the best compromise is to encourage collaborative assessment by allowing students to interact with others, to delay grading as long as possible, and finally to grade only what students select as their exemplary work. To extend Delores's analogy, if we want students to hop, we should demonstrate how we want them to hop. We should discuss with them whether we want them to hop far, or high, or steadily, or beautifully. We should give them ample time to practice hopping, and we should encourage them to have peers evaluate their hopping. We should take care that we do not discourage them from developing their own style of hopping. And finally, if they stumble when they try to hop, we should help them back up and encourage them to continue, not just confirm that they fell.

Works Cited

Bartholomae, David. "Writing with Teachers: A Conversation with Peter Elbow." *College Composition and Communication* 46 (1995): 62–71.

Belanoff, Pat. "Myths of Assessment." *Journal of Basic Writing* 10 (1991): 56–66.

Bridwell, Lillian S. "Revising Strategies in Twelfth-Grade Students' Transactional Writing." *Research in the Teaching of English* 14 (1980): 197–222.

Calkins, Lucy McCormick. "Children's Rewriting Strategies." *Research in the Teaching of English* 14 (1980): 331–41.

Elbow, Peter. "Reflections on Academic Discourse: How It Relates to Freshmen and Colleagues." *College English* 53 (1991): 135–55.

Gross, Janine B. *Inventory of Writing Assignments.* Grinnell: Grinnell College, 1995.

Hourigan, Maureen M. *Literacy as Social Exchange: Intersections of Class, Gender, and Culture.* Albany: State U of New York P, 1994.

Minock, Mary. "The Bad Marriage: A Revisionist View of James Britton's Expressive Writing Hypothesis in American Practice." *Taking Stock: The Writing Process Movement in the 90's.* Ed. Lad Tobin and Thomas Newkirk. Portsmouth: Boynton/Cook, 1994. 153–75.

Moran, Charles. "How the Writing Process Came to UMass/Amherst: Roger Garrison, Donald Murray, and Institutional Change." *Taking Stock: The Writing Process Movement in the 90's.* Ed. Lad Tobin and Thomas Newkirk. Portsmouth: Boynton/Cook, 1994. 133–52.

Peim, Nick. *Critical Theory and the English Teacher: Transforming the Subject.* New York: Routledge, 1993.

Sommers, Nancy. "Revision Strategies of Student Writers and Experienced Adult Writers." *College Composition and Communication* 31 (1980): 378–87.

Wallace, David L., and John R. Hayes. "Redefining Revision for Freshmen." *Research in the Teaching of English* 25 (1991): 54–65.

Wiggins, Grant P. *Assessing Student Performance: Exploring the Purpose and Limits of Testing.* San Francisco: Jossey-Bass, 1993.

Interlude

There are lots of ways to avoid grading student papers. Check-plus/check/check-minus; comments only; self-assessment by student, meaning student decides (probably within certain guidelines) how good the work was; conferences; pass/fail; satisfactory/unsatisfactory; groups rank members' work according to rubrics they (or you) develop. Evaluation is a necessity, whether you use grades or not, because in order to reach audiences, satisfy readers, convey our thoughts, get what we want, we have to observe certain conventions and be familiar with certain requirements. Grading is an art, not a science, but I don't think we need to apologize for, or slight the necessity of, making judgments. To praise student work indiscriminately cheats students of the chance to achieve. To withhold judgment lies to them.

—Deirdra McAfee
  Henrico High School
  Richmond, Virginia

9 Writing at Reading: How a Junior Year in England Changes Student Writers

Mary B. Guthrow
Randolph-Macon Woman's College

Mary B. Guthrow is associate professor of English and director of the writing program at Randolph-Macon Woman's College in Lynchburg, Virginia, where she teaches courses in American literature and academic writing, supervises the Writing Lab, and spends twelve hours a week in Writing Lab conferences with student writers from across the curriculum.

When one considers the benefits of a college junior year abroad, the strengthening of academic writing skills is probably not what first comes to mind. Most students and most advisers would think instead about the new perspectives that come with immersion in another culture or about opportunities for travel between terms or about improving foreign-language skills. At Randolph-Macon Woman's College, however, one of the prominent features of a long-established junior year in England is the writing-intensive experience it offers to participants. Because this program is conducted on a pass/fail basis and in a modified tutorial setting, it provides an interesting laboratory for considering the effects on college student writers of a nontraditional system of response and evaluation.

Every year since 1968 about thirty-five students from R-MWC have spent their junior year at the University of Reading. The students live together in college-owned houses near the campus and have their meals in a university dining hall. They enroll in one yearlong common course (a British culture seminar) and in individual programs of study made up of regular university courses and/or tutorials conducted for R-MWC students by British faculty at the University of Reading or, in some subjects, at Oxford University. While they are at Reading, students write three seminar papers of fifteen to twenty pages, one in each ten-week term, and about thirty shorter essays for their tutorials and university courses. If a student joins a university course in which tests are given, she must take them; but most students in this program will take no tests or exams in England, and all credits for the year's work are awarded on a pass/fail basis.

Part of the mystique that surrounds the Reading group when they return to the Virginia campus as seniors has to do with their enduring reputation as able student writers. Through many student generations, faculty have characterized Reading students as typically independent and self-directed in their senior studies; and in the formal evaluation of student writing skills that takes place at the end of each semester, names from the Reading group consistently appear in the lists of those whose academic writing has been judged "excellent" by at least two of their instructors. In conferences and in conversations with my own students and advisees, I have found myself enthusiastically echoing the standard advice: "If you want to learn to write, go to Reading."

Although the transforming effect of the Reading program on academic writing skills has long been part of R-MWC's campus lore, there had been no systematic examination of the experience. Perhaps this was so because the consistently pleasing outcome seemed so utterly predictable. Admission to the Reading program is competitive and self-selective; the sophomores who apply are above-average, motivated students who know that the program will be writing-intensive. Those chosen to attend will spend a year in a university system designed for a student elite (the top 6 to 8 percent of their age group in the U.K.), where undergraduate studies are much less highly structured and require more responsibility on the student's part for her own learning. The experience of living in a different culture, far from home and familiar routines, would by itself encourage independent behavior and develop self-confidence. Finally, the year at Reading offers the writer-friendly advantages of very small classes and long blocks of unstructured time.

According to Stephen North in *The Making of Knowledge in Composition*, one of the sets of conditions under which practice can legitimately become inquiry is when "both the situation and approach are nonstandard" (33); and as I began to think about the Reading program in North's terms, my informal conversations with Reading seniors began to move toward a more systematic examination of their testimony and their texts. Following my practitioner's instinct to learn more about a program that "works," I concluded that a closer examination of the Reading experience might yield some useful insights about the development of academic writing skills. As I set out to establish with more precision exactly what had changed for these student writers during the course of their experiences abroad, I was particularly interested in two things: whether the writing *process* changes for these students and whether *response* to student writing is significantly different at Reading.

A comprehensive study of writing at Reading would be a long-term project, probably using case studies and a participant-observer approach to follow representative student writers and their texts from the home campus to Reading and back again for at least three years. The present study, limited by my leave time and resources to a single semester on the home campus, is based on the experiences of six volunteer informants, all seniors in their final semester at R-MWC. Five, with majors in English, creative writing, art history, politics, and economics, had been at Reading during 1990–91. A sixth student, another English major, had spent her junior year in Scotland, directly enrolled at St. Andrew's University; I included her because her experience provides an interesting contrast to the year at Reading. After an orientation session with the group of six, I distributed a two-page prompt sheet and scheduled a two-hour taping session with each student. In addition, I asked each participant to assemble a portfolio of representative essays from her sophomore, junior, and senior years, together with any attached evaluation sheets or comments from faculty readers in both settings. I was also able to schedule two two-hour taping sessions with the resident director of the Reading program and his wife during their annual April visit to the home campus.

The composite experience that emerges here, from the interview transcripts and from the collected texts and comments, reveals two enduring changes in these Reading group writers. While the individual writing process did not change significantly for any of these students, they did become much more comfortable with the process; they all talked about new fluency and confidence as being the products of a year of intensive writing in a pass/fail setting. In addition, these students developed a strong sense of ownership in their writing. Encouraged by a primarily oral system of response at Reading, one that balanced new freedoms with high expectations, these student writers discovered some powerful new roles for themselves. Although it would be difficult in most American classrooms to duplicate either the freeing distance from traditional systems of evaluation found in a junior year abroad or the kind of commitment that can develop over time in a small residential learning community like the Reading group, there are some elements in the Reading experience that could be adapted to more conventional settings.

When R-MWC students arrive at Reading, they are coming from a small college where writing has long been an important part of the liberal arts curriculum. What is so different about the year in Reading is that for most students, writing now becomes the only basis of formal evaluation; instead of a term paper or two or three shorter papers representing 25 or 40 percent of a course grade, writing at Reading will represent 100 percent of the work most of these students submit to the faculty for course credit. As one student observed:

> The concept of studying here [U.S.], I would think, is going over your notes and wondering what's going to be on the test; instead, in England, you *read.* You get a book and you read it. [It's] all completely reading and writing. And that's it! You just don't *do* anything else.

The result of this approach is, perhaps, writing across the curriculum in its purest form; writing at Reading becomes, to use William Zinsser's phrase, "an organic part of how every subject is taught" (vii). For example, in the required British culture seminar, a student writes brief responses to assigned readings, she submits notes on the presentations by guest lecturers, and she writes a research paper in each term on a topic she chooses, under the supervision of a university faculty reader in her field of interest. In addition, for each of her tutorials and university courses, usually two and sometimes three each term, a student will write about twenty-five pages during the ten weeks, again in a variety of forms. Among the writing assignments undertaken at Reading by the students in this study were a long paper written collaboratively with another student and during two terms for a sociology tutorial; three eight-page essays for a university course in the American novel; a comparison essay on different accounting systems; a series of critical summaries of readings for philosophy tutorials; a long paper on congressional reforms for a university course in American politics; case studies for a business law class; and three short papers in a modern drama tutorial to be read aloud to the class.

In his "Autobiographical Digression," the second chapter in *Writing without Teachers,* Peter Elbow describes a term in his junior year when, by mistake, he signed up for a combination of courses requiring two substantial papers each week: "After the first two weeks' crisis, I found I wrote fluently and with relatively little difficulty for the rest of the term" (17). According to student testimony, the intensive writing experience at Reading can produce the same kind of fluency. One student reported that she finally counted up the pages she had turned out in ten weeks for her four classes "to satisfy my own curiosity" and came out with "about 100": "It never bothered me. I like writing more than I do these tests and quizzes; and I felt like I learned more." She concluded, "You got used to it. That's what I liked about this because you got the writing experience…by doing so many that…it didn't matter…it was not impossible." By the end of the year, she said, "It went faster, and I felt less stressed about it," and now, in her senior year, "It's a lot easier.…I know I can get it done." A student who said she finished her last seminar paper three days early explained, almost apologetically, "That was because I thought it would take me longer to do it. It all came out. It was great! It was like being inspired to write poetry. It just came out."

However, student testimony suggests that new fluency and confidence are products not only of intensive writing practice at Reading, but also of a uniquely balanced system of response. It is response to student writing that sets the Reading program apart, both from other writing-across-the-curriculum or writing-intensive experiences at home and from other programs of study abroad. Response, as Sarah Freedman defines it in her study of teaching practices in secondary schools, "includes all reaction to writing, formal or informal, written or oral, from teacher or peer, to a draft or final version.…Response can also occur in reaction to talk about an intended piece of writing" (5). At Reading, response comes from both British and American readers, from faculty and from peers, in oral and in written forms, and from outside traditional systems of evaluation but within a kind of community contract. Because the program balances new freedoms in a pass/fail year abroad with new commitments within the Reading group community, it encourages risk taking and experimentation while it builds responsibility and a sense of ownership.

Response to student writing takes place in a variety of forms and contexts at Reading, but by far, the largest part of response is oral. With longer papers, response often begins in the prewriting stages. One student's seminar paper supervisor had her come in for fifteen minutes every week with a progress report, and eventually an outline was requested, something that was not normally a part of this student's writing process but which she admits she found to be very helpful. This supervisor never actually read any preliminary drafts: "She would just sit there and listen to me.…She let me go my way.…She never actually went through the poems with me and pointed out things at all. I did that all on my own." But the weekly contact was important: "She made it exciting for me. She made me *want* to do it."

In the first stages of the two-term collaborative project in sociology, the co-authors met with their tutor four or five times: "We would meet with him and go have coffee, and he would give us the names of books, tell us about the feminist bookstores in London." Then, as they read and took notes, the two researchers began to respond to each other: "What does this book say? Is there anything in this book?" Finally, after making a rough common outline, they took turns drafting on the computer, each reading and responding to what the other had written.

For many of the shorter papers, the first response comes after a complete draft has been submitted. In an American novel course for third-year university students, the professor invited his one R-MWC student to his office to discuss her papers:

> He would say, "When would you like to talk about it?"…He would talk about…if I'd made my point, what I could have done to make it better, what more detail I could have used…and we would just sit and talk, too. It was really nice! I was in there for about an hour for each paper. It was really helpful.

In tutorials, students often read their papers aloud, with response coming both from the tutor and from other members of the class: "We learned from each other." In the British culture seminar, response to student writing also comes in class discussion, but there the short essays on assigned readings are submitted the day before class, so that they can be used to organize discussion in small groups. Finally, at the end of the term, each student has an individual conference with the Reading program director in which they review her seminar notebook, the comments from her seminar paper supervisor, and the term reports from tutors. Here is another opportunity for oral response to the student's writing: "Dr. Ivy sat down with me [and said], 'You need to do this and this.' It helped me pinpoint [things to work on]."

Written response to student essays at Reading is limited, perhaps because there is so much oral response, but also because British faculty readers are not accustomed to close marking of surface errors or to focusing on problems in student prose. As the Reading program director observes: "Most university tutors presume that their students know how to write or ought to know how to write and mark essays very lightly." In his estimation, R-MWC students are "probably getting on average less actual advice about their prose than they would had they been on the other campus…not because they are American students…[but because] that is the *norm* at Reading." Students were quick to notice that their British faculty readers were primarily interested in "your ideas," in "*what* you said," in whether you had "a convincing argument," and that they "didn't care about grammar" or, at least, "didn't correct me."

Examination of the collected student texts generally supports this judgment. For example, in one short essay, the tutor did not mark lowercase letters at the beginning of two sentences, or a fragment, or a plural subject with a singular verb. He did place two question marks in the margin to indicate problems with logic, and he made brief comments on matters of content: "*Cf.* Mill's *On Liberty* for similar theme." In a seminar paper, the faculty reader made only eight marks in a text of fifteen and a half pages: one exclamation mark to indicate overstatement; three check marks to indicate important points; two underlinings under Latin phrases; one spelling correction; and one word circled, commenting on word choice. He did not mark misplaced commas, misuse of semicolons, or typographical errors in the works cited list.

In contrast, reflecting a different tradition of faculty response to student writing, one of two American faculty readers at Reading made twelve marginal comments in a seven-page paper, including: "This is a run-on sentence," "Avoid contractions in a formal essay," and "Make sure subject and verb agree." In addition, she wrote a full-page comment at the end, analyzing the essay's organization in detail. "I worked harder on her papers," the student writer said, because she realized this reader would be paying much closer attention to surface features than the British readers did. While some students found less attention to surface errors liberating, this student was grateful for help with usage and sentence structure: "I feel like I lost or have forgotten so much. You're thinking you're doing okay, even if you're not [when errors are not marked]."

Written responses from the tutors on the collected student essays often included letter grades, but students quickly recognized that such marks did not necessarily correspond to those on the home campus or to marks awarded to the British students. As one student put it: "Sometimes professors would think that they understood the American grading system and gave a student a B or a B+." The program director acknowledges that there is a kind of grade inflation for junior-year-abroad students, who are at the university for one year and who are not going to take final examinations for the degree: "It probably is the case that our students receive A's for work that would not be graded as A if a University of Reading student produced it." At the same time, any letter grade is going to be awarded outside the American system as well, because R-MWC transfers all credits for the year at Reading on a pass/fail basis.

This yearlong suspension of traditional grading, combined with the emphasis on oral response and the shift away from close marking of surface features, allows the Reading program students to think more about writing as a learning process and less about writing as a finished product. By the time she was writing tutorial essays in the third term, one student said, "I would just pick out something I thought was interesting and write about it. My first draft was it. They were all handwritten." Still, she was careful to assemble evidence to support her ideas, in case someone challenged her in discussion: "I knew I would have to back myself up." In her freshman and sophomore years, she had had a whole different set of concerns in her writing assignments: "I was worried about saying the right things, answering the question, coming up with what the professor wanted you to do, and making it long enough."

The liberating effect of a pass/fail year is an important component of the writing-intensive experience at Reading; nevertheless, as the program director points out, "It isn't a total suspension of the rules; they do care about the response they get." Because the students live together in very close quarters, they get to know each other very well, and this bond of close community extends to the resident director and his wife, Americans who live nearby and who interact daily with the students, not only as lecturers, tutors, administrators, and academic advisers, but also as personal counselors, mentors, honorary house parents, and friends. Randolph Ivy, who has been director of the Reading program since 1978 and is associate professor of English at R-MWC, teaches a Dickens course at the university. Judy Ivy, an art historian, is a John Constable specialist. They bring to the Reading program an American perspective on the varied backgrounds and needs of American student writers, and their response to student essays reflects their graduate study and university teaching experiences at Chicago and Pennsylvania. "I get to know them very well," Randolph Ivy says:

> Though they don't know their seminar paper supervisor well, they know *me* well. I mean, *we're* friends…and we're going to look at the report together. My regard for them becomes part of

their self-estimation…so that disappointing me would be disappointing themselves.…That becomes a certain spur to them, not
to drop below a certain level.

Even though they wrote for a full year without the pressure of
traditional grades, as one student put it, "We still felt like we had to do
the best we could do."

This commitment to a kind of unwritten community contract
was not part of the experience of the sixth student writer in this study,
who spent her junior year in Scotland studying independently at St.
Andrew's. Directly enrolled with third- and fourth-year English literature students in a junior honors program, this student attended three
lectures and one or two tutorials each week for three courses each
term. She wrote six papers each term for her tutors, two in each course.
She "never understood the grading system" at St. Andrew's, except
that no one got A's and "over 60% was really good"; so she, like her
classmates at Reading, soon stopped worrying about grades and
found that "really freeing." Also, like the Reading group, she concluded that her university faculty readers were "not concerned about
stylistics" but primarily "wanted to see your ideas." With only four or
five hours a week in class, she had time to read widely, and as a writer,
she "never felt rushed." But her writing "didn't get any better":

> You had these tutors—you didn't know them very well—you
> didn't see them very often…and for some reason a lot of my
> writing is wrapped in with what I think the other person thinks,
> whether they think I've done a good job. And because I didn't
> care that much about these people in terms of their opinion of
> me, I got kind of lazy. My process didn't change in my writing,
> but I got lazy about it.

Compared with the Reading experience, writing at St. Andrew's was
more specialized but less intensive; there was not as much response,
and the response was more impersonal. There was the same liberation
from concern about grades, with the same pass/fail transfer of credits.
But without the balance of response from committed American faculty
readers within a close residential community, it was reading, not writing, that was at the center of this student's experience abroad.

In his book *Writing and Sense of Self*, Robert Brooke applies theories of identity formation and negotiation, borrowed from social psychology, anthropology, and political theory, to his experiences in traditional writing courses and in writing workshop classes. He argues that
learning to write depends on "the identification and exploration of
writers' roles for the self, roles which need to be broader than the lim-

ited examinee-to-examiner traditional school roles" (140). He concludes that workshop classes teach writing more effectively than traditional courses do because they more effectively promote an understanding of the self as writer. In a workshop course, Brooke believes, the focus shifts "from grasping the concepts underlying teachers' assignments to deciding through practice how certain activities help or hinder one's own development of texts" (84). Brooke also presents testimony from students that workshop courses "affect students at an emotional and personal level—they feel changed by their experience" (112).

Certainly, every student writer in the Reading program feels changed by her experience there; and in several respects, the Reading group resembles the writing workshops that Brooke describes. At Reading, almost everyone is writing something every week, for the most part on topics of her own choice; there is a lot of mostly oral response; there are no tests; and credit is awarded on the basis of what ultimately amounts to a pass/fail contract to complete a certain number of pieces of writing. Brooke's observations about the workshop students could also describe members of the Reading group:

> Instead of having to demonstrate that they knew what the teacher knows through tests, essay exams, or a sequence of work to master…skills, students merely had to do a certain amount of writing per week, take part in class and small-group discussion, and finish a number of pieces they had started during the course of the semester. Once they caught on…students recognized that it was a simple contract, one which they controlled and were responsible for. (146–47)

Thus, like the writing workshop courses in Brooke's study, the program at Reading provides "cues" that shift learning "from a teacher-student examination context to a cooperative community context" (147).

As I reviewed the transcripts of the interview tapes, I began to notice what Brooke would call "patterns of identity transformation …whereby individuals change their behaviors and their understanding of themselves" (26):

> There was so much more of me in a paper in England.…I was doing it for myself, and I was doing it by myself. It was my own little project and I had to do it, and if I didn't do it, it wasn't going to get done.…It's like a piece of you, and you're so much more proud of what you produce because you motivated yourself to do it.

> I had more time to do research, so I did it. I felt like I was doing it for me because it was pass/fail. The professor wasn't going to *grade* me…so I was learning something and it wasn't for anybody but me. It made it more interesting.

> [The modern drama tutorial] was really five or six different equals, sitting around and talking about a play.

"When students and teacher can move outside the limitations of traditional examinee-examiner roles," Brooke concludes, "then kinds of learning become possible that were not possible before" (82).

At Reading, shifts in conventional roles allow changes in self-concept, and the growing sense of ownership in student writers can produce changes in behavior. The student who learned "you can't cram papers" when she came up short on time, sources, and text in her first seminar paper submitted an outline to her supervisor before she started writing the next one. The champion procrastinator in the group, who knew that others had been asking Professor Ivy to look at their rough drafts, completed a full draft of her third seminar paper in time to do the same. A student who began on her own to bring papers into Randolph Ivy's office did so, he said, "not because anyone had said her prose was bad, but because *she* wasn't happy [with her essay], so she came to me." During the course of the year, he observed that

> Simply the process of sitting with students and spending time with them on their essays makes them better self-editors. After we've been doing this for awhile, the rough drafts that are coming to me are already much cleaned up. The punctuation is more frequently in the right places; the typos are gone; a lot of the spellings have been corrected; [and] sentences have already been combined.

For a significant number of students every year, there is what Professor Ivy calls a "real sea change" in their prose when they learn how to coordinate and subordinate ideas:

> They come writing simple-level sentences….They can't make the shape of the sentence reflect the shape of the idea….A number of them are just at that point in their lives that if you show them how to coordinate and subordinate, they can begin to do it.

This is not, he points out, just a surface-feature change, because as they learn to coordinate and subordinate, the nature of their ideas begins to change as well: "Papers become more analytic. The thesis paragraphs really become thesis paragraphs." One student said, "I feel like I can say things in more understandable terms." Another reported, "I learned to make my topics more specific." "The ideas…were always there," Professor Ivy concludes; "I think they'd not been able to express them because they didn't have access to them."

For a senior returning to conventional studies after a year abroad, there is always tension between her newly developed sense of independence and that traditional college student/examinee role. The senior who had been at St. Andrew's described herself as overwhelmed by "way too many classes." In Scotland there had been "no syllabi telling me exactly what to do…I miss the freedom." A schedule suddenly crowded with classes and daily assignments for five courses also represents a major adjustment for the returning Reading students. One senior complained: "One of the problems I'm running into is that [since Reading] I *want* to do the reading [but] there's so much pressure to meet all the deadlines that I'm not getting the reading done. I'm doing surface work [because there is] not enough time to absorb it." Reflecting on her Reading experience, another senior confessed: "I was allowed to introduce my own ideas—I felt comfortable with that. I really developed that way. [Now] I'm worried about what grades I get. I wish *that* had been my senior year. I feel like I'm going back to my old ways."

Still, in senior-year writing assignments, the confidence, the fluency, and the strong sense of ownership that develop at Reading do remain. "Only twenty pages!" said the economics major:

> I felt confident in my writing. I felt like, yeah, I could write! I started early on my [senior] seminar paper.…I just wrote twenty-two pages all in one weekend. I didn't have any problems with getting it done, and he seemed to like what I wrote.

When a visiting professor announced that she wanted a paper of ten to fifteen pages in a Thai culture and society course, another senior reported: "Everyone panicked. And I thought, 'Well, I can do that.'" After writing at Reading:

> Here…it's like, you know, "Oh, I have to do a five- to seven-page paper on Gandhi." So, I'll read, and, you know, look things up and find the most important things and write a paper.

The R-MWC junior year in England was not conceived as a yearlong writing-across-the-curriculum workshop; it developed naturally out of a particular set of circumstances into its present form, guided by Randolph Ivy and his predecessors, who, he says, "must have unconsciously seen that it was working." Combining intensive writing practice with primarily oral response, and balancing a suspension of traditional evaluation with a high level of expectation within a close community, the year at Reading allows student writers to develop new confidence, independence, access to ideas, and sense of ownership. In Brooke's terms, it is identity transformation, a new "sense of self," that is at the heart of the Reading experience and that ultimately generates the changes in writing performance so long associated with this program.

Those practices, Brooke concludes, which "promote an understanding of self as writer are likely to 'teach' writing more effectively than practices which focus only on expanding writing processes or on internalizing formal rules" (5). Changing the test-and-grade-dominated culture on most American campuses to something like the Reading pass/fail tutorial model is clearly unrealistic; nevertheless, there are some alternative strategies and modifications of writing activities that might be successfully adapted from the Reading experience: more conferencing and oral response throughout the composing process, and less marking of drafts; more informal writing assignments, presented as a way of learning, as a starting point for discussion or for further reading; a shift in focus from mastery of forms to development of confidence and fluency through intensive writing practice; and development of close, supportive relationships among students and teachers as the basis for more shared assessment of drafts. It may be that for college juniors especially, student writers who have just declared majors and who are often just beginning to mature intellectually, such strategies are likely to be transforming ones, at home or abroad.

Works Cited

Black, Anne-Wyman. Personal interview. 5 Feb. 1992.

Brooke, Robert E. *Writing and Sense of Self: Identity Negotiation in Writing Workshops*. Urbana: NCTE, 1991.

Dolan, Brenda. Personal interview. 25 Feb. 1992.

Elbow, Peter. *Writing without Teachers*. New York: Oxford UP, 1973.

Ellinger, Ann. Personal interview. 7 Feb. 1992.

Freedman, Sarah Warshauer. *Response to Student Writing*. Urbana: NCTE, 1987.

Ivy, Judy. Personal interview. 7–8 Apr. 1992.

Ivy, Randolph. Personal interview. 7–8 Apr. 1992.

North, Stephen M. *The Making of Knowledge in Composition: Portrait of an Emerging Field*. Upper Montclair: Boynton/Cook, 1987.

Roberson, Brooke. Personal interview. 6 Feb. 1992.

Wille, Suzanne. Personal interview. 7 Feb. 1992.

Wolters, Nancy. Personal interview. 18 Feb. 1992.

Zinsser, William. *Writing to Learn*. New York: Harper, 1988.

Interlude

What is "cutting edge" in grading alternatives? I've
only been teaching for twenty-two years, but in that
time, most of these methods have come around at least
two or three times. "Cutting edge," for me, will be the
day there are not grades at all, at least in teaching
writing. On that day, the only thing students will have
to go by will be conferences with me or in the college
writing center and comments written to them as well as
peer comments. On that day, we will act like writers
rather than "students" and "teachers."

 —Latisha LaRue
  Clarke College

10 Assessment through Collaborative Critique

Sarah Robbins
Kennesaw State College

Sue Poper
Mountain View Elementary School, Marietta, Georgia

Jennifer Herrod
Simpson Middle School, Marietta, Georgia

*Sarah Robbins teaches English and English education courses at
Kennesaw State College. She has written for journals such as* English
Education, English Journal, *and* Signs *about portfolio assessment,
student-centered literature instruction, nineteenth-century women's
teaching and writing careers, and negotiating authority in the classroom.
She is also director of the Kennesaw Mountain Writing Project.*

*Sue Poper is a fourth-grade teacher at Mountain View Elementary
School in Marietta, Georgia. She was one of the founding fellows of the
Kennesaw Mountain Writing Project in the summer of 1994. As a
teacher-consultant, she focuses her staff development work on assessment
of student writing.*

*Jennifer Herrod taught middle school language arts for four years. She
has left grading behind entirely by moving from teaching school to
writing and editing textbooks on insurance and financial topics.*

I n 1994, we were participants in the initial summer institute of the
Kennesaw Mountain Writing Project, a National Writing Project site
located just north of Atlanta, Georgia. Though we came to the five-
week workshop from different, recent teaching experiences—high
school and college (Sarah), elementary grades (Sue), and middle
school (Jennifer)—we found that we shared many beliefs and interests.
At the institute, we discovered how valuable it is for teachers of writing to have substantial time to develop *themselves* as writers—to have
intense, yet communally supported, opportunities for writing, sharing, and reflecting. In addition, we learned through *studying* writing
instruction and by *doing* many, varied kinds of writing together which
we were strongly committed to making a key part of a socially nurturing learning program for our students. Ideally and, perhaps, not sur-

prisingly, by the end of the summer we felt that the best kind of writing program for our students would look a lot like the NWP institute we'd just experienced. It would be a risk-free environment with many opportunities for idea-sharing discussions and for writing in a wide variety of genres about personally and intellectually meaningful topics. It would be a community committed to both individual and group reading interests. It would emphasize the *process* of learning to communicate; the products created in our classrooms, in other words, would be made to promote and assess learning rather than to provide artificial evidence of schoolwork done for a grade.

However, as fall approached, we realized we couldn't exactly duplicate the writing project in our regular classrooms. Though our respective institutions place a high value on student-centered learning, they also require teachers to turn in grades at the end of each marking period, so we could not entirely escape the role of "scorer" of student writing. Building on our NWP experience, we wanted to integrate the practice of writing and its assessment more fully and constructively, promote students' ongoing evaluation of their own writing processes, and move as far away as possible from the role of teacher as red-pen-wielder, judging student texts by way of decontextualized standards (Robbins et al., "Negotiating Authority"; Johnston; Elbow). But we also knew that working in places where quantifiable measures of student progress were receiving increasing support from stakeholders—such as local school board officials and state test writers—complete elimination of grades from our writing programs wouldn't be feasible—yet. Still, we hoped to be assertive communicators to our students, their parents, and the school administrators about the value of ungraded approaches to evaluating writing. And we suspected that one of the best ways to begin winning others over to our viewpoint would be to have them see some of the benefits of such writing up close.

Seeking a Socially Nurturing Writing Experience

Besides sharing these goals for writing pedagogy, we had discovered, in our discussions during the summer institute, that we held a common interest in classroom research and a related belief that allowing students to be active participants in inquiry-based curricula could enrich their literacy and their critical thinking (Stock; Fleischer). We believed, for example, that the intensive, critique-focused reading, writing, and discussions we'd shared had been supportive of our own development as writers and teachers of writing—in ways that neither a punitively grade-conscious classroom, on the one hand, nor a totally unstructured out-of-school literacy experience, on the other, could have been. We had just been "back to school," in fact, but in a self-consciously challenging, yet supportive, setting where the *process* of learning was something we constantly questioned together, and where our many diverse written products were continually evaluated in terms of context-specific goals but not scored. For instance, we had all written round-robin computer responses to an oral performance; letters to each of our colleague teacher-presenters, identifying strengths and weaknesses in their demonstrations; personal literacy narratives; brief writing-to-learn exercises, such as texts where we wrote word pictures "like a camera," recording something we observed; and a polished piece of our choice for the institute's anthology. Though none of these had received individual grades, each had been constructively assessed in a variety of ways by a number of readers, including, of course, the authors. All of these supportive social literacy events had belied the school-versus-real world dichotomy we had sometimes seen others invoke during arguments calling for radical reconceptualizations of school-based literacy.

At the core of our shared beliefs and goals, then, was a related commitment to pedagogy as a nurturing enterprise in a nonhierarchical, noncompetitive environment consistent with feminist and social constructivist theory (Grumet) and with our recent positive experiences as writing project teachers and learners. So, despite the differences in our teaching sites, as the 1994 school year began, we were all three seeking to make literacy practices in school more authentically and constructively social. We intended to do so not by throwing out the intellectual rigor of studying English/language arts in favor of doing just "real life" activities, but by integrating the two via collaborative evaluation of the learning process itself, rather than discrete grading of particular student products (Robbins et al., "Using Portfolio Reflections"; Willinsky).

With these ideas encouraging us, we felt that a cross-level research project, centered around ungraded writing, could support our ongoing efforts at classroom-level and systemic instructional reform, while at the same time helping us to further develop our thinking together. Specifically, we decided to work *with* our students on a project to make school writing more constructive and less stressful—to create at least some opportunities for them to experience the kind of challenging, yet grade-free, writing we had enjoyed at our institute. We read several action-research studies as models (Dyson; Jensen; Lipson; McWhirter; West) and *The Art of Classroom Inquiry* (Hubbard and Power) to help frame our questions and to explore possible approaches for involving our students. Then we developed a tentative set of "wonderings to pursue" (Atwell 315). We wondered if we could guide our students through classroom-connected, but ungraded, writing tasks that would effectively support both the specific curriculum objectives of our three different teaching settings *and* our broader common goals for writing instruction. After discussions identifying the major points of overlap between our shared aims and the level-specific instructional objectives we knew we would need to document, we chose cross-level letter writing as the particular focus for our project; the informal, friendly letter seemed to be a genre not only well suited to giving our students challenging ungraded writing experiences, but also adaptable to the particular material conditions of our teaching situations.

We planned to have students from Sarah's college and Sue's elementary school write on multiple occasions to the same class of Jennifer's middle schoolers, who would send a number of letters back to both groups. The letters themselves would *always* be ungraded, but we would use the occasions of composing, revising, and small- and whole-class review of our writing to discuss and critique such concepts as audience, genre traits, dialogic composing, formal versus informal language, and the effects of a text's appearance on the reading process. We would share our research questions and what we learned with our students and the K–12 students' parents, while inviting them to help us build some new knowledge growing out of the constant reflection on the writing processes we were exploring. One aspect of this sharing involved our *own* letter writing—a note to parents which explained our reasons for devoting class time to ungraded writing. The letters sent home to parents also requested permission for us to share students' writing samples from the letter writing research with audiences beyond the classroom, such as other teachers at staff development workshops and the readers of this essay. (Sarah secured similar releases from her college students.) Only one participant from the three classes preferred not to have her writing samples shared publicly. The three of us met regularly for ongoing evaluation of the project, but throughout its life (until January for the college class, longer for the K–12 participants), we each continued to teach within our individual writing programs, which included having students produce other texts that could be evaluated in more traditional ways.

Beginning Our Classroom Research Project on Ungraded Writing

In the fall of 1994, all three of us were striving to reconcile our personal goals for writing pedagogy with mandates shaped outside our classrooms (Duffy). Sue was lead teacher in a fourth-grade "inclusion" classroom at Mountain View Elementary, where a major aim was to improve the writing of students with widely diverse learning disabilities. Consistent with the elementary language arts curriculum for her district, Sue would be centering her writing instruction around a folder-to-portfolio system that allowed her students to write in a variety of genres and looked toward the new state-level writing assessment for fifth graders as a major measure of her program's quality. Jennifer was working at nearby Simpson Middle School, where she would be teaching eighth-grade language arts using a county-mandated curriculum that called for increased emphasis on spelling and vocabulary instruction (with spelling to have a separate report-card grade). This curriculum also called for teachers to begin using writing folders with multiple revisions of student texts toward year-end portfolios to help the middle schoolers take more control over their own assessment. Like Sue, Jennifer was well aware of the state-level writing test for her grade level, which asked students to write a personal narrative that is scored like the elementary instrument. Sarah, meanwhile, was teaching an integrated English/language arts methods course that included a six-week on-campus component, meeting twelve hours per week, followed by four weeks when students were assigned to a high school classroom three hours per day. Since a major focus of Sarah's course would be to help her students consider how to develop an effective writing program in their own teaching, the class members would try out and evaluate a wide variety of writing assignments. They would also continually reassess their own texts, both through peer response and individual reflective writing, and then assemble a course portfolio which included work from the on-campus and in-school portions of the class. Although Sarah's students had already successfully passed the Georgia Regents' Test of writing ability required of undergraduates in the state, they still faced the TCT (Teacher Certification Test), an exam of their knowledge of "English" as their teaching subject, which included questions to check their writing ability and their understanding of writing process pedagogy.

As our research project was about to begin, each of us tried to make certain that our experiment would support, rather than undermine, the context-specific writing instruction goals of our distinctive teaching sites—even those we might not have chosen if left to our own devices. (This concern about ethical considerations faced in classroom research also led us to frame separate research questions for each of our sites and to inform our students and administrators fully about the specific goals and strategies we had in mind for the project.) Starting with the broad "wonderings" we had generated together, we each outlined classroom-level research questions as well. The following excerpts, taken from reflective writing we did during the project, are descriptions of those questions and the early implementation of the pen-pal research in our respective classrooms. Re-viewing such memos now, we can see how this writing-for-research learning reflects both similarities and differences in the ways we incorporated the ungraded texts from this cross-level enterprise into our overall writing programs:

Sue

In particular, I wanted to answer the following questions: (1) Will the students be more enthusiastic about writing? (2) How will the quality of their writing change with regard to handwriting, spelling, punctuation, and capitalization? (3) Will there be a change in the level of detail and content of their writing? . . .

When school began in the fall, I explained to my students, in our get-acquainted process, that the main focus of my summer had been the Writing Project. I had made some wonderful new friends, and I wanted to stay in touch with them during the school year. One of the teachers I felt especially close to was Mrs. Jennifer Herrod. Mrs. Herrod, I told the students, taught at Simpson Middle School, just a few minutes away from our school....I explained that I would very much like for our class to write to Mrs. Herrod's class, and after we had established a relationship with our pen pals, I would like to go to Simpson for a short visit. My students were very excited about the possibility and wanted to write immediately.

[Preparing to start] the first exchange brought out all of the insecurities of my students about their writing. They asked me questions such as, what should I write about? Who should I write to? How should I begin my letter? I decided to take my students all the way back and begin with a friendly letter format and the parts of a letter. I modeled what I would write in a letter to Mrs. Herrod. Using the overhead projector, I thought aloud while my students "listened in." I was surprised how little letter writing experience the majority of my students had had. Besides their apprehension of writing in general, they were unsure to whom their letters should be addressed. We decided as a group to use the "Dear Pen Pal" greeting for this first exchange. I explained that once our letters were received, our pen pals would know our names and be able to address us more personally....Again, through a whole-group discussion, we decided that the letter should serve to introduce each of us to whoever received our personal letter. We decided that the contents should be general. Questions about what the eighth grade was like, or what they were studying, would be good topics because people usually like to talk about themselves.

Revisiting Sue's research memo now, we are struck by the complex writing issues her students started considering as this ungraded writing experience began, and by how closely their student-centered concerns matched Sue's own research questions. Their immediate queries about who to write to suggested an awareness of audience that might not generally be attributed to fourth graders and offered a tentative answer to her first question about enthusiasm for this writing task. Although "the first exchange brought out all of the insecurities ...[her] students [had] about their writing," her class was still "very excited" about beginning the project "and wanted to write immediately." Meanwhile, Sue's strategy of modeling a first letter on the overhead, thinking aloud and *along with* her students, helped set the stage for her third research question, as she demonstrated for them the way that the "detail and content of their writing" in this case could be dialogically shaped by both what they wrote and what they received back. At the same time, in focusing initially on content rather than on "handwriting, spelling, punctuation, and capitalization," Sue signaled to her students that in crafting a writing product, they need not be overly concerned with correctness issues early on. Nonetheless, by tackling the question about "to whom their letters should be addressed" as soon as it was raised, and by contextualizing her answer within the lesson about the friendly letter, Sue stressed the close relationship between content and form so that as they experienced an authentic writing task, her students were beginning to explore the multilayered aspects of genre formation. After all, while the "Dear Pen Pal" greeting fit a "correct" standard for opening letters which had been set outside their classroom, this specific variation also showed the students that they were part of a particular writing community that could establish nuanced adaptations of "rules" unique to their own group.

Though Jennifer's and Sue's specific research questions were quite similar, curricular concerns linked to her middle school setting led Jennifer to some notable variations in the issues she studied with her students through the ungraded letter writing and in the instructional strategies she employed for integrating the project into her overall writing curriculum:

Jennifer

I wondered: "What effect will cross-age pen-pal writing, consistent writing for a real purpose, have on my eighth graders' writing?" More specifically, I wanted to answer the following questions: (1) How will the students' affective feelings about writing change? (2) How will the complexity and appropriateness of their grammar and punctuation change? (3) How will the level of detail and complexity in style, content, organization, and sentence structure change? (4) What changes will I see in their higher-order thinking skills and metacognition in regard to writing? (5) How will the letters to the two different audiences (elementary versus college students) differ? . . .

I chose my second-period class to be pen pals to both groups of students. I based this decision upon several reasons. The class was my smallest (22 students as opposed to 29 or 30), and the time of day our class met would coordinate best with possible visitations from Sue's and Sarah's classes. Also, this class was a particularly cooperative and insightful group, and using the same group of students to write to both classes would allow us to compare their writing intended for two distinct audiences. I introduced the idea to my students after I had already inundated them with stories about my involvement in the summer institute. The institute had a profoundly positive effect on me, and I couldn't help but share with my students stories of the writing and learning I had participated in. We read an essay by the young adult science fiction author Ursula Leguin, "Thinking about Writing," and I spent several days talking with my students about writers' purposes, audiences, and products. I introduced the pen-pal idea very generally, explaining that it would be fun, would give them an opportunity to improve their writing by writing to a real audience for a real purpose, and would also improve the fourth graders' writing and would help the college students become better teachers. . . .

My students had an opportunity to meet Sarah's in person when her class visited mine to observe....It was interesting to Sarah and me that her students seemed to gravitate toward students of mine with similar personality characteristics. After talking for ten minutes or so, the college students departed, and mine were free to talk about...the project. They were excited at the idea of having pen pals, but anxious about embarking on a new experience.

Jennifer's question about the possible "affective" impact of the project on her students paralleled Sue's wondering if composing the letters might make her students "more enthusiastic about writing." Similarly, Jennifer's second and third questions matched the content of Sue's, while allowing for more complex, specific instructional objectives for content development and surface editing at the middle school level. But Jennifer also had two other research questions geared to her classroom. Her exploration of ways to promote "higher-order thinking skills and metacognition" through the project reflected her awareness of her school's site-based teaching goals for the year. Also, her wish to have her students learn to adapt their writing to "two different audiences" was consistent with the state middle school curriculum guide and the Georgia eighth-grade writing assessment instrument's stress on writing for a variety of audiences.

Also like Sue, and in line with the experiential learning they'd shared at the summer institute, Jennifer contextualized the particular "fun" composing task of letter writing within a frame which invited her class to explore several key concepts that would carry over into much of their other writing—in and out of school. Thus, Leguin's essay was a way of underscoring the links between thinking and writing that they would continue to study through ongoing critique of their letter writing processes; especially since Jennifer planned to have her students both discuss (as in Sue's class) and write written reflections about their work for the project. Similarly, in suggesting to her class that participation in the project would allow them to teach both elementary students and adults (i.e., "it would...improve the fourth graders' writing and would help the college students become better teachers..."), Jennifer signaled to her students that this ungraded writing could have a serious social purpose well beyond the typical, limited goal of fulfilling an assignment and getting a grade.

Sarah's research questions and initial teaching strategies for the project were also tailored to her students' site- and program-specific learning needs:

Sarah

Because my class was made up of students on their way to being teachers, I was eager for the project to serve a dual purpose. I wanted my students to be able to reflect on their own writing and the way it's shaped by different contexts of past and current experience—for example, to consider what the "school" audience for writing is usually like, and how that pattern of single-teacher-reader may have affected their own academic and personal writing....But I also wanted them to use the letter writing project to explore issues related to their upcoming *teaching* of writing. Along those lines, the main questions I wanted us to

address combined writing-centered and teaching-centered concerns: (1) How does audience affect writing, and how can we
provide a variety of real audiences for our students' writings?
(2) How does repeatedly writing to the same audience shape
writing, and what are the implications of sustained writer/
audience relationships for classroom writing programs? (3)
How does an understanding of genre shape writing? For example, what effect does guided exposure to models have on writing? How can/should teacher modeling and instruction in
genre be used to support student writing? (4) How might texts
be shaped by collaborative reflection on a particular writing
process? Assuming that individual and/or group reflection of
this kind might help writers, how can teachers provide opportunities for students to reflect upon writing as a social practice?
(5) What is the role of "correctness" in writing? For school? In
other sites? How can writing for authentic purposes support the
learning of correct spelling, punctuation, and usage?

We first wrote to other students involved in the project after
our visit to Jennifer's school. I was interested when, during
class the next day, several of my students said they were a little
worried about writing a letter the middle schoolers would *want*
to answer. We used that comment as a springboard for a discussion of audience, focusing for awhile on Bakhtin's conceptions
of dialogue. We discussed ways of building on what the eighth
graders had said during our visit to make each of our letters
unique. We then spent a good deal of time on what seemed at
first to be a trivial issue, but turned out to be quite productive:
whether my students should sign their own first names or the
more "teacherly" first and last names. This question led us to
discuss several issues, including modeling, the effect of hierarchies on writing relationships, and ways my students' own
transitional identities affected their writing.

Rereading Sarah's reflections on the early stages of the project,
we can see that some of her critique of writing processes with her students was more explicitly theoretical and centered around pedagogy
(versus writing itself) than the talks in Sue's and Jennifer's classes.
Nonetheless, in the major questions to be explored, if not in the exact
vocabulary used, there may have been at least as many similarities as
differences across our three research sites. All of us were intrigued by
questions about audience, the effects of social composing on text, and
the relative importance of correctness and other kinds of standardiza-
tion in writing communities' work.

By critiquing their writing processes for the letters, like Sue's
and Jennifer's classes, the college students themselves continued to
call attention to worthwhile issues for the whole group to consider. As

noted, an especially fruitful phase of our work was the start-up of correspondence. Sure enough, brief freewrites—typed in the computer lab on the day they turned in their letters for the middle schoolers—not only described the college students' at-home composing steps as initially requested, but a quick rereading of their own and others' reflections also encouraged them to propose topics for whole-class discussion stemming from the problems, questions, and observations they saw in more than one reflection. These reflections on their own letter writing, like the reflections Jennifer's students and we three teachers composed for the project, were obviously ungraded as well. In a sense, then, our project made use of rather complicated layers of ungraded writing—including ungraded student writing to assess ungraded student writing.

As revealed in their reflections, one difficulty the students had faced was making their two letters distinctive from each other. (Each methods class member wrote to two eighth graders.) Besides noting some of the various strategies they had used (e.g., different stationery, sealing the first envelope after writing the first letter to discourage copying), we also discussed why it had seemed important to diversify. We noticed, in addition, that several students had trouble deciding how carefully to proofread their letters. On the one hand, Deborah had commented in her freewrite that she "started off writing on a separate sheet of paper so that if I made a mistake, I could correct it." But she quickly reconsidered: "After the first several sentences, I decided that this was a waste of my time and that I should just write. After all, isn't this what letters are for? I don't prewrite when I write my parents or friends." On the other hand, while Deborah's comments suggest she was constructing herself as a friendly peer correspondent, Yvonne's description, when reconsidered by the group during our critique time, seemed to represent more of a teacher-as-modeler conception of her writing task. After all, she had explained in her freewrite that she felt she needed to write "a rough draft" of her first letter, then move to "revising" and recopying, and that she had "tried to sound as friendly and sympathetic as possible" without "sounding overly chummy." Contrasting Deborah's and Yvonne's decisions helped us to discuss the authorial stance for a "friendly" letter written to a middle schooler by an adult who was, and yet was not exactly, a teacher figure. Some students speculated that the eighth graders might share the letters they received with their parents, and thus they worried that that potential audience might be put off by surface errors rather than seeing the texts as calculatedly informal. Significantly, even those who argued that they had purposely tried to avoid seeming too teacher-like realized that, as initiators of the letter-exchange process, their texts might be more effective if prepared as models of conversational writing. Along those lines, another student's freewrite was representative of the class members' concerted efforts to invite response:

> I tried to remember who I was writing to....I wanted to make the letter personal and warm so that they would feel more comfortable opening up to me, when they wrote back. So I used more of a conversational type of language than a formal one. I first wanted to provide some background information about myself in hopes that they might do the same in their letter. After that, I asked them questions about what their view of a good teacher is and what was their favorite teacher like. I basically wanted the letter to be a kind of starting point.

Apparently, this set of letters provided a positive "starting point" indeed, as Jennifer reported later that more than one student had sent in a reply though absent from school on the day the responses were due. In the meantime, like Sarah and Sue, she had devoted some productive class time to discussing the writing process for the first letters the eighth graders would write. The coincidence of having received letters on the same day from both their younger and their older pen pals may have promoted many of their insights, and Jennifer was impressed by the way her class used comparisons and contrasts between the college and elementary letters to examine together several issues related to their own response writing. One of the first differences several class members noticed was that the college letters were "more personal" than the elementary ones, and after a brief listing of some examples, she and her students surmised that one reason might be that the college students had already met them and could refer to topics discussed during their recent visit. Since the ones from Sue's students were addressed simply "Dear Pen Pal," Jennifer let each of her students randomly select one. The eighth graders enthusiastically read these letters, with many describing them as "funny" or "cute" while sharing them with each other, often working together to decode some of the "creative" spelling. Commenting on the relatively "simple" vocabulary and sentence structure of their mail, the eighth graders discussed how they could adapt their usual writing voices to respond effectively to the younger writers. In considering together some topics to be included in their letters, the middle schoolers pointed out comments about hobbies and school interests and dislikes which appeared in some of the younger students' writing. Other issues that class members discussed prior to writing back included one student's suggestion that they all print rather than write in cursive, and another's proposal that they limit the length of their letters to match the approximate length of what they'd received.

Interestingly, while the college letters were addressed to particular, named correspondents and, as noted above, to more "personal" topics, almost all of them also included elements the middle schoolers judged to be more school-centered, such as questions about how to be a good English teacher (and specifically how to teach writing effectively), suggestions for books that should be taught in secondary courses, and queries about positive and negative experiences the eighth graders remembered from their schooling. Though she pointed out that some of the common topics in these letters might be more the result of all the authors preparing to student teach soon, Jennifer also began to introduce concepts related to reading and writing communities, and she speculated with her class about the kinds of genre-shaping talks the college writers might have had *as a class* before composing their letters.

Overall, the middle schoolers were eager to write back to both their elementary and their college correspondents. Most took advantage of class time to compose their responses to the younger writers, but they worked on their letters to the methods class students at home, where they could access stationery and spend more time preparing far longer letters to mirror what they'd received from the older writers. This careful attention to the physical appearance of their letters to the adults was expressed not just in efforts to write neatly and/or use personal stationery instead of notebook paper, as the elementary school students had done. From their first exchanges, the eighth graders also mimicked, following the college models (Randolph, Robbins, and Gere), such diverse techniques for embellishing, and thereby further individualizing, the physical text itself as adding drawings, stickers, or stamps; varying the look of their cursive and handwritten lettering for emphasis; playing with margins and text placement on the page; and enclosing letters in envelopes. (Interestingly, these attentions to textual presentation soon spilled over into the middle-to-elementary school exchanges as well; see Figures 1a and 1b.)

From the beginning of the project, we three teachers had explained that we would never be grading the letters, and that any student who wished to keep the correspondence private could do so. We had decided that sending the message that some school-based writing could be private was important, so that having received parent

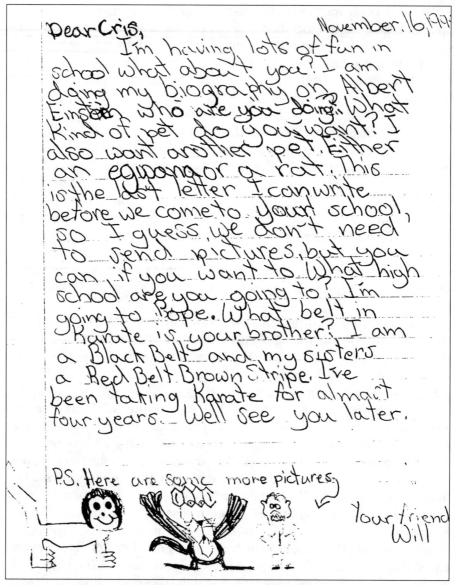

Figure 1a. Will's attention to textual presentation.

permission for the K–12 students to participate, and having held class
discussions about appropriate content, we could risk not censoring letters. None of our students disappointed us in this regard. Along those
lines, Jennifer did not screen the letters before sending them. She did
give her students time to read each other's, if they liked, and to make

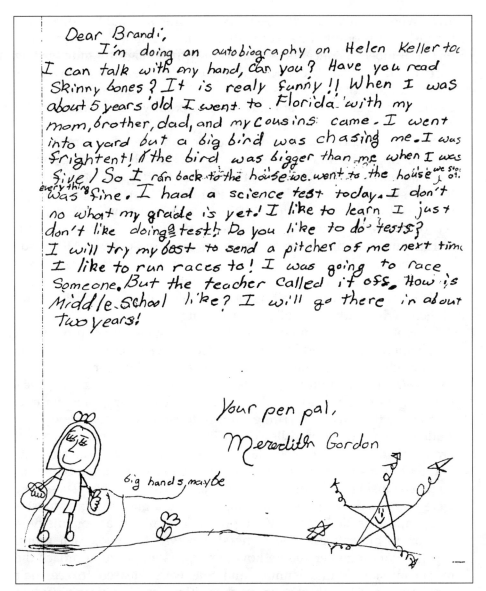

Figure 1b. Meredith's attention to textual presentation.

suggestions for dealing with frequently expressed concerns about length (usually worries that a draft was too short for college responses or too long for elementary), handwriting (i.e., legibility), and content (clarity and interest). Subsequent chances for students to write reflections on their own writing process—for the two different audiences and a whole-group debriefing—helped Jennifer see that this dual writing task had prompted her students to consider, in a meaningful context, a number of concepts central to the official eighth-grade writing curriculum of her district and to the state assessment program's goals for middle school writing instruction. She later created several lessons connecting these first letters and the collaborative classroom critique of them to specific elements of the eighth-grade writing-assessment instrument (e.g., composing for a specific audience, developing ideas fully, editing for surface errors), which she knew her students would soon be encountering as part of statewide testing. In other words, though she never graded the letters, Jennifer did use them as points of reference to guide instruction. Noting trends/patterns in the various sets of letters, for example, helped her to draw some inferences about learning needs and interests in that particular class (e.g., specific kinds of recurring spelling problems the students identified themselves when editing their letters, and writing subtasks they seemed to especially enjoy—such as co-writing projects like the serial stories several of them wrote with their college correspondents).

Noticing the popularity of those dialogic writing projects, in fact, helped Jennifer and Sue plan for an effective meeting between the middle school and elementary students later in the year. Adapting a "Magic Monster Activity" presented by one of their writing project fellows at the summer institute, they decided to try having their students respond to that creative writing prompt together during the younger students' visit to the middle school in December. Working in small groups that included representatives from both schools, the students first took turns drawing a series of lines (connecting, intersecting, or scattered), using different colors for each group member. Then they were asked to develop their drawing, turning it into a Magic Monster who could be called upon by the president to rescue astronauts on a mission to outer space. Once the sketch was finished, each group began a story together, telling how their monster would approach the rescue mission. While Jennifer and Sue were pleased to see their groups writing together, even more exciting was the strong student enthusiasm for continuing the stories in back-and-forth form in future letters. We also found it interesting that, in exchanges after this December visit and drawing-to-writing exercise, the middle school and elementary letters tended to make far more frequent and elaborate use of drawings within, around, and at the end of their texts.

That both this particular ungraded writing task and the ongoing letter writing were meaningful and productive for her overall writing program was quite clear to Sue when she and her students returned to Mountain View that afternoon. After she invited the students to write about their experience meeting their pen pals and visiting the middle school, the room was intensely quiet as they all worked away, and the whole-group sharing of these reflective texts indicated that these very young students were developing understandings of key concepts related to the project (e.g., writing *with* someone and *to* someone as similar, yet different; the effect of writing to a known audience versus an abstract one). They were also, of course, enjoying the experience for its own sake. Especially excited about the continuing exchanges was Siana, who had found a special friend in her middle school correspondent Neha. Away from the letter writing project, Siana had been the class's least communicative student, so Sue was at first surprised to hear her ask if she could write an "extra" letter to her pen pal. However, once Siana explained that Neha was also a recent immigrant and commented that they had a lot to write about to each other, Sue reminded herself that ungraded writing can simultaneously serve many worthwhile purposes—not all of them reflected easily in official lists of curricular objectives.

Nonetheless, like Jennifer with her classwork on the state writing assessment, Sue also found that traditional school tasks could acquire a new life with the support of ungraded writing. Later in the year, when a batch of letters from Simpson asked questions about another assigned writing task the middle schoolers were beginning and also solicited practical help from the elementary group, Sue's class could hardly wait to oblige. The eighth graders were preparing to write children's books, complete with illustrations as well as narratives. Surveyed about their favorite books and asked for tips for creating a "good" story for young readers, the elementary school correspondents not only reminisced in return letters about familiar, beloved stories, they also went to the library to find titles and details from sample "old favorites," thereby doing group research to identify traits of a genre that—until then—they'd taken for granted.

Evaluating Our Classroom-Based Study of Ungraded Writing

What advantages to using ungraded writing in school emerged from our work? First of all, we found that, partly because the project allowed our students great flexibility in their letters' content and style, we were often able to draw upon samples from their work to address curricular goals during mini-lessons. It seemed that whatever a particular day's or week's instructional focus was, we were easily able to find an appropriate student text to serve as a model or to provide an example of a particular problem/error we wanted to illustrate. In Sue's and Jennifer's classes, especially, the state's standardized writing assessments for fifth and eight grades have been crucial shapers of the school district's specific instructional goals for upper-elementary and middle school writing. At both the elementary and middle school levels, that test calls for students to produce a single timed-writing text, which is evaluated by trained scorers who judge it according to several criteria—topic elaboration, audience awareness, use of language, and surface-editing skills—to rank the author somewhere along a continuum of "emerging writer" [stage one] to "extending writer" [stage six]. Significantly, we believe, Jennifer and Sue were both able to use their students' letter writing for multiple lessons aimed at various elements in that standardized assessment (e.g., audience shaping content, editing for usage). So, our ungraded writing actually supported, rather than impeded, the learning of traditional basic writing skills.

One potential problem some naysayers had mentioned before we began did not, in fact, materialize. Although having the letters remain ungraded might have been expected to encourage our students not to take their project-related writing tasks seriously, all of them expressed in their oral and written reflections (and in the letters themselves) a high degree of commitment to doing their best work. In some cases, in fact, students at all three participating sites at times put more effort into their letter writing than into their regular school-based, graded writing. We might argue that this tendency rebuts the idea that students won't perform unless they receive a score for each product. But we're hesitant to overgeneralize on the basis of this single and, we realize, very informal experiment. We're also hesitant to overgeneralize about our students' ability to accept without complaint or apparent discomfort the fact that, in Sarah's and Jennifer's classes, some graded writing products also had to be prepared. Specifically, Sarah used a number of assignments in her methods class to allow students chances to try out various formative and summative evaluation techniques, such as preparing and self-scoring a rubric for I-Search papers. Therefore, throughout the quarter, the students were producing many ungraded pieces—e.g., informal reflections on reading composed in the computer classroom, descriptions of school-site visits, and daily lesson plans—as well as a range of texts they graded for themselves and each other, and a few which Sarah graded using a variety of summative systems. Perhaps because they saw practical advantages to trying out so many models, the students said they appreciated the chance to have both graded and ungraded writing within the same program, rather than finding this blend disjunctive. Similarly, despite their enthusiasm for the project's letter writing, the eighth graders did not question why some of their other pieces had to be scored. Sophisticated already about the necessity their teacher faced of having to report a grade for them, they realized that graded papers had to be a part of their school experience as long as Jennifer had to represent their work with a symbol on a computer printout every few weeks. Here, as in other aspects of the project, we may have been blessed with unusually amenable students, but we were still impressed with their ability to accommodate both graded and ungraded writing as part of one program.

Nonetheless, our enthusiasm for the results of this project should not obscure its very real limitations. Both the personal and the more traditional academic gains made by our students might well be difficult for those outside the context of our shared learning to appreciate or even, in some cases, to see. One of the lessons we three collaborating teachers have learned from this study is that assessment of sustained student writing is so highly contextualized that we need to develop new and complex ways of reporting our student progress (Flinders and Eisner). For instance, one exchange series—between Sasha and Erin—documents a positive answer to Sue's question about whether letter writing could help her students produce longer and more audience-aware texts; for Sasha began the year as a reluctant writer but, through her letters to Erin, gained confidence and skills (see Figures 2a and 2b).

Eager as we are to provide examples of such productive ungraded writing from our classrooms, we're also well aware that the samples, on their own, can be deceptive. How, for instance, would a reader who didn't know the context of Neha's and Siana's recent immigration experiences evaluate their letters? For us, though, the scattered surface errors in Neha's December note to Siana are much less significant markers of that text's meaning and value than her sensitive efforts to praise her younger immigrant counterpart, respond to one picture with another, and invite more letters (see Figure 3.)

Similarly, many readers might note how middle schoolers Neha and Erin both quickly imitated some aspects of college student Donna's early letters. For example, after receiving a note from Donna which began with the salutation "Hi! What's up?" Neha responded by

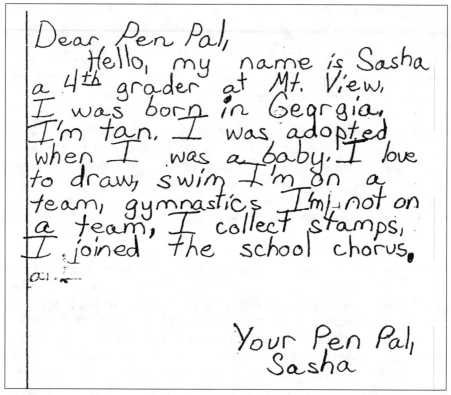

Figure 2a. Sasha's first letter to Erin.

using the same opener for her first letter back to her older pen pal. Neha also organized the body of her letter to match the content and order of Donna's, answering, in careful sequence, each of several questions Donna had posed. While any reader would probably see those parallels, equally significant for us would be the more subtle evidence of growth in Neha's subsequent letters to Donna. Over time, these exchanges seem to have promoted greater self-confidence, fluency, and experimentation with a more relaxed personal voice than a red pen and grade applied to Neha's early effort might have. And, we believe, a key factor promoting Neha's developing writing abilities over the course of the project was the supportive voice Donna was able to assume in her responses to the eighth grader's writing. Donna frequently represented herself rhetorically as beginning to assume the identity of a teacher (e.g., "Have you had many teachers who did activities outside?…I'd like to know because I would love to have some classes outside!"). Yet her comments *about Neha's texts* focused

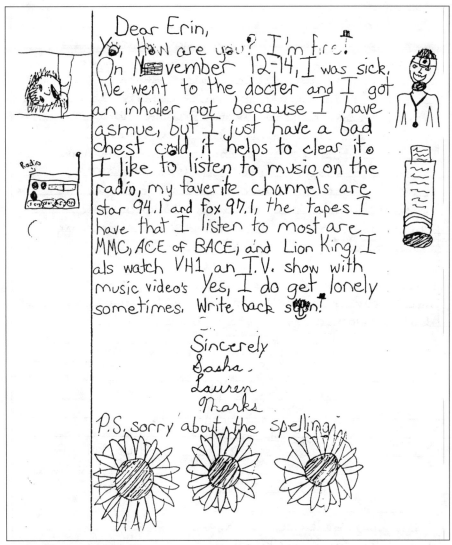

Figure 2b. Sasha's later letters to Erin are longer and more audience aware.

on encouraging more thinking, writing, and sharing of ideas rather than on correcting "faults" in the younger girl's letters. For instance, she begins one response to Neha by saying:

> I was SO excited about getting your letter! I have to say thank you for answering all of the questions I asked you, and thank you also for giving me titles of books. I want to have a library in my classroom, and thanks to you—I can add a few more titles to

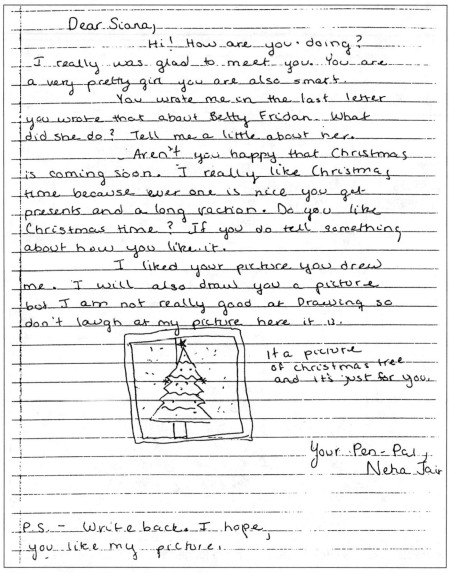

Dear Siara,

Hi! How are you doing? I really was glad to meet you. You are a very pretty girl you are also smart.

You wrote me in the last letter you wrote that about Betty Fridan. What did she do? Tell me a little about her.

Aren't you happy that Christmas is coming soon. I really like Christmas time because ever one is nice you get presents and a long vaction. Do you like Christmas time? If you do tell something about how you like it.

I liked your picture you drew me. I will also draw you a picture but I am not really good at Drawing so don't laugh at my picture here it is.

It a picture of christmas tree and it's just for you.

Your Pen-Pal,
Neha Jair

P.S. - Write back. I hope you like my picture.

Figure 3. Neha's letter to Siara.

my collection! It was funny that you mentioned R. L. Stine, because almost every student I have spoken to says Stine is really good.

Along those same lines, perhaps any casual reader would value the clear parallels between college student Emmanuel's sharing of drawings from his syndicated cartoon strip with a middle school pen pal and her pictures responding back. After all, who wouldn't stop to enjoy the clever samples of Emmanuel's "Sibling Revelry" strip, which he enclosed with his first letters, along with a funny explanation of how cartooning and English teaching go together? And who could fail to appreciate Dara's clever visual reply at the end of her first letter back, where she drew her own distinctive character and dubbed it "Potpourri the Cat"? But could a hurried school official—one used to scanning assessment reports that can be tightly graphed in quantitative scores—also be counted on to read several later letters? Could an administrator appreciate the way Dara then followed Emmanuel's lead even further when she began to make similar use of pictures in her letters to her elementary school correspondent, who in turn adopted the same technique for embellishing his letters back? What does this seemingly simple, shared composing process say about discourse communities, genre development, relationships between verbal and pictorial texts, and links between individual and group audiences? How, in other words, can we classroom teachers find adequate time and expertise to report and interpret such "data" from our research on ungraded writing in ways that will honor the complexity of these learning experiences?

Finally, as our essay title suggests, the conversations and informal written reflections that were a part of this project may have been at least as important as the letters themselves (Kearns). The shared critique of our writing processes, both within and across our various classrooms, helped all of us shift our rationale for assessing writing away from scoring it for a specific grade to collaboratively evaluating and assessing it in terms of ongoing learning goals (Schwartz). But there are still few reporting opportunities available for teachers to share such "results" of their work on ungraded writing with high-level curricular decision makers. We hope our essay and the others in this collection represent a good start.

Works Cited

Atwell, Nancie. "'Wonderings to Pursue': The Writing Teacher as Researcher." *Literacy in Process: The Heinemann Reader.* Ed. Brenda Miller Power and Ruth Hubbard. Portsmouth: Heinemann, 1991. 315–31.

Duffy, Gerald, and Laura Roehler. "Constraints on Teacher Change." *Journal of Teacher Education* 37 (1986): 55–58.

Dyson, Anne Haas. "Confronting the Split between 'The Child' and Children: Toward New Curricular Visions of the Child Writer." *English Education* 26.1 (Feb. 1994): 12–26.

Elbow, Peter. "Foreword." *Portfolios: Process and Product.* Ed. Pat Belanoff and Marcia Dickson. Portsmouth: Boynton/Cook, 1991. ix–xvi.

Fleischer, Cathy. "Researching Teacher-Research: A Practitioner's Retrospective." *English Education* 26.2 (May 1994): 86–124.

Flinders, David J., and Elliot W. Eisner. "Educational Criticism as a Form of Qualitative Inquiry." *Research in the Teaching of English* 28 (1994): 341–57.

Grumet, Madeleine R. *Bitter Milk: Women and Teaching.* Amherst: U of Massachusetts P, 1988.

Hubbard, Ruth Shagoury, and Brenda Miller Power. *The Art of Classroom Inquiry: A Handbook for Teacher-Researchers.* Portsmouth: Heinemann, 1993.

Jensen, Julie M. "What Do We Know about the Writing of Elementary School Children?" *Language Arts* 70.4 (Apr. 1993): 290–303.

Johnston, Peter H. *Constructive Evaluation of Literate Activity.* New York: Longman, 1992.

Kearns, Jane A. "The Player's Vision: Students Writing about Their Writing as Writing." *English Journal* 80.2 (Feb. 1991): 62–66.

Lipson, Marjorie Y., et al. "Integration and Thematic Teaching: Integration to Improve Teaching and Learning." *Language Arts* 70.4 (Apr. 1993): 252–63.

McWhirter, Anna M. "Whole Language in the Middle School." *Reading Teacher* 43 (Apr. 1990): 562–65.

Randolph, Rebecca, Sarah Robbins, and Anne Gere. "Writing across Institutional Boundaries: A K–12 and University Collaboration." *English Journal* 83.3 (Mar. 1994): 68–74.

Robbins, Sarah, et al. "Negotiating Authority in Portfolio Classrooms: Teachers' Use of Assessment Theory to Critique Practice." *Action in Teacher Education* 17.1 (Spring 1995): 40–51.

Robbins, Sarah, et al. "Using Portfolio Reflections to Reform Instructional Programs and Build Curriculum." *English Journal* 83.7 (Nov. 1994): 71–78.

Schwartz, Jeffrey. "Let Them Assess Their Own Learning." *English Journal* 80.2 (Feb. 1991): 67–73.

Stock, Patricia Lambert. "The Function of Anecdote in Teacher Research." *English Education* 25.3 (1993): 173–87.

West, Jane, and Penny Oldfather. "On Working Together: An Imaginary Dialogue among Real Children." *Language Arts* 70.5 (Sep. 1993): 373–84.

Willinsky, John. *The New Literacy: Redefining Reading and Writing in the Schools.* New York: Routledge, 1990.

Interlude

Grades interfere with my ability to teach. What I want students to do is to try new things, to take risks, to do things that stretch them and push them. But they're too afraid of making mistakes and getting a bad grade, so they resist my attempts to push them beyond their comfort level.

I've tried to relieve this anxiety by assuring them that if they do the things that I suggest, they will earn a B in the class, which is, to tell the truth, what most of my college students are seeking. I try to make criteria very clear, but I also ask students to talk with me when they have alternative approaches to assignments. I also try to model openness and flexibility in the classroom so that they can come to trust me. I have to go through all sorts of gyrations to establish my credibility as a teacher/evaluator/coach, to show that I'm flexible, that I won't just invite them to experiment and then nail them with a bad grade.

Grades interfere with my ability to teach.

—Suzy Shumway
Prescola University

11 What Grades Do for Us, and How to Do without Them

Marcy Bauman
University of Michigan–Dearborn

Marcy Bauman is on the English department faculty of the University of Michigan–Dearborn.

I have chosen not to grade students' writing any longer for a very simple reason: I have found that grading just doesn't work in helping people to learn to write more effectively. In my experience, no matter how much I try to make the assignments "real," no matter how I try to encourage students to write for their own purposes and to make their own discoveries, no matter how easy I make it for students to take risks, as long as I'm the one grading their papers, students tend to understand the writing situation as one in which their task is to please me so that they get a better grade. When I give grades, they tend to ask questions like "How can I make this paper better? Why didn't it get an A? What do you want me to revise?"—all questions that indicate to me that they haven't seen the writing of that paper to be a communicative act, but rather a demonstrative one. They have written to produce what Anne Freadman might call "an example of" something, rather than the something itself.

I see several problems with this state of affairs. The first is that it portrays what is to me a false notion of what writing is and what purpose it serves, because it obscures writing's communicative function (sometimes beyond recognition). The cycle of write, revise, get a grade, write, revise, get a grade tells students that writers write primarily for the purpose of being evaluated, not for the purpose of conveying information or attitudes about a subject that they care about, and certainly not to change anyone's mind, or to move anyone, or to make them angry, or to get them to laugh; that writing is typically produced and evaluated in a vacuum, divorced from genuine communicative intent or function or a genuine real-life situation to prompt it; that the purpose of writing is to produce fixed texts which serve no function beyond providing the writer with occasions to produce them; and that the end point of writing is for the writer to receive varying degrees of approval or disapproval. This is a bit like suggesting that the point of growing vegetables is to win prizes at the county fair. Prizes are (arguably) nice, but they don't put food on the table.

Furthermore, if students are concentrating on their grades at the expense of thinking about their writing as a communicative act, they are being given a false model of how people actually develop as writers. They are laboring under the delusion that learning to write is simply a matter of being told what to do and then doing it, that if the teacher could but only provide the necessary bits of information (or if they could only manage to learn all the right rules), they could generate flawless texts every time. If students are intent on getting a grade, they don't see much of the necessary cognitive work involved with learning to write; they don't come to understand that to a large degree, they will have to learn by trial and error—and that they themselves, not some outside authority, will have to determine where the error lies, that they themselves will have to determine what to do to correct it. They may come to think of learning to write as a process with an end point which the teacher has achieved and they have not. Or worse, they may think of learning to write as something only a few people can accomplish; and they will never develop the habits of mind which will enable them to continue to grow as writers for as long as they care to. This is really my chief objection to using grades and teacher-generated assessment and evaluation to teach writing: It denies the cognitive work about assessment and evaluation that has to become part of every writer's repertoire. What's important isn't that *the teacher* thinks that a student has done well, but that *the student* knows how to determine if she's done what she set out to do in a particular piece of writing (which may or may not include getting a good grade on it).

Finally, a grade-driven model of writing prevents students from engaging a great deal of what they already have learned about communication and language and how they function in the world. Students come to school with a number of years of rhetorical experience. They come to us with a host of language-learning behaviors that have served them since infancy. While I would not claim that learning to write is identical to learning to speak, I would argue that the two are similar enough that we ought to apply what we know about language learning in general to the classroom in particular. I would also argue that by not doing so, we deprive ourselves and our students of rich resources for learning to write—and that our students' development of writing skills is considerably hampered as a result. But explicit correction or evaluation of the kind provided by grades plays an extremely limited role in natural language-learning situations, which instead provide intricate, multilayered avenues of feedback and support for the language learner.

How Not to Grade?

I have tried many different arrangements for arriving at grades without my actually having to grade students' work. I have used various kinds of portfolio assessment methods; I have had people evaluate each other's work; and I have used contract-grading schemes. At this point, I have arrived at a method which suits me and which seems to allow for more of the kinds of learning I value than do the other methods I've used.

My approach is two-pronged: I try to create writing situations that simulate natural, out-of-school language-learning situations as closely as possible, and I shift the tasks of assessment and evaluation to the writers themselves in as many ways and as many different contexts as possible. What I actually do to determine students' final grades is really quite simple: I assign grades solely on the basis of the amount of work that a person does. Thus, in the freshman writing class that I taught in the fall of 1995, for example, I required that students

- read and annotate about 200 pages' worth of articles, culled (by them) from popular periodicals for the first half of the term and from scholarly sources for the second half;

- write one-page article recommendations (whose purpose is to convince others in the class to read the article they recommended) about once every other week (a total of five);

- write one-page responses to articles which had been recommended by others (they wrote six of these in all);

- produce a draft and final copy of a five- to seven-page typewritten, double-spaced midterm report;

- produce a draft and final copy of a five- to seven-page typewritten, double-spaced final report;

- write one-page responses for the authors of five to seven other midterm reports;

- write one-page responses for the authors of five to seven other final reports;

- write five 150–200-word "colleague acknowledgments": statements about the writing of classmates whose writing they respected;
- write a three- to five-page self-evaluation at the end of the semester.

Anyone who did all of those assignments to the length requirements specified got an A. Anyone who did 80 percent of the work (counted as total numbers of pages specified) got a B. Seventy percent of the work got a person a C, and so on. Missing a major assignment (I defined the midterm and final reports, the colleague acknowledgments, and the self-evaluation as major assignments) got a student's grade lowered by a whole letter.

Let me elaborate a bit. The scheme above called for 200 pages of reading and a minimum of thirty-six pages of writing. If students did at least 90 percent of that—180 pages of reading and thirty-two pages of writing—they were assured of getting an A in the course, assuming they'd not missed a major assignment.

This sort of grading plan creates a lot of paperwork; it's necessary to inform people early and often about where they stand. It also involves a lot of discussion, particularly at the beginning of the semester, about matters such as what constitutes a page, and so on. Sometimes those discussions get tedious—but they are no more tedious than the discussions I used to have about what makes a "substantive" revision, or what "better" means, or why certain changes haven't improved a piece of writing.

Actually arriving at the students' final grades for the course is only the tip of the iceberg, though; it doesn't take much work or thought to devise a scheme and to keep track of who has done what. Anybody could do this, once they'd decided to; it's pathetically easy to determine a final grade on the basis of quantity instead of quality. That's not the interesting part. The real trick is to create contexts where people are motivated to work and learn—where they take the work of the classroom seriously—in spite of the lack of grades on papers.

What Do Grades Do for Us?

As I have experimented with different ways of not grading writing, I've developed a healthy respect for the myriad functions that grades serve for both teachers and students in our classrooms—functions that relate to a student's performance and behavior in the classroom, even as they have little to do with that student's mastery of the subject of the class—and for the difficulty of replicating those functions in the current context of American schooling. It is not enough simply to take the specter of grading away and then to expect that students, liberated, will soar into new realms of language development and risk taking in their writing, and that teachers, released from the burden of evaluating and grading, will become coaches, mentors, and friends. Take away grades and you also take away the traditional means whereby students are motivated to work hard; you take away the chief mechanism through which they get feedback about their writing; you take away the means through which they learn how successfully they write compared with their classmates and others; and you take away their sense of accomplishment and reward. Similarly, when you take away grades, you take away the familiar lens through which teachers are accustomed to viewing students, themselves, and everyone's respective roles in the classroom—even what goes on in the classroom. If we choose not to grade student writing, that choice sets in motion a chain of causation that necessitates a number of other decisions as well.

If we take away the prop of grades, then, we need to see to it that the functions served by grades (albeit poorly served, for many people) are met in other ways. In the rest of this essay, I want to discuss those functions and the other means by which I've been trying to meet them. I also want to provide a small glimpse into how my role in the classroom has changed because I am no longer grading students' writing.

Motivation

It is undeniable that grades motivate many people. The problem, as I see it, lies in what grades motivate *for*. Grades provide people with extrinsic rewards, which work at cross-purposes with intrinsic motivations. There are numerous studies which show that extrinsic rewards severely inhibit intrinsic motivation (summarized in Kohn). Furthermore, extrinsic motivation doesn't lead to intrinsic motivation. Once the extrinsic reward is removed, people do not generally continue to engage in the behavior for which they were rewarded. Extrinsic reward doesn't lead to long-term, lasting changes in behavior (Kohn).

And long-term, lasting changes in behavior are precisely what I want to foster in my writing classroom. I not only want people to get response and feedback from their peers for the fourteen weeks in which they are enrolled in my course, I want them to continue to see getting a reader's response as a valuable addition to their repertoire of writerly tools. I not only want people to engage in extensive reading and research when they write papers in my class, I want them to come to understand that research really means extended engagement with the academic conversation, not finding five sources to quote for a paper. I want people in my classes to find reasons to be motivated to read, write, and research—and I want them to be able to find those reasons when they write for other classes later on (even if those classes are graded traditionally).

As I have experimented with different ways of not grading in my classrooms, I've come to see motivation as the result of a complex interrelation between activities and reasons. Paris and Turner argue that it is misleading to think of motivation as a "characteristic of people or a property of events" (213). Instead, they propose that "analyses of motivation should consider the characteristics of individuals in specific situations because a person's motivational beliefs and behavior are derived from contextual transactions" (213–14). They identify four characteristics of academic tasks which motivate learning:

- choice ("the ability to choose among different courses of action, or, at least, the freedom to choose to expend varying degrees of effort for a particular purpose") (222);
- challenge ("success without effort is a cheap reward and quickly loses its value in the classroom") (224);
- control ("Once students have chosen personally interesting and challenging tasks, they must exhibit control and autonomy to reach those goals in classrooms....Despite...[the] benefits of student control and autonomy, teachers often provide little genuine freedom in classrooms") (225); and
- collaboration ("Social guidance and cooperation in classrooms have now been recognized as fundamental for motivation") (226).

Setting up situations where students have motivated reasons to write without grades is tricky and risky. It requires second-guessing the sorts of tasks that will interest students and being willing to change or modify expectations in midstream if interest is waning. It requires setting up mechanisms whereby people are held accountable for doing their work. It requires giving students as much control as possible over the circumstances in which they write, while at the same time providing enough structure so that they can get help if and when they need it.

At first, engineering a classroom that provides students with choice, challenge, control, and collaboration seems like a dizzying, impossible task. One imagines a room full of twenty-five students pursuing twenty-five different agendas—with a teacher writing twenty-five lesson plans, twenty-five sets of feedback, and going home each day to twenty-five nervous breakdowns. Happily enough, I've found, creating such situations is largely a matter of "less is more." You start with one or two organizing principles or overarching pedagogical goals and move out from there. In my case, I am determined that all the writing my students do will be dialogic—they will write to people who will answer their writing, either by writing back, or by using it as the basis for further research, or by trying to do what it asks, or whatever—because I believe that those uses of writing illustrate most clearly what writing is for and why people do it. I want my students to perceive that they are writing out of their own genuine need to communicate something to someone who really wants to know what they have to say. A writing classroom without grades cannot function without this condition being present; otherwise, students will know that there is no reason (real or otherwise) for them to do the required work, and they will become bored and frustrated.

My task, then, initially becomes to find real audiences for my students' writing, or to make the situation in the classroom real enough that students care about reading what their classmates have to say. I try to find one large task, encompassing many smaller tasks, that will engage people for the duration of the semester—in short, I try to find what Frank Smith calls "enterprises." In the past, I have had freshman writers collaboratively investigate Henry Ford, the auto industry, and their impact on the southeast Michigan region where I teach; I have had technical writing students create discipline-specific Internet guides for humanities faculty; I have had technical writing students create World Wide Web pages for departments on campus; and I have had ESL students write a booklet designed to tell students new to the U.S. and to our campus about strange or baffling customs and university procedures. In each of these cases, the primary audience for the writing was someone other than me and someone outside the classroom, but I have also had success with having students work in groups to investigate specific topics and present the results of their research to their classmates by means of a class book.

If students' anonymous and confidential end-of-semester evaluations are any guide, the enterprises work at motivating people:

> I liked the way we were assigned to write documents that were actually going to be used. This not only helped to motivate me in doing the work, but it also gave me a sense of accomplish-

ment knowing that what I was spending so much time writing wasn't going to be read by the instructor, graded, and then thrown out.

The freedom that we had during this class's [electronic] discussion also motivated me. It would be easy to say that my personal involvement in my writing has taught me that what I write has great meaning and it created a passion to write rather than a boring and bland analytical writing assignment where I am struggling and just jumbling words onto paper to reach the professors' requirements. I wanted to write, I wanted to send e-mail messages, I wanted to make my point, I wanted people to notice and understand my writing. The freedom to choose our own research topic also pushed me to write with a definite goal and an absolute interest to make my point.

When I read those self-evaluations, I hear the voices of students who did find motivation in the situations I created for them.

Such is not always the case, though, and those other circumstances are troubling. The flip side of grading as a motivator for students is that grading can be a means of punishment, or at least of control, for a teacher. Giving a low grade can be a way (a not very specific way, to be sure, and hence not very threatening to the teacher) of signaling to a student that she needs to buckle down and work harder. Not giving grades on writing means that instructors have to find other means of informing students that their work is substandard and that they need to pay attention to it. I hope that the enterprises I've constructed will create means whereby a student will become publicly embarrassed if she does not complete her work on time and correctly—the need to fulfill an obligation made to group members or to other faculty on campus often does keep students more conscientious than simply completing an assignment for me.

Feedback

Grading is a crude substitute for many of the mechanisms that provide feedback in naturally occurring language-learning situations, and yet, as feedback mechanisms, grades are extremely poor. Even when teachers (or peers) offer extensive commentary in addition to grades, the presence of grades distorts the feedback, influencing the way the writer hears it. Giltrow and Valiquette, for example, showed that while students in their writing center recognized that instructors' comments on their papers constituted a specific genre which it was important for them to understand, the actual comments themselves confused and sometimes angered the students, who didn't know what they were supposed to do on the basis of them. Giltrow and Valiquette found that students most often read the comments as justifications for the grade on the paper, rather than as specific suggestions for improvement.

Other research, too, shows the dubious value of teacher comments on students' papers. Summarizing the research, Sperling writes that

> The emphasis on response has motivated much research on the comments written by teachers on students' papers. A large number of investigators examining the effects of such comments on students' writing have concluded that comments alone do not affect students' work (see review by Hillocks, 1986). One study of college teachers' comments showed them to be so facile and vague as to be mere "rubber stamps," interchangeable from text to text (Sommers, 1982). Other studies have shown comments to carry meaning for the teacher but not for the student, to be ignored by students and thrown away, and to be discounted by students who see in such comments their teachers' "confused readings" of their papers rather than their own writing weaknesses (e.g., Butler, 1980; Hahn, 1981). (66)

Sperling further notes that most of those studies were conducted on the basis of analyzing comments apart from instruction; there is evidence that comments may function best when embedded in process-based instruction. Even here, though, Sperling issues a caution, pointing to research that suggests that "student writers and teacher readers abide by complex and context-bound assumptions about one another that comments may not help to mediate....When students read teachers' responses to their writing, they may face, in part, the task of unpacking this complex of orientations" (67).

By contrast, in natural language situations, feedback is inherently easier to understand because the language always is intended to *do* something, to provoke some sort of a response in a hearer or reader. In such situations—a toddler asking her father for a glass of juice, for example—there is no need for grades; the person making the utterance knows if it succeeds by whether or not her hearer acts in the way she intended for him to act. Actions, of course, need not be restricted to physical movements; it is often the case that people talk to each other in order to evoke emotional reactions in their hearers, or to get others to share their point of view on a particular topic. Much research (Polanyi; Labov) shows that the point of a conversation is, in fact, to negotiate the meaning of the conversation, to settle on an interpretation of the facts and events being discussed. Thus, in the normal course of language-learning events, the ability to cause a specific action or to negotiate a certain meaning with our hearers provides feedback about the success of our efforts at communicating.

Naturally occurring language-learning situations also provide feedback to the learner specifically about particular utterances. For example, children learn the grammar and syntax of their native language largely by trial and error, and explicit correction from adults is comparatively rare. (Usually, in fact, it is restricted to specific formulaic situations—"Say thank you for the gift"—or to a small percentage of a child's utterances—"Don't say 'ain't.'") When correction occurs, though, it almost always occurs subtly and in the context of a meaningful discussion. If, for example, a child's utterance is unclear or ambiguous, a listener will ask for clarification, possibly offering alternatives, as in the following example:

> *Child* [looking at a car in a parking lot]: Mom, look at how that one's shaped.
>
> *Mother:* Shaped?
>
> *Child:* Yeah. It's all banged up. Look. It has rust.
>
> *Mother:* Oh, what shape it's in.
>
> *Child:* Yeah, what shape it's in.

In situations where an ungrammatical utterance does not interfere with meaning, usually no explicit correction is given. However, adults will sometimes repeat the structure of the utterance in a later utterance of their own.

Grades alone, of course, come nowhere near to offering this kind of subtle example or reinforcement to learners. Grades only tell students whether or not their work has met an acceptable level of competence, without helping them to know in what ways their communication has failed or succeeded and without providing alternatives which might have worked better. As a result, students come to believe that all that really matters is a sort of crude acceptable/sort of acceptable/not acceptable rating; they lose interest in the finer distinctions about performance.

Furthermore, grades teach people not to care much about what linguists, in reference to spoken language, call "repair"—about modifying or expanding on their work so as to clear up any initial confusion that resulted from it. For most people, once the grade is given, the transaction is concluded. Even in writing-process classrooms, the opportunity to revise for a higher grade is often seen by students as an opportunity to raise a grade, not to clarify the communication.

In the classroom, again, enterprises help to structure situations that provide for a fuller and more meaningful range of feedback for writers. As a result of structuring situations where written language will actually be used—to persuade or inform readers, who will use the information or arguments to carry out further tasks or to construct counterarguments—writers' and readers' feedback is always embedded within a context where the writing is expected by everybody to be immediately meaningful and pertinent. In such cases, the ways in which the reader uses the information that the writer has presented, or the sorts of counterarguments that readers advance, tell students the ways in which their written discourse is effective or ineffective. For example, if the enterprise in the class is to teach faculty members how to use the Internet, a guide that is incomprehensible to the faculty member for whom it was written is clearly ineffective. The situation provides the feedback; the faculty member clearly cannot follow the instructions the student has written because the faculty member is doing the wrong thing at the wrong time. The writers are pushed to clarify their statements and to find other ways of expressing their thoughts. The communication is not finished until a successful negotiation has occurred.

The standard set by negotiating understanding is at once more demanding and satisfying than working for an A. As one student put it:

> At the start of the semester the only thing I was looking forward to was the end of class....But with the group work...I notice that from reading other people's materials and just actively listening to what is being said amongst the groups that the quality of my work is improving. When I can look at my work and honestly tell that it is getting better, I try to dig deeper to get more facts or look at the topic from a different viewpoint to make it more interesting. Also, when I see people actively discussing my paper and arguing it vigorously, it is sometimes hard for me to believe that I wrote it.

And in an anonymous, end-of-semester evaluation another student said:

> I learned to be persuasive with my writing. The class discussions on the e-mail were very helpful. Not only did I get to express myself but often times students questioned my opinion and I had to explain in more depth the exact meaning of my statement. Which skilled me with the technique of persuasive and supportive writing.

Evaluation and Reward

Perhaps most obviously, grades are also a crude way of evaluating a person's performance and rewarding people for a job well done. Grades enable students to know where they stand in relation to others in the class, and they (theoretically) are supposed to give outsiders— employers or graduate school admissions committees, most likely—an objective measure of how an individual ranks in comparison with some Platonic standard.

This notion of standards is problematic. On the one hand, we want students to be aware that there *are* standards, and yet their understanding too often takes the form of wanting precise rules. If there's a standard way of doing things, why don't we simply tell them about it, so they can get on with it? A too-rigid conceptualization of standards reinforces a cookbook-style approach to writing: Follow the recipe and you'll succeed. Even though we as teachers know that blindly following recipes for good writing almost always leads to disaster, students are more often than not resentful at our refusal to provide recipes because they think we're holding out on them.

In the same way, although we might promote the idea that standards are really quite flexible (by saying, for example, that there are many types and kinds of good writing, or that there are many ways to approach a particular assignment) and that they are negotiated within a particular community (and thus, not really a product of a particular teacher's whims), students invariably understand standards as instantiated in particular classrooms at particular times by particular individuals. Thus, they ask, "What do you want on this paper?"—not "What does the academic community at large consider acceptable on this paper?"

Thus, if students are writing primarily to get a decent grade, then their focus must necessarily be on writing in a way that conforms to the standards held by the grade giver. To the degree to which they are writing in accordance with what the grade giver thinks of as good writing, they are denied the opportunity to learn to make their own value judgments about writing. Grades deprive students of the need to do the cognitive work involved in figuring out what constitutes appropriate writing in a given genre or discourse community. I want to be clear that this state of affairs applies simply because of the presence of grades in the classroom, irrespective of what any particular teacher does or does not do. As long as the teacher is passing judgment, the teacher's judgment will matter more than the student's.

But it is neither possible nor desirable to sidestep judgment altogether. In a class where grades are not given in the traditional manner, students still need to know how their performance compares with that of their classmates, to get a sense of how their writing works overall, out in the real world. Rather than provide such evaluations myself, however, I try to construct situations which will enable students to learn to make them. Learning to assess their strengths and weaknesses in comparison with others' is, to my mind, a crucial ability for writers (at any level) to develop and nurture. Good writing starts with the admiration of and respect for others' good writing.

To satisfy the writer's need for evaluation, and also to give people the chance to make their own judgments, I use a process of colleague acknowledgments, which I have borrowed and adapted from Russell Hunt (1993–1996) at St. Thomas University. At several points during the semester, I ask students to write me a note, telling me which (three or four or five) of their classmates' writing is particularly effective. I vary the wording of this assignment, depending on which rhetorical features I want them to think about. I might ask them to explain which pieces of writing have challenged their beliefs or perceptions, I might ask them whose writing is the clearest, or I might ask them whose style they most admire and why. I might ask them to quote specific bits from others' writing in their explanations.

I then redistribute these acknowledgments (anonymously) to the people who have been acknowledged. Thus, students in the class gain an understanding of whether others see their work as valuable, and if they do, what exactly about their writing strikes people as worthwhile. I love distributing the acknowledgments; people usually find them far more affirming than any grade could be—and since the acknowledgments are freely given, they are read by the recipients as being much more sincere than even the sincerest praise coming from a teacher.

The acknowledgments always make for interesting reading, both for me and for the people being acknowledged. I am frequently amazed at the diversity and subtlety of what students notice about each other's writing; I nearly always get a fresh insight into what's really going on in class for the students—what they value about writing and the class, what they're coming to value, as well as what they're not seeing or understanding. Mostly, though, students' acknowledgments are often specific and perceptive as well as complimentary, as the following example shows:

> Jennifer is a very talented writer; she is very expressive and heartfelt in her papers. I especially enjoyed reading the article on corruption in America's P.D. She is very persuasive in the presentation of her topic, and doing so on a level that is of interest to us, young college students. I thought that her point-of-view was the same as mine, or vice-versa, in that, "What distinguishes an officer of the law from the average person?" and "We do not need close-minded corrupt police officers taking away individual rights and creating chaos." I admire the fact that she is strong-minded and will put it in her writing. I am always afraid of what other people would think, and tried to avoid any type of controversy. After reading Lisa's papers, however, I realized that your view won't always be like someone else's, but it is a good way to make a discussion. I have learned to be more expressive from Jennifer's example.

Sometimes, even if the acknowledgments are not particularly specific, they display an honesty which is not available to me as a teacher to show:

> Kerri puts a lot of effort into her work; you can tell she doesn't B.S. her way through writing assignments and she does a good job making her topic sound important and meaningful.

> Sandy's writing is never confusing; she always gives great detail and gets right to the point. I can read her papers without getting completely bored.

> I thought Laurie's topic proposal on stress was very persuasive compared to most of the other proposals. She made a somewhat boring topic sound pretty interesting.

Also, sometimes it is clear that the acknowledger understands that her acknowledgment is written primarily for the writer, although she knows that I read them, too:

> I think that Danny R. is an excellent writer for a variety of reasons. He manages to write casually, without losing the basic sense of grammar or the point of the assignment. I enjoy reading his writings because they are interesting as well as informative. I like what he did to the encyclopedia article. He used his imagination to get around the obstacle the article presented. (He knows what I mean). I respect his writing because he gives his opinion very openly, yet at the same time, it is never offensive. I hope he keeps this writing style because it is persuasive, and I think we will find it beneficial to the group.

It often happens that not everyone in a class will receive acknowledgments. In order to increase the learning that is possible from the acknowledgments, I have used a variety of strategies to make it possible for others to read them. One strategy is to ask people who've been acknowledged to send me, via e-mail, the acknowledgment they value the most, along with a short explanation of why it was meaningful to them. I then reproduce those notes anonymously and pass them out for the whole class to read. At that point, we can discuss in more general terms what makes for effective writing—and what makes for effective acknowledging. People thus have the opportunity to see what kinds of qualities their classmates have acknowledged in others' writing, as well as how others have effectively expressed their admiration; the whole notion of what makes for good writing can thus expand beyond any one person's ideas.

Another strategy that I have begun to use is to ask students to post their acknowledgments anonymously via computer using a World Wide Web-based bulletin-board program called HyperNews. The advantage here is that as the acknowledgments are posted, other students can read them. I'm hoping that being able to read what others have said, just before they post their own acknowledgments, will give students another context for learning strategies for effective writing. I also hope that the ability to read others' acknowledgments will help to develop a classroom climate of appreciation—rather than criticism—for the writing being done in the class.

Replacing Grades with Learning

Finally, then, deciding not to grade students' writing has had a far more profound impact on my classroom than I ever imagined it would. In the process of noticing that removing grades was also removing many positive elements from the classroom, and of trying to replicate those positive elements in other ways, I have had to interrogate many of my longest-practiced teaching techniques in light of my most deeply held assumptions about the nature of teaching and learning. I have begun to question nearly everything that goes on in classrooms—in mine and others'. I think that I'm on the right track with what I am doing now. The kinds of learning I see in my students lead me to believe that if a class is structured to provide the elements that grades supply, not grading students' writing really can free them to take more control over their work.

I'd like to close with comments written by two students on their end-of-semester self-evaluations:

> I think I have reached new heights in self-expression this semester. Sometimes when I write for classes I am afraid of my point

of view offending people. This semester I think I have overcome that fear. A lot of what my group was writing about is considered controversial and I was aware of how strong my views are about the topic, but I overcame that and wrote what I felt should be written. It was especially rewarding when people agreed with my strong opinions and enjoyed my writing because of them. In other classes I would have toned it down a bit. I really felt that there would be no negative consequences from writing "from the heart" so I went ahead and did just that. I didn't have to worry about being graded down for offending the professor. Because of the lack of grades, I was able to concentrate completely on my writing and not what I thought the professor wanted to read.

Through high school I had always done well in English but I never really got the opinion of other students on my writing. In this class I found that all those A's in high school didn't really mean anything if other people can't understand your writing, find it boring, or have many questions about what you wrote.

These evaluations, and others like them, let me know that the payoff for upsetting the apple cart is that at least for the space of time that they're in my class, people have the chance to learn what it means to write for themselves.

Works Cited

Freadman, Anne. "'Genre' and the Reading Class." *Typereader: The Journal of the Centre for Studies in Literary Education* 1 (1988): 1–7.

Giltrow, Janet, and Michelle Valiquette. "Student Writers and Their Readers: The Conventions of Commentary." Paper presented at the Conference on College Composition and Communication. Mar. 16–20 1994. Nashville, TN.

Hunt, Russell A. Personal correspondence. 1993–1996.

Kohn, Alfie. *Punished by Rewards: The Trouble with Gold Stars, Incentive Plans, A's, Praise, and Other Bribes.* Boston: Houghton, 1993.

Labov, William. *Language in the Inner City: Studies in the Black English Vernacular.* Philadelphia: U of Pennsylvania P, 1972.

Paris, Scott G., and Julianne C. Turner. "Situated Motivation." *Student Motivation, Cognition, and Learning: Essays in Honor of Wilbert J. McKeachie.* Hillsdale: Erlbaum, 1994. 213–37.

Polanyi, Livia. "So What's the Point?" *Semiotica* 25.3/4 (1979): 207–41.

Smith, Frank. *Essays into Literacy: Selected Papers and Some Afterthoughts.* London: Heinemann, 1983.

Sperling, Melanie. "Revisiting the Writing-Speaking Connection: Challenges for Research on Writing and Writing Instruction." *Review of Educational Research* 66.1 (1996): 53–86.

Interlude

I remember once bringing home a report card from elementary school. I had straight A's except for one A-. My father looked at the card and said something like, "What's the matter with you, this A-?" Now my dad was a fairly stern parent and wanted us to achieve in school. I was crushed, and to this day, I don't know whether or not he was joking.

—Nancy Warthan
University of Nevada, Reno

12 Seeing How Good *We* Can Get It

Kelly Chandler
University of Maine

Amy Muentener
University of Southern Maine

Kelly Chandler taught high school English before entering a doctoral program in literacy education at the University of Maine.

Amy Muentener is a first-year undergraduate in the Russell Scholars program at the University of Southern Maine, where she plans to major in biology.

For the past two years, I have taught English at Noble High School in Berwick, Maine. Amy Muentener was my student in English 10, a heterogeneously grouped class required for all sophomores, and "Literature Seminar," an upperclass elective. She was also a two-year member of my summer book club for students. With my recommendation, Amy decided to enroll in the senior advanced placement English course for the 1995–96 school year. That July she was writing one of her A.P. summer assignments when I gave her a call about the book club:

> "Hi, Amy, this is Ms. Chandler. I'm calling to get a head count for the book club meeting. Did you read the book?"
>
> "I'm not quite done, but I've been busy writing my *Catch-22* paper for A.P."
>
> "How's it going?"
>
> "I know it's going to be good."
>
> "How do you know?"
>
> "The ideas are there. I still need to ask myself some questions, though. Am I backing things up with text? Is it staying with the question? It's almost like you're here standing over my shoulder, saying 'Why? Explain.'"

When I hung up, the details of this five-minute telephone conversation seemed minor to me. I realized after some reflection, however, that it revealed a great deal about Amy's development as a writer. Without teacher assistance, she could identify the strengths and weaknesses of a piece in progress and devise strategies to address the flaws. Having internalized the process for herself, she no longer needed a conference with me to move from a first to a second draft. Although she told me that she could hear my voice in her head, what she really heard was her own writer's voice. She had achieved Arthur Costa's "ultimate purpose of evaluation" by teachers: the student's ability to evaluate herself (Rief 45).

As I pondered Amy's progress, I wondered how she had gained this independence. What steps had she taken? What support had I given? I couldn't answer those questions alone. Further, as I considered the professional literature I'd read and the conversations I'd had about the assessment and evaluation of student writing, I realized that the piece missing from many of those discussions was the student's perspective. For this reason, I invited Amy to be my co-author for this piece, to share both her own story as a writer and her insights on assessment and evaluation.[1] As we considered these issues while writing this essay, we agreed that one-on-one conferences were the most powerful teaching and assessment method for Amy. The following pages explore the kinds of conferences that we had and the effect that they had on Amy's development as a writer.

"Big Picture" Conferences

When Amy walked into my classroom two years ago, I never would have predicted that she and I would become partners in a writing project. As she remembers, she "didn't like to write. I hated English. I dreaded going to that class more than any other." Poor grades and red pen bleeding all over her papers had convinced Amy that she was a poor writer. And, indeed, her technical skills were weak—her punctuation haphazard, her usage erratic, her spelling more creative than correct. Much of her previous writing had been graded harshly because of these errors in mechanics. No one had made it clear that her lack of control over surface features didn't make a text meaningless. I could tell from one of her early papers, a richly detailed descriptive piece about a barn, that she had something wonderful to say. Nonetheless, she was shy about saying it: reluctant to share her work, insecure about its worth, and convinced that she was a far better reader than she was a writer:

> I have always been a reader. I remember when my family would go on trips and I would pack bags of books, instead of clothes....My mother is the one person who really influenced

my reading habit. She's also addicted to reading. Although I read a lot, writing was never one of my strongest abilities. It's something I need to constantly work on. I was never encouraged to try harder at writing until my sophomore year in high school.

Encouraging Amy was what those first conferences were all about. Because of her previous negative experiences, I needed to "deprogram" her, to use Zemelman and Daniels's phrase, from her expectation that her work would be evaluated for its correctness, not its content (227). I needed to provide her with an interested, supportive audience, to convince her to keep going when she was inclined to give up on a piece. According to Amy, "students want their teachers to listen to and care about their writing. I find that it means a lot more when the teacher wants the paper to be good, not just done." I had to convince Amy that I was one of those teachers. Consequently, I did not pick apart her early pieces of writing. Instead, as Amy recalls, those early conferences were focused on the "big picture" of the piece, "looking at the whole paragraph to see if it said what I wanted it to say, making sure I had all the elements of the paragraphs and of the whole paper—introduction, conclusion, thesis." I asked questions during those conferences, rather than giving instructions.

At the end of the first quarter in English 10, Amy's class had a portfolio share day. Students had selected three pieces from the term's worth of writing to revise and polish. Their portfolios, with accompanying letters of self-evaluation, were graded on their overall quality and on their improvement from first drafts to final drafts. Each student read his or her best piece aloud on the share day. Even though her piece about the barn had vastly improved from its first draft, Amy was still reticent about reading it in front of her peers. In fact, she refused to share it unless I read it. When I did, her classmates were unanimous in their praise—which Amy did not expect. "I was surprised that they liked it and that they thought it was good," she said. "I had never really shared a piece of writing before. It was neat that others also enjoyed something I liked."

Editing Conferences

About midway through that year, Mrs. Muentener called me to ask if I would give Amy some extra help with grammar and mechanics. Although she was pleased about her daughter's new confidence in herself as a writer and impressed by some of the pieces Amy had produced, she was still worried about how Amy would perform on upcoming standardized tests. I agreed to spend some extra time with Amy once a week on Thursdays. Instead of completing grammar exercises from the textbook (at which Amy was already quite good), we decided to work on her position paper, which argued that women should to be admitted to the Catholic priesthood. Although engaging and passionately argued, the piece was weakly organized and littered with errors. It had received a B- in English 10, but Amy knew she could produce a much better final draft.

At first, Amy remembers, she was motivated to work on the position paper merely because she "wanted to see how good we could get it, how many problems I could work through, how clean it could be." Her desire to fine-tune the piece is evident here, as is her expectation that "we" would do it together. By this time, she saw us as equal partners; I was no longer the authority and she the recipient of my knowledge. Amy says that "during that time we worked *together,* sharing ideas about how to make my writing better and ways for students and teachers to collaborate better."

After two weeks of tightening and clarifying the paper, Amy decided to apply to SEARCH, a discussion program for high school students sponsored by the University of New Hampshire. The SEARCH application required a writing sample that explored a controversial issue and took a stand. Once Amy decided to submit her position paper, she worked even harder in our conferences. "It was not going to be graded," she remembers, "but it *was* going to be judged, and that made me want to make it clear and finished." Because she had a real-world goal, she was able to sustain her initial desire to improve the piece for its own sake. She had also overcome her fear of allowing other people to read her writing.

From these conferences, I learned a great deal about teaching and evaluating skills within the context of a student's piece—something I'd previously preached but not really practiced. Paragraph by paragraph, we edited Amy's position paper, eliminating surface errors. Trying not to overwhelm Amy by pointing out all the errors she had made, I learned to focus on one skill at a time until it was mastered. For example, I sometimes selected a paragraph and told Amy that there were three comma errors in it but not what or where they were. She worked until she fixed them, reviewing rules concerning commas and ignoring any other errors she encountered. Another weakness we addressed was spelling. Amy's misspellings were often so bizarre that the spell checker could not provide her with the correct choice. To remedy this, I showed her how to pay closer attention to initial sounds and to count syllables in order to better approximate the word. Her proofreading improved dramatically.

From these Thursday conferences, Amy mastered some specific strategies for improving the technical quality of her work. Because I modeled working on one kind of error at a time in our conferences, she began to focus her independent editing as well. She learned how to identify her own particular demons—inconsistencies in verb tense or omitted words—and how to isolate those mistakes when reading a draft. In time, she was able to self-correct a much larger proportion of her technical errors. She also learned the power of precision and accuracy in her writing when she was accepted to SEARCH and the adviser told me that Amy's essay was among the most impressive of the applications.

No Conferences

Amy and I continued this kind of intensive coaching the following spring when she took my course entitled "Literature Seminar." In the fall of her junior year, however, she was not my student. Instead, she was enrolled in English 11, a yearlong heterogeneously grouped course taught by another teacher. Amy did not flourish in this class; she earned an 82—the numerical equivalent of a C—for the third quarter, and once she even received a midterm failure warning. Amy's most significant criticisms of English 11 concerned assessment and evaluation. She particularly resented the teacher's practice of grading final drafts without having seen the previous stages. According to her, when he gave an assignment, "He didn't talk about it at all. There were no conferences about the paper. It was just due. A week later it came back with a grade on it."

Interestingly enough, Amy did not seem to question the teacher's basic fairness or his knowledge of writing. She was more angry about his lack of knowledge about *her*. She complained that "all he saw was the finished product, not what I did to get there. Probably if he'd seen what I started with and where I ended up I would have gotten a better grade." She believed that effort and improvement should be factored in with the quality of the product. She also wanted her teacher to be actively involved with her work in progress. As she put it, "in order to really grade students' writing, the teacher needs to talk with the students and follow them through their writing process."

Although Amy views the lack of conferences in English 11 as a negative experience, I see a positive result. I believe that part of her ability to articulate the conditions she needs to grow as a writer came from their absence in English 11. Amy missed daily support as a writer so much that she pursued outside resources. "I found myself wanting and needing one-on-one conferences and seeking out Ms. Chandler just to talk about a paper or idea for my other teacher," she says. Amy came to appreciate—even demand—a process-oriented approach that included conferences only when she was denied it. She also learned how to get the help she needed even when it wasn't readily available.

I cannot condemn Amy's English 11 teacher, however, for his practices. I, too, struggled in English 10 to balance whole-class instruction with individual instruction, reading with writing, content with skills. In my writing program, I sometimes spent more time on brainstorming exercises and revision activities than I did on coaching students through a piece of writing. Although I never graded first drafts and structured conference time into my lesson plans, those conferences were neither frequent nor sustained enough. Most students in my English 10 classes were not getting the personalized attention that Amy had in our Thursday sessions.

In addition, my grading practices were inconsistent in English 10. I tried new techniques frequently but could not find anything with which I was completely comfortable. Sometimes I asked students to participate in the evaluation process; sometimes I graded their papers without their input. During some marking terms, I required students to keep portfolios; sometimes I graded individual pieces after they had been through a couple of drafts. On occasion, the students and I developed a rubric together to score an assignment; more often, I articulated the criteria for quality only to myself. Not surprisingly, my students weren't developing as writers as successfully as I wanted them to do.

When I saw how much progress Amy could make with regular coaching, I realized that I needed to spend less time on my couch with my comment pen and the student's paper and more time in my classroom with the student and the paper. The following year I began to explore a format for my upperclass elective, entitled "Literature Seminar," where I could replicate our tutoring time as closely as possible. Amy signed up for that course, and our partnership continued.

Analytic Conferences

The basic requirements of the literature seminar were simple, designed to provide maximum choice and individualization for students: each quarter, students read a minimum of four books of their choice, completed at least two polished papers or projects related to their reading, participated in conferences and discussions, and wrote weekly letters to me about their progress. At least half of each eighty-minute block was reserved as workshop time for the students and me to read, write, and—most important—conference. For the first time in my teaching career, I was able to give *all* of my students the kind of focused, personalized instruction I had given Amy on Thursdays.

In the course, Amy read novels such as *Sula, Cold Sassy Tree*, and *One Flew Over the Cuckoo's Nest*, and then wrote several papers in response to her reading. Having established a relationship of trust with Amy, I was able to address more sophisticated issues in her work during that second year. Although she met with me at various stages of her writing process, depending on her needs, we usually sat down for a full-fledged conference only after she had completed a first draft. Then we critiqued her writing together in almost the same fashion that one would close-read a literary text. I call this kind of student-teacher interaction an "analytic conference," where the purpose is to analyze the piece for meaning on both the sentence level and paragraph level while making sure that the entire piece hangs together. Amy made big strides using this approach. As she explains:

> The course that helped me the most in writing was the Literature Seminar. The method that benefited me most was sitting down with the teacher and picking the piece of writing apart, not only looking for grammar errors but also questioning thoughts and ideas. This time was spent reading each line and asking, why was that put in? What is its importance? Does it make sense with the rest of the paper? I found that it helps when someone questions my ideas because that makes me think of a better way to justify myself.

By this time, Amy had learned to accept criticism constructively. She needed fewer "big picture" conferences for validation and more analytic ones for sharpening and polishing her pieces. She had moved far enough from her previous negative feelings about writing that she no longer took feedback personally. At this stage, Amy became more independent because she "could do the first draft on my own. I didn't need to talk to you all the time. From having had similar conferences before, about the same kind of weaknesses, I knew what to do and how to change them."

Self-Evaluation Conferences

In "Literature Seminar," unlike English 10, I did not grade individual pieces of writing. In fact, I didn't grade anything at all, at least not on my own. Twice per quarter, students and I conferenced about their progress to that point and negotiated a grade for their midterm progress and quarter reports. Before they came to meet with me, students letter-graded themselves in four categories—reading, writing, use of time, and participation—that we had discussed as a class on numerous occasions. Then they wrote explanations for the grades they felt they had earned. In the writing category, students needed to address both process and product in evaluating themselves.

I completed the same procedure for each student. In the evaluation conference, we shared our sheets and converted our letter grades to numbers.[2] If there was a discrepancy, we negotiated it. This happened very infrequently; during the four sets of self-evaluation conferences I had with the twenty-four students in the course, I disagreed significantly with students on only three occasions.

When Amy and I met for a self-evaluation conference during the first quarter, our numbers differed by only one point. As she described it, "We didn't really negotiate. Our ideas were just about the same. You knew me, knew how I write, what I went through to get what I handed in." Because we had conferenced so frequently, I did know her and her work. I had been assessing her progress continuously throughout the quarter and giving her feedback. Final evaluation was not an abrupt stop in our continuum of teaching and learning; it was just another step.

These conferences allowed me to have a less adversarial relationship with my students. Grading was no longer something I did to them; it was something we did together. Instead of quibbling with me about how much a given assignment was worth or whether they could pass in long-expired homework, they were discussing themselves as readers and writers. When the grading process was demystified and they were consistently included in it, students could focus on their learning, not on "beating the system." With decreased anxiety also came increased insight about themselves as individuals. Like Linda Rief, I discovered from self-evaluation conferences that students know themselves as learners better than anyone else. They set goals for themselves and judge how well they reach those goals. They thoughtfully and honestly evaluate their own learning with far more detail and introspection than I thought possible. (47)

This was certainly true of Amy. In preparation for our first grading conference, she wrote a self-evaluation that was honest, fair, and critical in the best sense of the word. Giving herself an A for the quarter in writing, she described her improvement: "I have become more independent with my writing, knowing what you want and doing it, not just waiting until you tell me what the next step is." Other strengths she listed were backing up her points with specific text from the book and adding detail in subsequent drafts. She wanted to work on her weakness of "leaving my ideas too open-ended. I want to refine my thinking skills and complete my ideas." I couldn't have said it better myself.

Preparing for self-evaluation conferences forced Amy to articulate her strengths and weaknesses, her accomplishments and goals. She couldn't rely on me to tell her how she had performed during the quarter. She had to think for herself. I believe that this process was instrumental in moving her toward the self-reliant writer who talked to me on the telephone.

Conferences with Herself

Amy has demonstrated remarkable progress as a writer in the two years I've known her. Her first drafts are clearer and cleaner than they used to be, and she needs far less help to improve them. She says that she "now enjoy[s] writing about books and expressing my own thoughts and feelings for other people to read" and attributes that transformation to being questioned about what she put down on paper. Her eagerness to collaborate on this piece shows me how confident she has become about the worth of her ideas and her own ability to communicate them. Accepting the challenge of an A.P. English course is another indicator of her growth. I believe that Amy's story shows the worth of Susan Sowers's advice to teachers: "Ask questions you want students to ask themselves, so that they may have…individual conferences with themselves. What they can do with you today they will do on their own later" (140–41).

In the real world, writing doesn't receive A's and B's. When Amy leaves school, her work, like her SEARCH essay, will be judged, not graded. She will no longer have a teacher with whom to conference, although I'm sure she will always seek people from whom to get feedback. She will need to be able to evaluate the quality of her work for herself, to decide if a piece is clear enough and clean enough for its purpose. I believe that one-on-one conferences are both the best way I taught her to make those decisions and the best assessment tool I had for determining if she had learned those lessons.

Notes

1. For the sake of clarity, I use the first person in this essay and quote Amy. Nonetheless, we collaborated on every aspect of the writing of this piece. According to Amy, "After Ms. Chandler suggested working together, I had the feeling that she would just be using some quotes from me to back up her thoughts and ideas. After we met to discuss the project, I saw that she was making me an author, too." Both of us wrote separately about a series of broad questions concerning writing, assessment, and evaluation. These musings became our raw material. Meeting twice before we could narrow down a thesis, we roughed out the general outline of this piece while riding a bus to a Shakespeare play. On my own, I wrote a skeleton of that draft, which we developed more fully in a marathon conference that incorporated elements of our "big picture" and analytical conferences. Several editing conferences later, we were finished. As Amy puts it, "This paper is the result of two people working in a partnership to produce a piece of writing that might help others who are distressed about their writing or teaching."

2. At that time, Noble High School reported numerical grades to parents each quarter. Because I was more comfortable with letter grades, which I considered broader and more holistic, I assigned arbitrary numbers to the letters at the end of the term. Since the range for a C was 78–84, a student who earned a solid C for the quarter would receive an 81 on her report card. A B was an 89, and an A was a 97. All my students knew how to do the conversions, and no parent or administrator ever commented on how strange it was that my grades were almost always odd numbers.

Works Cited

Rief, Linda. "Eighth Grade: Finding the Value in Evaluation." *Portfolio Portraits*. Ed. Donald H. Graves and Bonnie S. Sunstein. Portsmouth: Heinemann, 1992. 45–60.

Sowers, Susan. "Reflect, Expand, Select: Three Responses in the Writing Conference." *Understanding Writing: Ways of Observing, Learning, and Teaching*. 2nd ed. Ed. Thomas Newkirk and Nancie Atwell. Portsmouth: Heinemann, 1988. 130–41.

Zemelman, Stephen, and Harvey Daniels. *A Community of Writers: Teaching Writing in the Junior and Senior High School.* Portsmouth: Heinemann, 1988.

Interlude

My seniors want grades...but they have been "side-tracked" to earn the rank of "Completion Attained." They were getting confused on what assignments they'd done, and what was left to do, so I got an elementary school sticker chart. They love it! I use (I can't believe I do it, but I do it) smiley-face stickers, a different color for each completed assignment. They read that *#$!$%& chart every day to see if they've got 'em all in, or who's done more. This took so much heat off grades! The goal is to turn in ten quality pieces of writing in one semester—I require certain types, and some are free choice—but completion = passing. They really work!

> —Marcie Woods
> Northview High School
> Grand Rapids, Michigan

13 Grading on Merit and Achievement: Where Quality Meets Quantity

Stephen Adkison and Stephen Tchudi
University of Nevada, Reno

Stephen Adkison is a graduate student in rhetoric and composition at the University of Nevada, Reno. He is associate editor of Halcyon, *a journal of the humanities, and a co-director of the Truckee River Project, an interdisciplinary summer institute for teachers held annually at the University of Nevada, Reno. He is particularly interested in writing instruction, interdisciplinary and environmental literature, and the implications of brain research for language-learning theory.*

Stephen Tchudi (introduced on the Editor page) chaired the NCTE Committee on Alternatives to Grading Student Writing.

"Kneel before the judge," orders the bailiff, a rough-looking dude who reminds us of a football player from an English 101 class.

"All others please rise," he continues, and we become aware from the shuffling that there's a large crowd in the hall behind us.

Through a window to the left, we are shocked to catch a glimpse of a guillotine, sunlight glinting off its razor-sharp blade. To our right, we see, is a jury, and we gradually realize that it seems to be made up of former students of ours. We smile at them, happy to see familiar faces. They do not smile back. Our gray prison garments stick to our sweaty bodies.

"The charge, your worship," says some lawyer-type guy decked out in a sharkskin suit, "is that of grading inequity."

He smooths his slick black hair with his palms, and the jury nods at him. He paces toward the jury box and continues: "The question is one of fairness and equity."

Somebody in the jury says, "Amen, brother!"

The lawyer raises his fist in a rhetorical flourish: "A question of specificity and honesty."

Somebody else shouts, "Right on!"

The lawyer crosses back over to us and glares: "A question of just how it is one gets an A in this course."

"So how *do* you get an A?" sneers the lawyer, "or a B for that matter, or a C plus, or even . . ." (and here he pinches his nose while speaking) "add Evv?"

We finally understand what's happening and speak up.

"Well," one of us says, "we're modern writing teachers, so we give A's for things like *ideas* and *structure* and *personal voice*."

"Yeah," the other adds, "like, we don't grade for grammar or mechanics or things like that. We want to encourage our students to write."

"Encourage?!" sneers the lawyer, while the jury giggles. "So tell me Mr. Wiseguys, just what's an 'A' *idea,* as opposed to a 'B'? What's a 'C' in *voice?*"

"Well, that's a little hard to say," we begin.

"Hard to say?" asks the lawyer, imitating our intonation. "Don't you grade for *clarity?* For *specificity?* For *details?* Please be *clear, specific,* and *detailed.* Tell us the difference between an A paper and a B+, or B- versus a C+."

"Well, clarity is, you know, clear," one of us says, and the jury listens, waiting for more. Somebody snorts.

"And voice," we say, "we can easily recognize it in student writing."

"Just give us a writing sample."

"And a rubric."

"We can show you."

"You see!" screams the lawyer, whom we now recognize as that prelaw kid to whom we gave a C- a few years ago, "They don't know! They really can't tell us what those grading criteria are. 'Guess what I like,'" he mimics, "'and I'll give you your A.'"

"I've heard enough," screams the judge, "Off with their heads!"

Thus ends our living nightmare of putting letter grades on student writing.

There are may good reasons *not* to grade student writing, ranging from the psychological to the pedagogical. In this essay, we'll concentrate on just one of these: the rhetorical difficulty of articulating grading standards—in advance, with clarity and detail—that tell students exactly what one believes to be "good" writing; what kind of writing the teacher will reward with an A; why a paper, after going through the proper stages of the writing process, might still wind up as a C. We will offer our rationale for what we call "achievement grading," an approach that allows us *not* to put grades on individual papers, and we'll illustrate and discuss problems with this system through anecdotal evidence from our university classes. By articulating our approach to grading, we hope to end our nightmares, or at least, to face the jury with a clean pedagogical conscience.

Writing quality, we have come to realize, is virtually inseparable from the context of writer, audience, occasion, and content. From the beginning of rhetorical history, scholars from Aristotle to Quintilian and beyond have tried to describe the abstract or general traits of writing. They have spoken of organizational structures and patterns, the characteristics of good style, and matters of language purity and propriety. Yet much of the writing advice that one finds in current-traditional handbooks—our inheritance from the classical and neoclassical traditions—seems to us empty and unhelpful. What is a good topic sentence as opposed to a bad one? A solid reason or piece of evidence as opposed to a shaky one? Clear, concise, and coherent prose as opposed to the unclear, inconcise, or incoherent? Although the rhetorical generalizations are interesting, none of these descriptions seems to us precise enough that a well-meaning writing teacher can explain to students, in advance, just what an A paper will be. The rhetoricians would have as difficult a time in court as we would.

We believe that until a writer begins drafting—trying to hammer out a poem or essay or story about elephants or mermaids or his or her life—the criteria, rhetorical or evaluative, remain vague. Once the process is under way, the teacher/rhetorician may be able to offer advice—"You seem to need more evidence about elephant memories"—or even grading hints—"This seems to be shaping up as an A paper." But before the fact and before the judge, one is limited to vague generalities, to waving rhetoric books and rubrics at one's students.

The solution we have explored in our own teaching is what we call "achievement grading." (We hasten to add that we see this only as a partial solution to the grading dilemma.) In simplest terms, the approach awards higher grades to the students who complete a wider range of work or who go into ideas and topics in greater depth than their peers. Achievement grading has its roots in so-called "contract grading" and "point" systems, where students receive credit for completing tasks successfully and do not receive grades on papers per se (see Kirschenbaum, Napier, and Simon; Knowles; and O'Hagan, this volume). Actually, we have to say that our first choice in teaching would be not to grade at all, but to have the schools—or, at least, English/language arts classes—run on a pass/fail or credit/no credit system. Achievement grading attempts to implement what amounts to pass/fail within the confines of the grading system:

- All work is "graded" credit/no credit (or pass/fail or successful/unsuccessful).
- The requirements for credit are stated in terms of *tasks* or *assignments* to be completed. The criteria for credit usually specify both the amount of work to be done (quantity) and the kind of thoroughness and polish required for acceptance

(quality). The teacher may be the sole determiner of tasks and criteria, but usually students are involved in the negotiation of both.

- Students get points, grades, or other rewards on the basis of how much creditable work they do.

One sees a kind of achievement grading at work in Mark Twain's *Tom Sawyer*. In Tom's Sunday school, the children are given colored ribbons for reading Biblical verses. Ten ribbons of one color can be turned in for one ribbon of the next hierarchical color; ten of those can be converted to a ribbon of a third color; and ten of those can be exchanged for the big prize, one's own Bible. Tom shocks the Sunday school superintendent by turning in the necessary ribbons to earn the Bible, even though he acquired them through bartering, not reading. (Achievement grading, like the Bible ribbon program, needs to include various checks and measures to keep students on track and within the rules.)

In fact, Tom's experience with reading ribbons in Sunday school parallels the more recent summer reading programs for young readers found in public libraries nationwide. Though varying in specific details, these programs typically recognize readers as they reach reading goals based on how much they've read throughout the summer, rather than on whether they've digested what this librarian or that considers "essential" to their young minds. One scale we're familiar with openly encourages young readers to undertake voyages of discovery by designating four successive levels: "vagabond," "adventurer," "explorer," and finally, "discoverer." The youngsters must read ten books to gain "vagabond" status and then ten more books for each successive level afterward. Achievement is recognized at each level with a certificate indicating that the recipient has met the requirements for that level and is acknowledged to be an "adventurer" or "explorer" and so forth. The youngsters are encouraged to read and then to read more; each book encountered and completed adds to their progress up the scale of the reading program. Certainly, by summer's end, different readers will end up at various points along this scale (as do students engaged in achievement grading at the end of the term). Freed from grade tyranny (but having their good work praised), many children read more than they otherwise would have, and many read a prodigious amount. Better yet, most of these programs are set up so that the young readers are not only rewarded for reading, but are encouraged to choose what they will read, discovering their own motivation to read.

Then there's scouting—both boy and girl—which plays a major role in the lives of huge numbers of young people, an *educational* role, we might add. In the scouts, a hierarchy of tasks is arranged. The more of these one completes, the higher up the ranks one goes. The tasks are clear and explicit: "Cook a meal on an open fire." "Do a safety inspection of your house." There's no puzzlement over A's and B's or the fine gradations of a C+. A mentor adult or older scout monitors the process to make certain the job is well and thoroughly done. In scouting, learning is self-paced, incremental, and interdisciplinary; the rewards are clear and unambiguous. Without idealizing the program (there *are* problems in the merit badge approach to learning and rewards), it has occurred to us that the schools could do worse than to convert the curriculum to something like the scouting awards program:

> You want a diploma? You want a Bible? You want to be a "vagabond"? You want to go to college? You want to prepare for a job? Here's a list of things you can do to qualify.

This list of tasks required to qualify for a specific grade forms the backbone of our approach to achievement grading. The tasks spell out, in concrete terms, what is expected of students in the classroom. Rather than struggling to master vague and context-dependent concepts—"structure," "voice," "clarity," "specificity," and the like—students are shown a number of assignments that must be completed during the course of the semester. All tasks are pass/fail or credit/no credit, with the possibility that unacceptable work can be redone until it is creditable. (We'll tackle the obvious problem of defining "creditable" before we complete this paper.)

We have found that, given a set of tasks that must be acceptably accomplished, students spend less time trying to determine what we, the teachers, prefer and more time working on the tasks before them. In short, students encounter less ambiguity surrounding teacher expectations and course requirements, and they find focusing on the course easier.

For example, here is how Steve Adkison structures the achievement grading in his freshman composition class, English 101, a required course in the University of Nevada's core curriculum. Conceptually, the aim of English 101 is to encourage student development in various levels of the intellectual process through writing and other whole language activities, a sequence of writing that moves from *observation, interpretation,* and *analysis* to *integration* and *synthesis.* Since most of the students entering freshman composition classes are new to the university community, many come to the 101 class anxious about both the course itself and college in general. They are worried about "making their grades" for a premed or other grade-conscious concentration, and some are simply concerned about passing the course and staying in school. Grade consciousness often outweighs any interests they might have in developing their writing and thinking skills through an active exploration of the writing process.

In an attempt to break the ambush these anxieties often spring in writing courses, Adkison establishes a performance-based evaluation system in his 101 classes. The system is based on specific requirements for both B grades and A grades; though some students do end up receiving C grades (mostly for failure just to do the work or to come to class), this emphasis on B's and A's helps focus students on higher rather than "acceptable" goals. In fact, any students who normally pursue, at best, C grades often find themselves actively working for higher grades than they would have in a traditionally evaluated classroom. To earn a B, students must:

- attend the class regularly, coming prepared to participate actively in class discussions, readings, and small-group work; more than three absences will lower the final grade one full letter;

- maintain an informal writing journal, responding to all assigned readings as well as both in-class discussions and out-of-class field trips. Journal entries are made both in class and assigned as homework;

- complete several (from five to seven, depending on the specific syllabus) out-of-class field trips which form the basis of several in-class activities. (As an example, one of the field trips requires the students to find and observe someone that interests them in some way and to write a description of that person and what he or she is doing. The descriptions are read and discussed in class as a way of looking at significant details and how they function in specific writing contexts);

- complete five formal essays assigned during the course of the semester. Though these essays are generally structured to move students through the overall course aims, the specifics of each assignment are open-ended and broad enough to allow students a wide range of approaches and possibilities; and

- develop a final portfolio consisting of further revisions and polishing of two of the five formal essays. The students choose which of the two essays they will revise, and include all draft materials, the essay as it was originally accepted, and the final polished revision.

Moving beyond the basic requirements for a B in English 101, the requirements for an A encompass all of the B requirements and also encourage students to push themselves beyond the work done in the classroom. The A grade requires students to develop a project that they pursue independently over the latter half of the course. Suitable projects might range from a sixth formal essay to reading projects that are designed to immerse students deeply in a particular interest they wish to explore. The particulars of these projects must be negotiated individually with the instructor and completed according to agreed-upon criteria. This A approach reinforces the idea that A grades are reserved for work that goes beyond the baseline effort required to complete the course.

None of the requirements—for a B or an A—is graded, per se, but rather all work is evaluated as either "credit" or "no credit." Since the 101 students are not pressured to write "A" papers—papers the instructor will "like"—most spend much less time struggling with what they think the instructor wants and more time creating their own approaches and developing their essays. As a result, the vast majority of work turned in by these 101 students is creditable the first time around. And creditable work is by no means merely marginal work but must be complete and thorough.

A wonderful example of this work occurred during a segment of the course in which the class focused their discussions and writing on western land and water issues. One of the students, a former C student in his high school English courses, committed himself to an A project—arguing that control of federal lands in Nevada should be turned over to the state—a view decidedly at odds with most of the rest of the class, including the instructor. Because his initial drafts were emotionally loaded patchworks of evidence cookie-cuttered from various media sources and merely pasted together, he at first failed at moving his classmates to take his argument seriously in group discussions and peer workshops. Rather than retreating to a position which he knew to be safer and more acceptable with both his classmates and the instructor, he instead decided to work harder at being heard and understood; he scrapped his original approach and went on to develop an appealing argument supported by carefully considered evidence drawn from both his original media sources and personal anecdote. The essay he turned in for "credit" had evolved far beyond his original cut-and-paste report approach and was, in fact, a model of original synthesis. In the end, though he did not sway the whole class, his voice was not only heard and understood, but also respected by his colleagues. This experience motivated him throughout the rest of the course as well and was reflected in the high quality of all the work he did. His A project in achievement grading turned him into an A student.

Overall, this approach to evaluation presents course requirements in specific, concrete terms focused on work to be accomplished, which helps allay from the beginning the anxiety and dissonance many students experience in the course of trying to "figure a class out." Moreover, lack of ambiguity in expectations is only the beginning of several other benefits we have found with achievement grading. One student wrote on a 101 course-evaluation sheet that the achievement grading system allowed him "to worry less about what the teacher expects and concentrate more on doing my work. Since I am free to try different things for different assignments, I care more about what I am doing. I *want* to get all my work done. I *want* to do a good job." Another wrote that she "was able to focus a lot more on the 'quality' of my work, rather than simply making sure I did it." Yet another was sure that "I've written some of my best essays in this class because of not having the burden of a grade resting over my head. This helps bring out the true writer in you because you're not writing to please the teacher." All three of these freshman writers echo much the same thought—given the prospect of a set of tasks to accomplish rather than a teacher to satisfy, students often discover motivation within themselves to work that does not exist when they perceive themselves as pursuing a grade rather than getting work done.

We have found that, without grade-driven pressures, students are more likely to take risks in their writing. Sometimes the risks the students take are successful and sometimes not, but whether the risks work, the students are actively learning about "voice" and "details" and "clarity" in rich, context-sensitive ways that are much harder to attain in grade-driven classrooms. This ability to foster personal contexts created by the students themselves is at the heart of achievement grading. Though we argue against ambiguity of expectations, a healthy ambiguity drives the creation of these personal contexts. Since students are presented with a set of tasks to accomplish rather than rigid requirements for completing course assignments, they must decide for themselves how they will accomplish these tasks, what they want to achieve, and how to go about getting the work done. The ambiguities they must resolve are not between themselves and a teacher's vague expectations, but between themselves and a task they must achieve. Thus is born commitment to the task at hand rather than to the hoped-for grade-at-end.

> "But hold on," says a classroom lawyer. "All this talk about 'creditable' and 'noncreditable' or 'criteria' for projects sounds the same as conventional grading. What's the difference?"

Thanking the lawyer (and noticing that he has straw coming out of his shirt sleeves, as do most straw men), we quickly acknowledge that, yes, there are elements of subjectivity in our criteria. Furthermore, we can't always state in advance how the criteria of acceptability will work out for particular papers in particular contexts. The critical point is that we have shifted grading away from sliding scales (from F to A) and that we describe criteria in terms of completion of the job rather than abstract rhetorical traits. In addition, the system shifts the development of criteria away from the professor toward the students. The question is not so much "What does the prof want?"—although some of that inevitably enters in—as "What do the prof and I think has to be done to make this a creditable paper?"

Of course, our expectations as teachers do play an essential role in this process; we decide what is and is not "creditable." However, since we negotiate these expectations with students individually, our expectations are refined and attuned to the particular contexts each student has created instead of being thrown, blanket-like, over the entire course. Not only is this easier for our students to grasp, but we also find ourselves struggling less to define what is and is not acceptable for a given grade in our classrooms:

> Want an A in this class? Here is a list of tasks to complete for the grade. Now decide how to approach each task and we'll talk about whether your approach is creditable for each task in turn.

Most important, perhaps, is to observe that in the vast majority of cases, the work that is submitted *is* "creditable." We find that freed from the vise of traditional grading, students feel free to do their best. We talk candidly with our students about traditional grade pressures, and we tell them that we respect their maturity and refuse to use a carrot-and-stick approach. We tell them that we want their best efforts, regardless of grades, and we feel that our students respond well to that opportunity and invitation to operate under their own sense of values. We occasionally receive work that shows evidence of being done the night before or just before class or having simply been poorly executed or conceived, and we send it back. But for the most part work comes in well executed, so we can praise it, credit it, and move on to the next task.

Furthermore, achievement grading breaks down an important barrier by placing the teacher on the same side of the evaluation fence as the student. That is, relieved of the responsibility of being a judge, the teacher can face a much more interesting task: that of helping students do the right thing, to be the best that they can be. With achievement grading, the criteria for what makes something "creditable" or "noncreditable" diminish in the face of more important questions: "How's your paper coming, Samantha?" "Are you reworking the paper the way your discussion group suggested, Paul?"

Thus we move closer to being able to face the jury when the time comes to assign grades for the course. Because we've left room for the students to participate in deciding what they learn, we've also given ourselves the flexibility to enunciate our expectations relative to real contexts, not vague, unspecific cover-it-alls.

Designing this structure or, more accurately, flexibility of structures presents some of the greatest challenges in setting up a course based on achievement grading. Keeping in mind the essential principle that in achievement grading, more (quality) work is better, we have explored a variety of ways of issuing rewards, of moving from a collection of student work toward the grade that must appear on a transcript:

- In an intermediate writing course, "C" is the baseline grade for completing four papers (plus basic attendance, readings, participation, etc.); the B is awarded for maintaining a writer's notebook throughout the term; the A is tied to the development of an independent project.

- In a freshman seminar where the C, again, covers core course requirements, students can nudge their grade up through the pluses and minuses by completing self-designed mini-projects. One project moves you to C+, two to B-, six to an A. (We see this system as directly related to the scouts' merit badge plan, except that the students design the requirements for the badges.)

- In another intermediate writing course, we've used a straight contracting system in which (while completing the core requirements) each student designs and argues for a B project and/or an A project, or a single project that will carry the weight of an A, after the class has discussed the general criteria. Students write a proposal for their projects early in the course, including a discussion of their goals, their planned procedures, their timetable, and a set of criteria that they and the instructor can use to determine whether the project has been completed successfully.

- In a British literature/writing course, we created the "clock-watching option," where students, beyond the C, spend up to thirty hours in reading and in writing about their reading to move up to the B, and thirty more for an A. The students began searching the library vigorously to find books related to the course topic and read and reported on those books, logging in hours as they proceeded. The students were particularly appreciative of this system because, as they noted in evaluations, "some people read slower than others, and this system doesn't penalize you for that."

- In an undergraduate "capstone" seminar on children and children's language, the B and the A could be earned for reading varying numbers of young adult books, coupled with volunteer tutoring in the schools.

- In another freshman composition course, we used a point system: points awarded for attendance, for completing core projects, and for completing advanced projects. Points varied for a range of projects—writer's notebook entries, journal or diary entries, short "experimental" writings, work done on a family history, or extra work done on papers being submitted for other courses.

With these kinds of grading frameworks, we've been able to open up our writing classes to a wide range of activities and writing adventures. Among the projects we've been able to credit are

- writing one's own obituary in advance;
- creating a learning center on a Native American reservation;
- analyzing the power structure in an institution, including the university, one's family, or a job;
- mastering a new skill (cross-country skiing, elementary German) and writing a how-to book;
- interviewing people on a key topic;
- writing a string of letters to newspapers, public officials, university administrators on getting things done;
- examining the rhetoric of people who write letters to editors and public officials;
- creating media projects of all sorts: composing through film, video, photography, sundry magazines, or even the World Wide Web.

Recalling that our purpose as teachers is to assess and evaluate, not just to grade, we have discovered that achievement grading supports and even encourages us to extend the range of assessment devices and systems. Where conventional grading essentially requires that all students be processed with the same assessment tools, be they portfolios or standardized tests, a grading system based on accomplishment can use many different forms of assessment. In fact, part of determining what is "creditable" involves having the students design appropriate tests and measures. "What are your goals in this project?" we will ask frequently, "and how will we know whether you've met them?" Some students have problems with this process at first. We've had them say, "Well, I don't know, but I guess we'll know in the end" or even "Well, if you [the teacher] are satisfied, I'll be satisfied."

Those aren't good enough, and we push our students to think of other criteria, other measures. They may, at the conclusion of a project, want to survey their readers or audience and ask for response. They may establish publication (say, of a letter to the editor) as a measure of success. We encourage them to submit journals and notebooks and scrapbooks as evidence, to turn in drafts and revisions as proof of change; we've had them propose to keep project logs or diaries as part of the assessment process. In some classes, we even employ more-or-less conventional tests, if there is specific content that we think all students should know. (Tests are "graded" pass/fail or credit/no credit and can be reworked if students have not demonstrated mastery.)

Like any system, achievement grading has its problems. (Please recall our original assertion that if we could, we'd work exclusively under a pass/fail or credit/no credit system.) What follows are some hard and skeptical questions raised about achievement grading. As phrased, they may sound as if they were raised by negative critics, but in fact, these are critical questions we've raised ourselves over the years, as we've prepared ourselves to face the jury of our nightmares. Here then, are some foil questions, followed by some of the answers we've worked out for ourselves:

How can you justify completion of a "wider" range of work as leading to a higher grade? Would a composer of one piece of brilliant music be more brilliant if he or she composed twelve very different major pieces? We believe that breadth of experience is as important as depth in a limited area, in that students are exposed to a greater range of voices, perspectives, and techniques. This wider exposure, we argue, is instrumental in students' learning to situate their own perspectives in the broader worlds of academe and community. Indeed, this wide range of work has often resulted in greater overall depth of experience for our students than would have been possible in more narrowly focused situations. No, composers might not be considered "more" brilliant merely on the basis of the number of pieces they have composed. While some composers might be considered brilliant on the basis of a single composition, we feel brilliance is most normally recognized in those composers, and students, whose accomplishments span a range of areas and situate their work within a broader context. Thus, rewarding students for a wide range of work in fact rewards them for striving toward brilliance.

Similarly, how can "greater depth" be measured in such a way as to avoid vagueness? Vagueness regarding "depth" cannot be avoided if we attempt to measure it before the fact. We can, however, within the context of an individual paper on a given topic, measure relative depth. Generally, and vaguely, speaking, a given paper exhibits greater depth if the student has integrated a range of perspectives sufficient to synthesize her own position in such a way that it accounts for or explains the most possible variables surrounding an issue. The broader the range of experience a student integrates and synthesizes into his own context, the greater the depth of experience that will result.

What about the student who chooses *to work for a C or a B? Can one justify a system where students opt for anything less than the top grade?* Of course, we'd like to see all students get A's. (We don't worry about the alleged evils of "grade inflation" in a system we did not create.) But we have to be realistic—we teach mostly *required* courses that students might not have selected otherwise. We know that students have varying interests in signing up for a writing course. At the beginning of the semester, we urge students to consider going for top grades; we make it clear that even students who've never gotten an A before can do so under achievement grading. We then accept the students' decisions about the grade they wish to seek.

Doesn't this system overly reward the drones and worker bees? Possibly. We *have* had achievement-oriented students march through our courses cranking out required and optional projects at a great rate, sometimes almost mindlessly. Although drone-like work will sometimes be "unacceptable" because it lacks vigor or depth, we'd have to acknowledge that some worker bees effectively bypass course involvement. We also have to boast that we've had worker-bee types who set out to do the minimum, efficiently, and who got hooked on enthusiastic work, precisely because the system encourages students to think, act, and assess for themselves, something that the worker bees have previously failed to learn.

Clearly, not all work done in your courses is of the same absolute quality or quantity. Doesn't the system reward different amounts and qualities of work equally and thus inequitably? We worry about the student who does an exquisite project and gets the same final grade as a student who did an adequate job. We justify this to ourselves, though, in that we are seeking each individual's best work. Although there are clearly differences in the absolute quality of student work (which would be quickly marked up and down in conventional grading systems), what we're seeking is individual growth, not standardized or Procrustean growth or quality measured with a Platonic evaluation scale using vague criteria. Our final grades represent an ongoing assessment of each student, coupled with a final evaluation relative to that student herself or himself. The grade is individualized and not necessarily to class norms and certainly not to the vague norms of the larger, mostly conventionally graded, university community. We recognize that, just as one student's A in our classes may not represent the same quality as another's A, an A or a B or a C in our classes may or may not correspond to an A or a B or a C in a conventionally graded class. We make no apologies for this. Remember, under achievement grading, the most important tasks the students accomplish involve individual growth and motivation; these, not the final grades, are their true rewards.

What about late work, sloppy work, or work that just plain doesn't make the grade? We've built some safeguards into our system. We warn students that late work can lead to a lowered grade, as can consistently hasty work. We also make it clear to students that the higher grades—B's and A's—are available only to those who do a topnotch job at the core level. We are candid about this with our students, and an important ground rule in achievement grading calls for the instructor to confront students early on with work that is not up to par. As for work that is simply not up to minimum standards, if a student has some sort of learning handicap, we make allowances even as we seek help for that person. If the work is subpar and we think the student has the ability, we tell him or her so and hope for improvement. If that doesn't come about, we've been known to give failing grades, not as punishment, but for failure to achieve.

Aren't these sliding standards? Aren't you guilty of what you attacked earlier in this article—grades or marks that are created ad hoc, as the student writes, rather than a priori, before writing, when criteria are needed? We plead semiguilty. We do offer students generalized criteria before they write: We want writing that is clear and concise, shaped to an audience, well structured, filled with personal voice, carefully drafted, edited, and proofread. We then refine those kinds of criteria (involving the student as well) as a paper emerges. What we're doing, we think, is *acknowledging* the context specificity of most writing—that you don't really know what will make a good paper until you've written it—and thus demystifying it for the students.

What about the student who slides along all term and then does a dramatic finish? We also advise the class that we don't reward catch-up work, that the most spectacular finish in the world will not save the grade. There's no last-minute substitution or negotiation where B or A projects come to replace basic work that has been missed.

This system might be OK at the college level, where students are mature, but could it ever work at the lower levels? We've asked ourselves that, in part, because we do a good deal of work in the K–12 schools. In fact, Steve Tchudi first learned about and developed this sort of system when he was teaching public high school and working as a collaborative teacher in the middle school and elementary grades. Our experience is that achievement grading has the same successes and experiences the same problems at other levels. More important, we believe that because of its stress on goal setting and legitimate assessment (as opposed to grading), it helps teach skills of independent judgment and assessment that have, by and large, atrophied under conventional grading, K–College.

> The guillotine we saw from the courtroom looms before us. The lawyer stands beside it, his hand resting on the trigger that holds the blade poised aloft.
>
> "How's this for clarity?" he yells above the crowd, a cruel smile twisting his face.
>
> "Here, have some more detail!" screams another ex-student, loosing an overripe tomato.
>
> "Try this idea!" another bellows. "Is it developed enough for you?" he yells, letting fly a cabbage that smashes into the cobblestones in front of us, splattering our filthy gray clothes.
>
> The lawyer sweeps his arms wide: "Let's show 'em a sense of audience," he roars to the crowd gathered to watch our humiliation.
>
> "I was so confused I couldn't write for two years after I got a C in English!" shouts someone in the mob. "You're getting what all writing teachers deserve!"

"I tried to write what my teacher wanted," cries out another, "but all I was told was 'you need more voice' and 'be more specific.' What does that mean? I wish we could drag the whole bunch of them to the guillotine, and we will!"

"We were only trying to help, to give you ownership of your own writing, to help you discover your own voice," one of us pleads.

"Freedom; we wanted to give you the freedom to discover . . ."

"The freedom to discover what?!" another student screams. "That no matter what we try, it's never what we need to get an A!"

"You don't understand," we beseech the crowd. "We meant . . ."

"That's just the point," interjects the lawyer. "We *don't* understand; we *never did*. And it's your fault and the fault of every English teacher who ever dished out a C- or D+!"

A hooded executioner moves us into position under the guillotine blade and straps our necks to the block. The bailiff places a basket under each of our heads.

"Ideas, Structure, Voice!" half the crowd begins chanting as the other half responds with "Clarity, Specificity, Details!"

The lawyer grins and cracks his knuckles.

"Any last revisions before we turn in the final draft?" he sneers.

We look at each other hopelessly; we've only got one card left to play and we're not sure about it. One of us shrugs at the other and begins anyway.

"W . . . w . . . well, we could, like, just not give grades on essays at all; you know, kind of a credit/no credit approach."

"Yeah, we could try giving you a list of tasks to complete for the final grade."

"And you could decide how to approach each task and talk with us about whether your approach is acceptable in each case," the other chimes in. "We'll negotiate one on one to clarify the ambiguities."

A frown crosses the lawyer's face; his hand trembles on the guillotine's trigger. He gestures to the bailiff: "Let them up; we need to hear more about this."

The bailiff unties us from the guillotine, and we stand, hands still bound behind us. The crowd looks at us expectantly. We look at the lawyer. He's waiting.

"We want to give you room to participate in deciding what you learn," one of us begins.

"We'll give ourselves the freedom to create standards based on real papers, not vague unspecific lists of goals," continues the other.

The lawyer is resting his chin in his hand, thinking. The crowd is hushed.

Suddenly it dawns on us that we had good answers all along, that we could have faced the jury with a clean conscience. We could be graded on our own achievement! A smile splits the lawyer's face. He signals the bailiff to release us as the crowd begins chanting, "There's no grade like an A!"

Works Cited

Kirschenbaum, Howard, Rodney Napier, and Sidney B. Simon. *Wad-Ja-Get? The Grading Game in American Education.* New York: Hart, 1971.

Knowles, Malcolm S. *Using Learning Contracts.* San Francisco: Jossey-Bass, 1986.

Interlude

Talk of power redistribution in the classroom has been popular for the past few years. But it is just talk if the teacher still retains the final evaluative say, which in the classroom is the single most powerful tool. Grades are a vortex around which all classroom activity whirls, pulled inexorably toward. They create a vacuum around which power and classroom politics cling, mooshed to that empty center by centripetal force. And at the same time, learning flies centrifugally to the farthest edges of the classroom environment.

I know lots of teachers are working their tails off to mitigate the effects of the grade. Portfolio systems are becoming more popular, in part, because they compensate for part of the ill effects by putting a bit more evaluation responsibility on students (at least in those systems where students compile their own portfolios), and they disperse a bit the authority teachers have by bringing colleagues in on the evaluation process.

I think, though, that as long as the teacher retains the final say, each effort to get past the grading barrier is going to be crippled to some extent. As long as teachers reserve that right, contracts and any other attempts to reconfigure authority can be undercut and even be disingenuous. I think if we're going to share authority with students, it's got to be authority and really shared. They have to have a real say in what grade they get, or it's just a sham and it's worse than the good old honest straightforward teacher-as-sole-judge-and-jury system.

—Eric Crump
University of Missouri-Columbia

14 Total Quality: A Farewell to Grades

Charles McDonnell
Piedmont Technical College

Charles McDonnell, a native of South Dakota, earned his B.S.E. from the University of South Dakota–Springfield and his M.A. from the Bread Loaf School. He is co-chair of the Department of English at Piedmont Technical College in Greenwood, South Carolina.

Remained, no pleasant images of trees,
of sea or Sky, no colours of green fields,
But huge and mighty Forms, that do not live
Like living men, moved slowly through the mind
By day, and were a trouble to my dreams.

—Wordsworth, *The Prelude* ll. 395–400

One day, back when I was in school, I suspected trouble brewing when one of our two teachers began to cry. "Grades are so unfair," she said, turning away. Her fellow instructor agreed and shocked us all by announcing that they had decided to give one student an A and the rest of the class A-minuses. To my classmates' credit, they remained civil for the remainder of this, our final class meeting. After class was dismissed, we soon determined, through a process of elimination, which student received the A, and some ugliness surfaced.

Although this experience did not change the admiration I felt for the instructors both then and now, it did alter my thoughts about graduate school and has been a constant trouble to my dreams. It took many years, and much more grading experience, before I fathomed what happened.

The instructors' hands had been tied, probably by an unwritten school policy or code prohibiting teachers from awarding all students A's. As teachers, their choice was to defy school policy and use judgment, or follow policy and abandon it. What if they'd said:

You've been a great class. Your attendance is nearly perfect, your participation exemplary, your work ethic refreshing, and

> your attitude inspirational. You've done your reading faithfully
> and recorded it splendidly in the journals you've kept. We think
> you all deserve an A. However, school policy prohibits that. We
> did the only thing we could think to do: we drew one name out
> of a hat and gave that person the top grade. We know this
> sounds unfair, but the other way around is even more so. Thank
> you, and we're sorry this had to occur.

This incident stands for what many teachers feel about grading: there
is something discomforting and unfair about the process. Teachers
with significant experience know the student described above: great
attitude, fantastic work ethic, perfect attendance, cooperative spirit.
Yet after the final class, the grade averages out to 93.42. The cutoff for
an A is 94. Another student, who has few of the above qualities but
does well on timed tests, has a 93.46 average. Sound familiar?

My purpose here is not to prove that grades are unfair (that's
discussed elsewhere in this volume) but to provide an alternative. I
would like to discuss what "total quality education" (TQE) is, how it
works in the classroom, how well it works, and why it does.

What Is Total Quality Education?

The way he viewed grading is what first attracted me to the views of
W. Edwards Deming, the founder and best-known practitioner of the
total quality movement:

> Abolish grades (A, B, C, D) in school, from toddlers on
> up....When graded, pupils put emphasis on the grade, not on
> learning....The greatest evil from grades is forced ranking—
> only (e.g.) 20 per cent of pupils may receive [an] A. Ridiculous.
> There is no shortage of good pupils. (Deming, *New Economics*
> 148)

Deming's system—*total quality transformation*—offers an alternative to
teacher-centered grading. His system is based upon participatory
management. To understand the classroom implications better, let's
consider the opening anecdote: What if the instructors had explained
the situation and asked the students for input? I believe a better solution would have been found. Perhaps one student would have volun-
tarily accepted an A-. Perhaps a few, or all, would have. However,
TQE is not about outcomes; it is about competencies.

In my business English class, I am using competency-based
assessment delivered through a pass/fail (A/F) grading system measured in a portfolio outcome. That's a lot of jargon for one sentence, so
here's a breakdown:

a. Students take an active role in determining the purpose and vision of the class and are largely responsible for establishing quality standards.

b. Students have as many opportunities as they wish to do each assignment. When each project is completed successfully, they earn an A.

c. Students learn TQE as part of the course content, learning how to use tools for problem solving and statistical-process control to create continuous improvement.

d. Students assume responsibility for recordkeeping. At the end of the term, they must "document, defend, or demonstrate" (Langford, Lecture) the course competencies during a portfolio-review process.

Students want answers to three questions:

1. Why am I here?

2. What are we going to do today?

3. How will I be graded? (adapted from Langford, *Quality Learning* 8)

TQE addresses those three questions systematically.

How It Works

Day one: I use the first ten hours (seven of thirty-two class periods) to introduce TQE theory and the management/leadership tools. The first day of class, students are asked: "Why are you here?" Some students may be uneasy with the question, but if the first response is not what you hope for, try a *five-why process* (Langford, *Quality Learning*). If a student answers, "My curriculum requires it," simply ask, "Why does it require it?" By the fourth or fifth "why," the real purpose, learning, surfaces. Students receive note cards and are asked to answer another question: "What is the purpose of the learning in ENG 165?" They hand in the note cards and are asked to write a friendly letter listing their hopes and fears for the class. This is a rough draft, but they are instructed to do the best they can within the time frame (forty-five minutes). This becomes their diagnostic writing. While they write, I compile key phrases from the note cards on an overhead projector. The class consolidates these phrases into a general-purpose statement. We discuss ideas openly and meld them into one statement. To see the amount of agreement, we use a *consensogram process* (Langford, *Quality Learning*) to determine the student commitment. If the level is sufficient, we adjourn. If not, we revise.

Day two: A typed copy of the class-purpose statement is brought to class for discussion and final revision. After *operational definitions* (Langford, *Quality Learning*) are made and agreement reached, each student is asked to sign the statement. Students are given Post-It® notes and asked, "What do you need to know or learn in order to achieve your purpose?" This is called an *affinity process* (Langford, *Quality Learning*), and students, working in small groups, take all the responses and cluster them into like categories. One student is asked to record the responses. The others are excused.

Day three: Students complete a *purpose and vision process* (Langford, *Quality Learning*) by melding the results of the affinity process with the existing course guide (students will have the same competencies plus many more). Another consensogram is done to determine commitment. Students are introduced to the *flow tree process* (Langford, *Quality Learning*).

Day four: Students discuss a first draft of a *competency matrix* (Langford, *Quality Learning*), which reflects the types and amount of learning they have created through the affinity process. They receive a portfolio checklist. They use *imagineering* (Langford, *Quality Learning*) to design a "perfect" portfolio. The results of this focused brainstorming process establish the standards for portfolios.

By the end of day four, students know why they are here and what they are going to be doing each day. Participatory management is the cornerstone of TQE: "Create constancy of purpose toward improvement. . ." (Deming, *Out of the Crisis* 23). Students have agreed to learn, signed the agreement, and generated a list of projects they wish to do.

Day five: We study grading systems. For teachers, grades often represent a task to be completed at the end of the term. For students, grades are everything: They can mean scholarships, family financial support, self-esteem, loans, or grants. The way a teacher designs, delivers, and administers grades is an outward expression of an educational philosophy. When school policies become restrictive in any of those categories, the possibility of genuine, positive human relationships developing between the students and the teacher is severely undermined. If TQE represents hope for the future of our schools, it lies in this fact: *It is a better management system* for student/teacher interaction.

Day five begins with the *F-test* (Langford, *Quality Learning*). Students review all they know about the letter F. They review upper- and lowercase letter location (beginning, middle, end). They are allowed questions. A short (200-word) passage is placed on an overhead, and students are asked to count the number of times the letter occurs. They are given three minutes for task completion.

The example has thirty F's. No student has found more than twenty-nine; the mean score is usually around twenty-one. This brief activity sums up timed, basic-skills tests: Did the students have the competency? (Yes.) Did the teacher teach the test? (Yes.) Did the teacher do a good job? (I'd like to think so.) What went wrong? Why didn't students perform better? Did they care? (I gave a pep talk.) Did they try? (They knew their scores would be recorded.) Why didn't they perform better on a task asking them to review a competency they already had? Answers (the result of student brainstorming): The writing was small; the lighting was poor; the time limit caused anxiety; the focus was divided by reading and counting; some were tired; they had poor seating; they were distracted by movement and noise. All are defensible causes. My question is this: Wouldn't those statements also be true of any timed basic-skills test ever given?

To study the results of this test, students, working in groups now, are taught to record the results of the F-test on a *histogram* (Langford, *Quality Learning*). They are shown the *six sigma quality* (three standard deviations above and below the mean score). They are asked to grade their classmates' performance on the test, using the standard deviations. They are asked if they have problems with the results (most do have problems). They are introduced to *variation theory* (Deming, *New Economics*). They are taught that the only valid points on the histogram are the mean and the upper and lower control limits. All points that fall in between the control limits stem from common cause (see above). If any points do not, they may be considered to have special cause (i.e., the student is diabetic, her glasses are broken, etc.). The only valuable information a control chart gives is whether the system is stable (variation has common cause) or unstable (variation attributed to special cause). Regrettably, education has misappropriated the normal distribution aspect of control charts into a grade distribution method:

> Grading and ranking produce artificial scarcity of top grades. Only a few students are admitted to the top grades. . . .
>
> This is wrong. There is no scarcity of good pupils. There is no scarcity of good people. There is no reason why everyone in a class should not be in the top grade, nor at the bottom, nor anywhere else. Moreover, a grade is only the teacher's subjective opinion. This is so even for the result of an examination.

> What is the effect of grading and ranking? Answer: humiliation of those that do not receive top grades or top rank. The effect of humiliation is demoralization of the individual. (Deming, *New Economics* 151)

Students are then given the raw scores of their friendly letters (first-day diagnostic), asked to enter that data on a histogram, and draw conclusions about that.

Day six: Students are taught the *Pareto process* (Langford, *Quality Learning*) by categorizing the types and frequency of writing errors on their diagnostics. Their task is to locate which errors constitute 80 percent of all those made by students. I have labeled the errors for them. Normally, four types constitute 80 percent: format, paragraphing, punctuation, and spelling/usage. The others are normally trace elements. We use this information to create quality standards for our business writing assignments. The goal of total quality is "continuous improvement." In my experience, student-set quality standards will be high. We discuss the nature of the errors and decide to eliminate all format and paragraphing errors, restrict those involving punctuation and spelling/usage, and limit the others.

"In time management jargon, this…Pareto Principle—80 percent of the results flow from 20 percent of the activities" (Covey 156)—focuses on the large problems first, so that immediate results are seen. Later in the term, after form and paragraph errors are eliminated totally, we will do another Pareto process in order to focus on a "new" 80 percent. On a typical memo or letter, students may allow one or two errors, with zero tolerance for projects like résumés or cover letters.

Day seven: We conclude the theory and begin the practice. Students, working in familiar groups, study the pluses and minuses of working in teams. Teamwork cannot be overemphasized in the modern workplace or classroom environment. During a recent employers' day seminar at our school, a panelist was asked to name three skills a floor-level employee should have. The employer thought momentarily and replied: "Teams. Teams. Teams. For better or worse, teams." As schools move toward student-centered learning, as tech prep gains momentum, and as schools gravitate toward long-block scheduling, the ability of a teacher to employ learning teams in the classroom becomes a survival skill. Two-hour classes make lecturing less desirable—for students and teachers.

The student teams do a *force field analysis* (Langford, *Quality Learning*) to determine the societal pressures supporting and opposing the team environment; they use *multi-voting* (Langford, *Quality Learning*) to limit the list of opposing forces to the five or six most likely causes; and, they use a *relationship process* (Langford, *Quality Learning*) to determine the primary cause that prevents team success. Then, students are given three assignments:

1. As a team, write a persuasive memo which clearly states whether pass/fail (A/F) grading is inferior or superior to rating and ranking (A, B, C, D, F). Attach a *deployment flow chart* (Langford, *Quality Learning*).

2. As an individual, write a memo to the instructor informing him of which grading system you would prefer to be measured by. This is an authentic assignment; the memo is a contract.

3. As a team, write a procedural memo composed of two parts: a code of cooperation which all members can agree upon, and a list of roles each member agrees to perform on behalf of the group. Initial this agreement and hand it in to the instructor.

The rest of the class periods, days eight through twenty-nine (class periods thirty through thirty-two are set aside for group and individual portfolio reviews), represent a fairly typical English classroom, I suspect. Students, working in teams, begin the twelve to fourteen writing projects they have created for themselves. As facilitator, I limit lectures to fifteen minutes each day. Students have roughly an hour of unstructured team time during each of these class periods. They are not required to stay in the classroom; rather, they are encouraged to find work areas outside it. Our college has a lifelong learning competency for all students, staff, and employees. Students soon realize learning takes place outside the classroom. The first two memos have a word-processing requirement, so the computer lab becomes an alternate classroom for some students. I teach one member (the scribe) of each team how to enter data with a word-processing program, how to save it, and how to print it. That person assumes responsibility for teaching the other members of the team how to do the same.

The goal of this, and all of my classes, is for the students *to become independent learners.* Most days I stay in the classroom; on others, I move to the computer lab; near the end of the term, I spend time in my office in order to provide more individual conference time. Team members assigned the facilitator role are trained to build agendas, and each group member is asked to meet with me for a mandatory ten-minute progress report at least once per term.

How Well Does It Work?

As I said earlier, I am using this system in only one class, English 165: "Professional Communications," but TQE has forced me to reevaluate the way I grade in all my classes, and it has made me a portfolio fan.

To measure the success of the course, I use the *Shewhart cycle* ("plan-do-study-act") *for learning and improvement* (Deming, *New Economics*). I decided to analyze the results against two cohort groups: all classes at the college and all English classes. So far, I have data on 146 students from seven sections. I broke the results into two groups: successful and unsuccessful completion. Operationally, for a college student, I define success as A, B, C, while D, F, and W (withdrawal) are failures (see Table 1). While the numbers are encouraging, I wish to emphasize this: Even if the numbers were slightly below the two cohort groups, I would still be willing to state unequivocally that TQE is a *better classroom management system* because it is more humane and more fair.

The most frequent criticism I receive (from other teachers) is that this system leads to grade inflation. I respond to this argument by granting it. I say,

> Yes. I inflate grades by nine points. I'll admit it, if you will be willing to admit the possibility that your grades may be inflated by as little as one point. Now, if my students, who are receiving 94 percent, are, in reality, only earning 85 percent, what does that mean? It means the worst student in class is doing B- work. Now, what if one of your students received a 70 percent (D-)? Which of us has a stronger accountability argument?

Table 1. Analysis Results

No receiving	By TQE	In all English	In all classes
# of A: (%)	115 (78%)	196 (28%)	2,637 (34%)
# of B: (%)	5 (3%)	196 (28%)	3,174 (41%)
# of C: (%)	1 (1%)	103 (15%)	listed w/B's
# of D: (%)	0 —	28 (4%)	294 (4%)
# of F: (%)	9 (6%)	41 (6%)	294 (4%)
# of W: (%)	16 (11%)	126 (18%)	1,261 (16%)

SUCCESS/FAILURE RATIO:
  by TQE method: 82/18
  In all English: 71/29
  In all classes: 76/24

Source: College Office of Institutional Effectiveness.

Most good teachers know from experience that students will live up, or down, to teacher standards. Where should the standards be set?

I have always liked the writing process. An accept/revise system creates true process (see Figure 1). Students are no longer asked to revise because the teacher wants them to; they revise because they have agreed to. Participatory management is a key to what works, but this system has other benefits: conflict resolution, critical thinking, and *profound knowledge.* All play vital roles in creating a new classroom vitality.

Conflict Resolution

I asked a group of student development staff members to brainstorm the major sources of conflict between students and teachers. Their list included the following:

- personality conflicts
- design, delivery, or administration of grades
- deadlines/time management
- attendance/punctuality

TQE can help in all four areas, indirectly in the first and last. Personality conflicts are often the product of the second item, above. My grading system allows students to *choose* their grade. The success chart indicates only 6 percent have chosen to be rated and/or ranked. Students in the class have only one *deadline:* the class periods reserved at the end of the term for portfolio review. Instead of deadlines, I teach time management. One good method revolves around "Habit Three: Put First Things First" (Covey 145). The idea of working on matters that are "important, not urgent," is a good motto, so Covey's Quadrant II design fits the class perfectly.

Deadlines, whether we like to admit it, exist in education primarily for teacher convenience. We justify them on "real-world" grounds: They replicate the busy world of work that lurks out there beyond graduation ceremonies. Education, though, is a process, and students tend to view deadlines as an authority issue, regardless of our justifications. Factory-line mentality fits schools more poorly in the nineties than it did even thirty years ago. The underlying principle in the total quality approach is that *all students have the same capacity to learn, even if they don't learn at the same rate.*

By substituting time management for deadlines, we give students a skill more valuable than meeting deadlines: self-management.

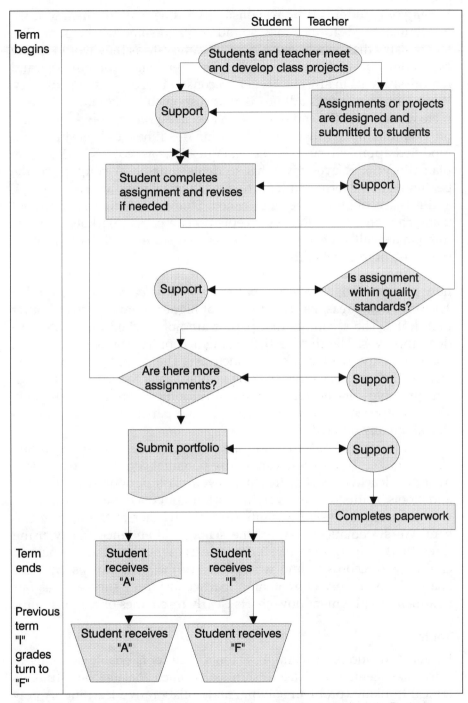

Figure 1. Flowchart of typical accept/revise grade system. (Lynda Rutledge, Spring Semester 1996.)

Freeing our students from responsibility is one way for them to learn it. Eliminating deadlines may sound scary to some teachers, but the fact remains that papers come in at the same rate as they would in any classroom but without the hassle. The percentage of efficient and mature students in any class will be a constant regardless of pedagogy. What happens sans deadlines is that responsible students will complete work before the end of the term and irresponsible ones will put it off. Sound familiar? Instead of dumping deadlines, I suggest trying a modified approach, such as the "no questions asked" (NQA) coupon plan (Reeves). Reeves gives his students four NQA coupons at the beginning of the term. Students turning in late papers attach a coupon, and it is accepted, no questions asked. Students are rewarded for not using coupons, while Reeves accepts no late papers without one. Try this. On a small scale, it offers evidence that students do have a collective sense of responsibility.

An important digression: For the teacher using TQE, the paper flow remains about the same, but *the paper load decreases dramatically!* There are many reasons. The first is that higher standards create better first drafts. The second is that papers are not marked unless the student approves. The third is that, using accept/revise, papers may be rejected orally, with comments such as "The heading is formatted incorrectly," or "I see three spelling errors. That's too many." This system promotes on-the-spot usage acquisition, which is an extremely effective approach. I do not normally take papers home. I can't say that about any other class.

Although *attendance* and *punctuality* can be sore spots in any classroom, the TQE system can defuse potential conflicts between student and teacher. During the first seven class periods (the "theory" and "tools"), attendance is very important, but once the students form work teams, responsibility shifts from the teacher to the team members. We systematically study the school's attendance policy using flow charts. By doing so, students learn who has the attendance choice, who records it, and who processes the withdrawals. Systems analysis can be very enlightening, particularly on issues such as fair treatment. Deployment flow charts clearly teach lines of responsibility.

Tools

Earlier, I mentioned several TQE tools. The tools enable students to learn management and leadership skills. Each tool teaches students critical thinking, problem solving, and collaborative learning. A new basic skills list ought to include those three. The tools teach all three efficiently (minimal cost, reasonable time and effort). The bibliography makes note of two sources that describe TQE tools in detail. *Total Quality Tools for Education* organizes each tool around five statements:

> What is it?
>
> What does it look like?
>
> When is it used?
>
> How is it made?
>
> Remember.

By using the tools, the classroom becomes student-centered areas for active learning. More important, the tools teach students processes for critical thinking, process analysis, and systems analysis.

Profound Knowledge

Deming notes that

> profound knowledge appears here in four parts, all related to each other:
>
> - Appreciation for a system
> - Knowledge about variation
> - Theory of knowledge
> - Psychology [of change]
>
> One need not be eminent in any part of profound knowledge in order to understand it and apply it. (Deming, *New Economics* 23)

Total quality helps students view the world as a series of interrelated systems. Profound knowledge could be summed up in the short phrase "appreciation for a system," except one also needs to understand variation theory and enough about human nature to realize people resist change. Deming insists that a person needn't be "eminent" in any of those areas. A person needs to know math, but needn't be brilliant, only conscientious. The tools explain what needs to be done to gather continuous improvement information. For students who understand the concept of profound knowledge (and it will not be all of them), total quality is liberating. It turns future workers into managers, future managers into leaders. Deming's system is for leadership development, to take us "out of the crisis."

Portfolios and Assessment

A note or two on portfolio assessment: The first time I tried using portfolios, I got burned. I know why. I kept them. I kept them for the students and in my classroom. I did not release ownership. Now, I have a new rule: Never, ever touch a student portfolio. Doing so not only violates ownership, but releases the student from responsibility for tracking his or her learning. I remember walking out of my classroom Friday afternoons with a fifty-pound cardboard box full of student portfolios that needed grading over the weekend. I hated portfolios.

Now I only see them during the final class periods, and I don't touch them. During portfolio review, students show me the documentation for all completed projects from their checklists. Students color code personal competency matrices to show the level of learning attained for each one listed. I may have handled each component part of the portfolio, but do not touch it. I like portfolios, now.

I also firmly believe that portfolios are *the only sane response to the accountability nightmare* obsessing our state education departments and legislatures. Standardized tests, achievement tests, and exit tests strangle our educational system. Deming opposes using tests for measurement (he feels their only purpose is prediction) and feels inspection/ regulation is counterproductive: "Cease dependence on inspection to achieve quality. Eliminate the need for inspection on a mass basis" (Deming, *Out of the Crisis*). He knows that mass inspection creates diminishing returns. We use systemized testing to rate and rank our teachers, administrators, schools, and states the way teachers do students. Not only that, as we invest more and more of our educational time, talent, and treasure in the process of designing, creating, fieldtesting, researching, selecting, promoting, delivering, administering, collating, measuring, evaluating, and assessing standardized tests, we lose time, talent, and treasure that could be spent on students, equipment, classrooms, and instruction. Legislators and bureaucrats rob our students' resources, yet they still have the temerity to hold schools accountable for improvement despite dwindling instructional support, staff, and equipment.

TQE and portfolio assessment offer a sane response to that: random samples of student portfolios are kept on record. The student demonstrates competency, the teacher displays standards, and the district shows responsibility. Teachers should not fear competency-based assessment, *unless we persist in rating and ranking*. We know what a good paper looks like and when one is correct. If we design processes that allow students opportunities to meet those standards, why worry about accountability? One student summed up her TQE learning this way:

The TQE system acknowledges that students learn, read, understand, comprehend, remember, and test differently, yet grades us equally, either by passing or failing.

When I have taken tests in other classes, I have been very reluctant to ask why there are so many check marks on my papers—mainly because I am afraid I may have been the only person to miss that question. In the TQE class, when a paper has been turned in, the instructor gives each student the opportunity for a one-on-one conference to discuss any errors and how to avoid making the same ones again.

TQE is a better method of grading and teaching. The students set the quality standards, not the "State." Students are more involved in this classroom than my other classes. There is actually more time involvement for the students but in the process of completing the projects, we become more like teachers than students.

Competency-based education may be the future of education (Barker). TQE gives us the opportunity to move from grading to learning, from assessment to accountability, and from management to leadership. Why wait?

Works Cited

Barker, Joel A. *Paradigms: The Business of Discovering the Future.* New York: HarperBusiness, 1993.

Covey, Stephen R. *The Seven Habits of Highly Effective People: Restoring the Character Ethic.* New York: Fireside, 1990.

Deming, W. Edwards. *The New Economics: For Industry, Government, Education.* Cambridge: MIT P, 1993.

———. *Out of the Crisis.* Cambridge: MIT P, 1986.

Langford, David P. Lecture. Quality Learning Workshop presented at Lander University. 8 Aug. 1994. Greenwood, SC.

———. *Quality Learning: Manual for Four-Day Seminars.* Version 2.0. Billings: Langford International, 1994.

Reeves, Bruce. "Turning a Major Headache into a Good Experience." *Innovation Abstracts* 15.8 (1993): n.p.

Total Quality Tools for Education (K–12). Dayton: QIP/PQ Systems, 1995.

Wordsworth, William. *The Prelude. The Norton Anthology of English Literature.* 6th ed. Vol. 2. Comp. and Ed. M. H. Abrams et al. New York: Norton, 1993. 205–86.

Interlude

Every child who walks into my room (whether in sixth grade, seventh, or eighth) starts out with an A on that first writing assignment. At the beginning of the year, I have my own personal expectations, but no expectations for them. They have responded (in some way) and so have I (with an A). Hey...they have success...some boast about it; some quietly fold their papers...maybe they never have had an A in writing before. Then, we get down to business. (This does not mean the A's will stop.) We, as a nation, as school teachers, as students, are programmed to A's and SOOOOOO for the first quarter everyone gets A's....They begin to feel that they could do more editing, more proofreading...more with ideas. . . more something. (By the way, we're working in English class on grammar and other skills—speech, reading—so grades for writing only count 1/4...not enough to slant the grades...but certainly enough to encourage writing.) If they feel successful, they will experiment...and if they experiment, there is a whole world of ideas for the next writing lesson, the next grammar lesson. Let them succeed for a bit before we begin carping...at least a quarter....

—Jeanette Werner
St. Brendan School
North Olmsted, Ohio

15 Using a Multidimensional Scoring Guide: A Win-Win Situation

Gail M. Young
Hillsboro High School, Hillsboro, Oregon

Gail M. Young lives in Portland, Oregon, and teaches at Hillsboro High School. As part of the International High School program, she developed "World Studies," a sophomore-level language arts/social studies integrated block class. She also teaches English in the special education department and has been active on the school-site council.

Thirty years and five states ago, when I began my career as an English teacher, a well-meaning veteran of the classroom warned, "The paper load will do you in!"

Many times during my years of teaching, I was reminded of her words as I struggled to keep my head above a pile of essays. Of course, I've experimented with a variety of shortcuts and acts of desperation, including holistic grading and the "check, check-plus, check-minus" method. I've tried to justify nearly anything short of dumping the pile into the trash by reminding myself of the words of another mentor in the profession who stated without a hint of guilt, "If you have time to evaluate everything your students write, your students aren't writing enough!"

But that wasn't good enough for me. I had to know for certain that whatever choices I made for teaching and learning in my classroom, my students would in fact benefit. I had to observe an improvement in their language skills and, hopefully, a growth in their appreciation of literature and language.

More recently, my experiments with classroom assessment have involved the use of a scoring guide (a "rubric," or grading system, that uses a set of described criteria). In my district and at the state level in Oregon, a scoring guide for writing is used each spring to assess the writing of all eleventh graders in six dimensions: content, organization, voice, word choice, sentence fluency, and conventions. In my classroom, I've created rubrics for specific assignments, sometimes in collaboration with my students, with both predictable and surprising results.

I've discovered that rubrics have three significant advantages. First, they motivate students toward top performance because they clearly define the elements of an excellent product. They also increase students' efforts toward improvement because they provide the language to distinguish between levels of accomplishment. A third advantage is that a rubric provides an explanation and justification of the grade to students, as well as to parents and administrators.

The experience which opened my eyes to the advantages of using a scoring guide was a poetry project for tenth graders. It was the culminating activity after a conventional poetry unit. I focused on oral presentations in which students (1) demonstrated their knowledge of writers' use of poetic devices; (2) showcased their ability to interpret and critique a literary piece; and (3) practiced their communication and presentation skills. These three purposes of the assignment became the dimensions of the scoring guide and were described specifically at four levels of achievement, from excellent to inadequate, corresponding to the values 4, 3, 2, and 1 (see Table 1). The grade for the project was a combination of a student's self-assessment, peer assessments, and my assessment. An average of all assessments (mine weighted equally) produced the score or grade. My students were fascinated that they and their classmates had a share in the scoring responsibility, which seemed to elevate their interest and involvement in the entire project.

Because I needed to know if and how the activity was beneficial for my students, I was eager to hear from them at the end of the experience. I asked for written responses to two questions: (1) Did the scoring guide help you with this assignment? How? (2) Did it help you assess the presentations? How?

Advantage 1: Motivation toward Top Performance

In their written responses, students told me that they clearly understood from the scoring guide what constituted an excellent product. From the guide they knew the elements of top quality:

> The guide helped me get organized and told me how to accomplish it.

Table 1. Scoring Guide for Poetry Project

	Excellent: 4	Good: 3	Satisfactory: 2	Inadequate: 1
Literary Knowledge and Application	Explains poetic devices in concise, sophisticated language that demonstrates full understanding.	Explains poetic devices in own words, appropriate for the audience, that demonstrate understanding.	States definitions of poetic devices that demonstrate partial understanding.	Names poetic devices used in the poem and attempts an explanation of them.
	Exhausts examples from the poem and explains eloquently their use as poetic devices	Recognizes numerous examples and explains fully their use as poetic devices.	Recognizes a few examples and tells how they are used as poetic devices.	Gives examples that fail to illustrate the poetic devices or overlooks examples from the poem.
Interpretation and Critical Thinking	States with conviction, clear idea of poem's intent.	Explains, in clear language, ideas of poem's intent.	Gives an idea of poem's intent which is vague in concept and expression.	Lacks an idea of the poem's intent.
	Uses specific passages and information to fully and convincingly support ideas of poem's intent.	Uses numerous passages and information to support ideas of poem's intent.	Uses one or two passages to support somewhat the idea of poem's intent.	Does not make connections between passages from the poem and the poem's intent.
Presentation and Communication	Incorporates a creative visual or auditory component which is appropriate to the poem and carries the presentation to a level of unexpected significance.	Incorporates a creative visual or auditory component which enhances the poem and the presentation.	Includes a visual or auditory component which is somewhat related to the poem.	Presents the poem without a visual or auditory component.
	Uses voice quality as well as eye contact and body to captivate audience.	Uses voice quality and variation, as well as eyes and body, to hold the attention of audience.	Frequently varies voice, uses satisfactory voice quality, and makes occasional eye contact with audience.	Reads presentation in a monotone of voice and body expressions.

> It gave me a basis for preparing. I could check to make sure my presentation had all of the necessary requirements.

> I liked having the guide when preparing my presentation because it showed me everything, exactly, that I needed to cover. It also let me know if I covered certain parts adequately.

It was obvious from their comments that students were motivated by the scoring guide's clearly stated expectations and then challenged to perform with top effort. Because they recognized the distinctions between a 4 and a 3 or a 2, they had guidance toward achieving excellence in their preparation:

> I really liked a guide in front of me while preparing my presentation. I automatically tried for a straight A and knew what was expected.

> It set my goals high on how to perform the presentation. I spent more time with it than most of my presentations.

> I really like the idea of having the concrete expectations for an assignment and to know exactly what I needed to do to get the grade I wanted.

> It assures you an A if you follow specifically.

Advantage 2: Guidance in the Plan for Improvement

The difference between a scoring guide and a more traditional grading system is most significant for the student. In many traditional systems, specific descriptors are given for the perfect product (an A), but a B, a C, and a D are simply percentages of the perfect product. On a scoring guide, each level of performance has its own distinct and specific descriptors. It is because of these distinctions that students know how to approach a plan to improve their work:

> I skimmed the 4 point guide before I started and then checked it again to see what grade I would get. Then I polished it up to the point where I thought I would get all 4's.

Using these specific descriptors for self- and peer assessments gives students the tools they need for their own improvement plan:

> I liked being able to grade my peers because it made me listen for things they do better than me. It gave me specific things to listen for and judge on.

> It gave everyone a fair chance to make a quality presentation because everyone was given the same guide to follow. I also

liked grading other people and myself. It gives them and me a second opinion on our work.

And from a student who often gets low grades:

It told me what needed to be done to get a better grade.

In this model, descriptive language from the scoring guide gives students the words they need for "Explanation and Comments" on the scoring sheets for their classmates (see Figure 1). They use words and ideas taken directly from the scoring guide to describe what is "excellent," "good," or "satisfactory" in a particular dimension.

By using descriptive language for peer assessments, students practice skills which are transferred to self-assessment and self-improvement. Improvement is facilitated when a student has the language to recognize and express the distinctions between excellent, good, and satisfactory. A scoring guide models that language. For instance:

On Literary Knowledge and Application:

You did pretty well with poetic terms used in the poem. You explained about four or five the poet used. (Score 3)

You mentioned personification and alliteration, but I don't think that that was really an example of personification. (Score 1)

On Interpretation and Critical Thinking:

The passages you chose persuaded me that you understood the poet's intent. (Score 4)

You had only one quote to support your idea about the meaning, and it didn't fit very well. (Score 2)

On Presentation and Communication:

I was really surprised by how well you presented. You really did "captivate" the class. (Score 4)

I had to give you a 2 because you read your paper and looked up only a few times. It ruined your poster because you didn't even refer to it—even though it was pretty good. (Score 2)

Advantage 3: Validation of Grades

Because students had specific feedback from their classmates, as well as from their teacher, and a voice in their own assessment, there was not one complaint or even a question about a grade. Grades were validated by the scoring guide. Explanation and justification were defini-

---

Evaluation Sheet: Poetry Project Presentation

Presenter: **Evaluator:**

Dimension: *Score:*   *Explanation and Comments*

Literary Knowledge
and Application

Interpretation and
Critical Thinking

Presentation and
Communication

Figure 1. Scoring sheet.

tive because of the scoring guide, and therefore the grades were satis-factory to them. Grades based on the specific distinctions of a scoring guide are equally clear to parents and administrators.

Other Thoughts

The three dimensions and the specific descriptors I wrote for each of the four levels on this scoring guide are, of course, somewhat subjec-tive, based on what I consider important for the assignment. I could have focused on logical organization, or well-developed support, or an attention-getting opening statement, or a creative element by ask-ing students to write a line of poetry related to the poem which they were assigned to analyze. For each of those I would have written descriptors to explain each score level. Or a scoring guide could address only one dimension, in which case the grading process would be simplified. Each assignment has its own focus, and for each would come its own unique scoring guide.

There are options, as well, for the grading aspect of the project. If I had wanted to emphasize self-assessment, I could have weighted the student's own evaluation more heavily in computing the average of scoring sheets. Or I could have asked students to evaluate only some of the presentations, had I wanted to encourage more elaborate written comments.

No grading system is a panacea. A variety of assessment and scoring methods is needed in a dynamic classroom. Using a multidimensional scoring guide for the presentation of a literary analysis to a group of teachers and learners is just one way of handling assessment.

The poetry project, in summary, indicates that students can be motivated by a scoring guide to reach for "excellent" as their goal. It demonstrates that they can learn to distinguish between excellent, good, and satisfactory and, more important, that they know how to improve their performance when they haven't yet reached their goal. Using this model, assessment and teaching are integrated activities throughout the project, from the initial assignment to the culminating grade.

A final word, just in case anyone missed the bonus advantage to the teacher: There is no risk of being "done in" by the paper load with this grading model. When the bell rings, the activity is complete. There are no papers to take home!

Interlude

I have been working in a writers' workshop style, and
I, too, am most frustrated in my reading of papers. I
want to reward a student for wondrous ideas/writing/
metaphors, etc., but then "what did I get?" comes up,
and I feel great frustration. I tried to do more port-
folio-type evaluating but found that students wanted
everything read by me, so I ended up overwhelmed again.
Hmmm...I know that the cross which we must bear is
that of grading all of those papers (so says my principal), but there has to be a way to keep each of us
fresh to the next great writer.

    —Mary Ellen McWhirter
      Saint James Academy
      Solana Beach, California

16 Students Using Evaluation in Their Writing Process

Jacob S. Blumner
Kent State University, Stark Campus

Francis Fritz
University of Nevada, Reno

Jacob S. Blumner teaches at Kent State University, Stark Campus, in Canton, Ohio.

Francis Fritz is a graduate fellow in the composition and rhetoric program at the University of Nevada, Reno and is involved in the Core Writing program's portfolio project and the development of the Student Core Writing handbook. He currently entertains a perverse obsession with grading and is initiating a research project involving peer evaluation.

"Here you are, Mr. Fritz. This one had a really strong focus," Christine told me.

"Great," I answered, handing her another folder. At this point in the class, students were nearly piling up on each other waiting to get the next folders to score. Even though I was busy with the effort of keeping the folders in order, making sure each paper got two different readings, keeping students moving along, I could still overhear bits of the conversations of the scoring partners: "I don't think so, Joe. This piece has a lot more originality than you say it has. Who would have thought to argue to legalize fake IDs?"

"Good point," Joe responded, "but are originality and craziness the same thing?"

I heard another pair speak: "But there's only one spelling error in the whole paper. I'd still give it a five."

"Yeah, but the paper is only two pages long. Are you sure it's worth a five?"

Two students suddenly shout simultaneously, "I'd give coherence a four!" They both laughed out loud.

Paul, stepping up to me to pick up another folder, sighs, "This stinks! It's really hard."

I smiled, happy to share this understanding with him, and handed him another folder. He looked at me again and sighed as before. On my left, two students were waving their hands and talking quickly.

"Some of these sentences I can barely understand. I thinks it's a three."

"A three? The introduction is pretty good. That first sentence about potholes is hilarious. It's at least a four."

"But what about...."

"Mr. Fritz, can you check this one? We can't seem to agree."

I shake my head and smile. "Sorry. Today it's your job. Just keep talking about it. I'm sure you can work it out." More students sidled up and handed me folders containing the papers they'd scored. I quickly exchanged them for one that required another reading.

Finally, Aaron stepped up, a student who had often shown his strengths as both a writer and a reader. He looked at me earnestly.

"Mr. Fritz, this is tough. Why do I have to do it, instead of you?"

We considered this same question as we prepared to teach our classes, because the comments we made on student papers, the recommendations for improvements in drafts, the explanation of why students received the grade we gave them seemed to us to be possibly work done in vain. Did students actually learn the kinds of writing strategies that would make them more effective writers, or did they merely learn how to give to us, the instructors, another version of the right answer? Did our comments actually invite them to contemplate the intricate weighing of rhetorical and cognitive possibilities, or rather, did they merely add to or subtract from their papers what they interpreted to be words and sentences we prescribed? Were our grading practices sufficient to instill in our students a sense of ownership in their writing, or did the opposite occur—ownership was neutralized by the very grading that we had been using for so long?

We began to think about what use our grading practices were compared with our efforts to create in our classes a greater awareness of writing possibilities, a stronger sense of ownership of their writing practice, a greater understanding of their role in a community of writers, and, most important, a deeper investment in what our students chose to strive for in their efforts to write. In an attempt to address these problems, we drank coffee and discussed how we might resolve these issues. We began by sharing our frustrations, our successes, and our ideal classrooms. While we debated our teaching practices, we discovered we were constantly returning to three major questions: (1) How can students become more integrally involved in the evaluation process? (2) How do we increase student dialogue and community? (3) How do we increase student ownership of writing?

One problem we see with giving grades is that grading can become the driving or sole purpose for instruction. In fact, evaluation can direct pedagogical practice in potentially negative ways (e.g., instructors teaching to a test). We decided to try to turn this idea on its head. What if we could find a way to make evaluation and grading serve our goals for instruction and process?

The purpose of our composition classes is to assist students in becoming more successful writers, not merely to generate grades. Therefore, we thought, why not involve students in the assessment and evaluation process? Already we have our students in their peer-response groups read and respond to their fellow writers' drafts. Why not let students—as a community of readers as well as writers—grade each other's writing efforts? Wouldn't they experience greater control and ownership over their learning and achievement (Williams 267, 274)?

As many teachers know, one apparent quality of evaluating student papers is its uncertainty. Each of us struggles to come to fair measures regarding what constitutes successful or poor writing. What teacher hasn't seen a complex mixture of both qualities in a single paper? Each of us comes to our own conclusions about what we measure and the degree to which we measure it against other qualities. We had come to believe that our students could only benefit from this same experience in their attempts to justly evaluate their peers: "The practice of peer evaluation would give students more responsibility for their own successes and failures" (Williams 267). Their struggles to come to decisions would encourage them to look more closely at what constitutes good writing, how readers and writers can talk about it, how we already continually judge its quality, and the consequences of those judgments.

Since assessing and evaluating student writing is difficult, we thought that it might be better if the students did it in pairs because this way, they could each read a particular paper and discuss the merits or weaknesses of the piece and share the responsibility for evaluating it. Beyond assessment and evaluation, students can develop a sense of community as writers with their partners; feel more secure in their decisions, which will eventually be shared with the rest of the class; and become more aware of, through articulation, why they make the choices they do as readers and writers.

After surveying a variety of approaches, we decided to experiment with a variation of trait scoring. We noticed that when students worked in peer-response groups, they were overly concerned with surface features, often overlooking organization and audience. We assumed trait scoring would encourage students to examine particular writing qualities, specifically thesis, organization, sense of audience and purpose, coherence, paragraphs, and surface structure. Next, we designed a generic six-point rubric in which we tersely described the qualities of each trait under each score (see Figure 1). Later efforts at composing guidelines for evaluation moved us away from a generic rubric and toward rubrics that are constructed according to the specific paper assignment. For example, students working on an interview paper created the criterion of "claim," which, in the context of the class, meant taking the interview material and using it for their own argumentative or contemplative purposes. In addition, students placed this criterion first on the rubric because they believed it was the most important one. In short, students combined our original criteria of thesis, audience, and purpose into one criterion because they saw these elements as integrally connected and central to a successful paper.

Understanding these problems, we knew that preparation was necessary before that day of evaluation. During the first week of classes, we had introduced students to the grading system we intended to use. We contemplated many possibilities, and although we saw many potentially successful methods for moving from scores to grades, we chose the following:

- The criteria to earn an A grade for the essay writing component of the course were that students needed to receive at least a 5 out of 6 on four of the six papers for the class, and no papers could receive below a 3.

- To earn a final grade of B, students needed to earn a score of 5 on two papers and at least a score of 4 on three other papers.

- For a grade of C, students needed to earn a score of 4 on four papers.

- In addition, final grades for the course included the evaluation and grading of participation, attendance, and journals. These were simply evaluated on a satisfactory/unsatisfactory scale.

Although we wanted students to be involved in the accountability of giving scores that would result in grades, we chose not to place specific grades on papers or equate scores with grades in any direct way so that they would not feel overwhelmed with their newfound responsibility. Each paper received scores from two different pairs of readers. If two or more groups gave a paper the same score, that score stood. In the event of a split score, we acted as final readers. Also, in the event that we felt a student paper received a particularly unjust score for a

Author's Code Name and Title:

Thesis	6 5 4 3 2 1
Organization	6 5 4 3 2 1
Audience/Purpose	6 5 4 3 2 1
Coherence	6 5 4 3 2 1
Paragraphs	6 5 4 3 2 1
Surface Structure	6 5 4 3 2 1
Overall Score	6 5 4 3 2 1

Comments (use back of sheet if necessary):

Evaluators' Code Names:

Figure 1. Generic six-point rubric for trait scoring.

number of reasons—including, for instance, the possibility of the evaluators' dislike of the topic—we would raise the score accordingly. We also told them we would never lower a score. We realized that by maintaining our role as final arbiters of grades, we could not fully give the class evaluative control, but we felt we needed to be able to have some direct influence on scores because students are inexperienced in the process, and the academic consequences could be significant. Thus, our right to raise scores operated as a kind of safety net against unjust scoring. Students could feel they had latitude in what they might give and receive, and we hoped students would still be willing to take risks in their writing as well as to evaluate honestly.

During the week prior to evaluation, we brought in a number of transparencies of examples of student essays from previous classes. We handed out our rubric and spent a short time reviewing the various descriptions. Students listened quietly, some nodded knowingly, and there were very few questions.

After having a student read the paper aloud, we walked through the assessment and evaluation process, attempting to model the kind of thinking and talking behavior we hoped our students would use. We continually moved from paper to rubric and back, keeping our evaluation focused and limited. Finally, we gave a number to a trait and then moved down to the next one, again talking through our process until we had completed our discussion of the paper.

Next, we placed a second paper on the overhead, asking a different student to read it aloud. At this point, we started a class discussion, asking our students questions about what they saw, making sure our questions were open-ended in order to encourage dialogue. We began with the general question "What is this paper about?" Students gave tentative answers, and we encouraged them to talk about those answers. As the discussion progressed, we guided students first to examine more global issues like organization, asking them questions about the specific arrangement of ideas, and then moved to more local concerns like the ordering of sentences in a paragraph, and finally concluded with talk about surface features. Our goal was to encourage conversations about papers, taking care not to rush them into making scoring decisions. We wanted our students to begin thinking through the scoring process, to practice talking about it, describing what they believed they saw, and what they felt worked and didn't work. Eventually, we did ask students to score each trait, knowing that asking them to commit to a score would increase their awareness of the complexities of scoring and the need for careful observation and deliberation.

It wasn't long before students began to see the difficulties in our rubric, and by extension, any rubric. First, they began to recognize that this method of scoring compartmentalizes writing qualities, denying the interconnectedness among these qualities and its inseparability from the content. Students persistently raised questions and made comments which addressed the inextricable nature of many of these qualities. For instance, they found decisions regarding organization difficult to evaluate without taking audience into consideration. Yet, the rubric asked them to do so. Of course, having them recognize this difficulty was one of our pedagogical goals. In spite of this problem, we still thought this method was most beneficial for the purpose of having students look closely at writing. One student claimed that he saw that his attention had mostly been on correctness, but that he gave little attention to an engaging thesis or sophisticated coherence. For this reason, we believe that trait scoring gave students specific directions for addressing the writing.

Second, students noticed that trait scoring with a generic rubric overgeneralizes the qualities it is asked to assess. Much class time was spent discussing, or "norming" (bringing the class toward agreement), what each quality might consist of for a particular paper. During these discussions, students reiterated the difficulty they had with the explicit definitions of the different traits. They had difficulty with the varying definitions of coherence. At first, students said coherence meant "flow." Through further discussion, they narrowed their definition to the presence of transitional words within a paper, such as "however" and "yet." But we asked the students, if a paper lacked transitional words, should the paper be scored lower for the trait of coherence? They quickly recognized that coherence was much more complex than the presence of transitional words. So they struggled with developing a definition that was specific but at the same time not so abstract that it became useless. Over time, the students in the class, as a community, began to come to decisions about what these traits should mean, above and beyond our own short descriptions. Essentially, they began to take ownership of the criteria for evaluation, testing them against their own experience with the piece of writing. Again, we see this type of discussion as vital to students' development as writers. So, though there is difficulty in what each term means in relation to a specific writing task, the struggles students go through, like those instructors go through, are part of the process we believe necessary to becoming a good writer.

Third, students quickly began to concern themselves with the value placed on the traits we had had them score. They recognized the problems in privileging some qualities over others, and many of them quickly came to realize that they held what one student called his "lopsided" idea of what good writing should be. When we first began to use peer evaluation in our classes, we selected particular traits to be evaluated. But by choosing and naming the traits we do, we inevitably devalue other traits that could be scored. For instance, we had particular trouble using *development* as a trait unto itself. We hoped that issues of development would be included in how students assessed other traits, but we realized we could not be certain that development would in fact be assessed. One response to this problem which we have begun to employ is to have students develop their own list of traits and a rubric to accompany them. We chose to do this because in the process of developing criteria as a community, students engage directly with the purpose of and goals for the assignment and define which elements might make a successful response to that assignment. In our reading of the literature, we also learned that "students and teachers tended to differ in the criteria they employed for deciding what constituted a successful completion of the task and in the criteria they employed for ranking the essays according to scoring criteria" (Ruth and Murphy 202). So, to address this problem, we simply decided to let students help in developing the criteria. This way we could, as both a class and community of writers, design what is valuable within the context of the assignment itself.

Fourth, our students often expressed dismay at being forced to score these traits on a linear scale. Students focusing on placing a paper somewhere along this scale have a tendency to move away from talking about specific issues in the writing—as they had been accustomed to in their peer-response groups. If students find that a paper exhibits strong coherence at the beginning but less at the end, in their effort to grade the paper they lose the possibility of acknowledging and discussing specific successes or weaknesses of that trait.

Finally, students had to take the scores they had given each trait and try to reduce them to one numerical score, and this required a relative value to be placed on each trait scored. This last step increased the frustration they had already experienced in their struggle to give each trait a score. In response, we invited them to develop a strategy for turning the trait scores into one value for the paper. Students attempted to find a mathematical solution, but they quickly found that no formula would fairly convert the trait scores into a single number. The students suffered from the same problem of subjectivity that instructors confront in their effort to evaluate. Through this process, students discovered that there were many possibilities for what readers value as good writing, and we think this is a useful realization for them to grasp as writers. And acting upon this realization, we assisted students in class discussion again, as a community, in using the trait scores to intuitively decide on an overall score for the paper.

After discussing the benefits and shortcomings with the class and modeling the kind of behavior we wanted them to use during the scoring sessions, we placed another student paper on the overhead. This time we asked students to talk with their partners about each score, recreating the dialogue modeled in class. We gave them two conditions: They couldn't give half scores, and they needed to come to an agreement on each. The chatter quickly rose as they struggled with making their evaluative decisions. Many students became animated, adamantly defending their choices, then shifting, reconsidering the evidence offered by their partner, finally making themselves decide upon a score. One student exclaimed, "I don't care if you don't like the topic. It's still well written. Find a place where it isn't." After many minutes of haggling, they reached an agreement. Encouraging this kind of dialogue, we gave them as much time as they needed. This didn't seem to be a process that could be rushed. When they were finished, we again opened up discussion to the class.

We wrote the name of each trait up on the board and collected tallies: Three pairs gave the paper's organization a 5; seven pairs gave it a 4; one gave it a 3. Pairs were asked to talk about their scoring. They were expected to give evidence, to point to specific examples of where they thought the paper succeeded or failed, and to explain why that success or failure deserved the score they gave it. We had begun to "norm" the readers, while simultaneously aiming them toward an even greater awareness of which qualities they were discussing, why they saw them the way they did, and how these qualities applied to successful writing. All throughout this discussion, the class returned to the inherent problems of scoring, but each time developing and expressing a greater sophistication about those problems and the potential solutions to them. The discussions in our classes have been lively, informative, and fruitful.

Given that students would be responsible for grading each other's work, we found it important to spend a good portion of class time having them score and then discuss their scores. The students in the class could see some of the dangers easily enough. Some pairs were repeatedly overly critical, ready to punish the slightest mistake in a paper with a low score. Others were all too ready to give a string of sixes. But as instructors, we exerted a helpful influence in how our students decided what constituted successful or less successful writing. We found class discussions an opportune place to share our opinions, as readers, of what we value in writing. In many instances, this provided the guidance students needed.

Before the day students were to score their classmates' papers, we had prepared them in the following ways: (1) discussed the use of rubrics, their benefits, and drawbacks; (2) facilitated students' designing of an assignment-specific rubric; (3) modeled assessment and evaluation; and (4) had students practice evaluation as a class and then with their partners. Because we believe that conversation is "the ultimate context within which knowledge is to be understood" (Rorty 389), during this process we fostered a sense of community by negotiating the terms for evaluation, honoring the various voices that contributed to the discussions.

On scoring day, students came to class with two copies of their papers in a manila folder with the names removed and a number on the folder and on the top of each paper to help us with identification. In addition, we provided forms on which they could record their scores. We handed out the folders to each pair. Each member received his or her own copy for easier reading. We asked them not to write on the papers.

And then they began scoring them, following through on the model we helped them to create through their practice in class. After they completed reading the papers, the chatter again rose up. This time students were much quicker about deciding what they believed the scores should be. As they finished, they came up to turn in folders and to take new ones. After all the hours of preparation the class had given to this task, the students approached the work with excitement and seriousness. Each time a student returned to pick up another folder to read and score, it became clear to us that they had made their decisions about their fellow students' papers in earnest. Rarely, it seemed to us, was a decision made lightly. With only a few folders left to be read, some of the students talked more openly about the difficulty of scoring fairly:

> Stephanie said, "This is hard. I've never had to read papers so closely and then argue about it."
> "Do you think this gives you a better idea of what good writing might look like?"
> Stephanie stopped for a moment, thinking about my question.
> "I think so. I think I see that I'll just have to be more careful when I do my writing. I can see I have a lot of stuff to think about."
> "Good, Stephanie," I smiled. "Here's your last folder."

Works Cited

Rorty, Richard. *Philosophy and the Mirror of Nature*. Princeton: Princeton UP, 1979.

Ruth, Leo, and Sandra Murphy. *Designing Writing Tasks for the Assessment of Writing*. Norwood: Ablex, 1988.

Williams, James D. *Preparing to Teach Writing*. Belmont: Wadsworth, 1989.

Interlude

In my collaborative/self-grading program, students "grade" only at semester's end—we don't do intermittent or paper grading. We *do* work at looking at how they view grades after midterm. Leading into the final essay, we talk about grades and how they see them, as well as how others see them. I want them to appreciate how difficult and complicated grades really are. We also spend time in class reviewing the evaluations and peer feedback they gave and received, looking for places where they captured in writing what they have learned about writing as well as where they have made improvements. The goal setting directly helps with this....Then they have to establish what criteria they are using for arguing for a grade: improvement; meeting goals; understanding what writing is; the ability to experiment and try things with their writing which may not have succeeded, but from which they have learned; and others. After establishing the criteria, they have to show how they have met them. They must refer to their writing and must be able to talk about it....After they argue on how well they have met the criteria—I call it "building value"—they then have to tell me what the value is worth in terms of a grade. They also expect or assume about them as writers on the basis of that grade. If they don't meet those traditional expectations, then they need to argue further why they should get the grade in spite of that. I read the papers and look at how well they've constructed the argument, noting especially the criteria and explication of how well they've met them. I prepare a response and we discuss it.

—Nick Carbone
University of Massachusetts at Amherst

17 Unlocking Outcome-Based Education through the Writing Process

Rick Pribyl
Blue Valley Northwest High School, Overland Park, Kansas

Rick Pribyl is currently English department chair at Blue Valley Northwest High School in Overland Park, Kansas, and is finishing his doctoral program from Walden University, conducting research in alternative assessment methods and critical thinking through writing.

. . . and you're going to do it over and over and over again until you get it right!

Thus concludes the punch line of a well-worn joke about a teacher and the persistence of repetition in education. We all laugh at this image, and even Hollywood films depict the stereotypical teacher as the strict Pavlovian disciplinarian, tapping his or her wooden pointer on the desk, reciting rules of learning over and over.

As I entered my senior "Modern Literature" class the past few years, armed with the latest tools from the National Writing Project, I was challenged with how to break away from some of these traditional stereotypes that have hindered progress in education. I discovered that perhaps not all the traditional ways had to be thrown out. In fact, the idea of "doing it over and over again" provided the necessary step in my classroom to tie the writing process to the concept of "Outcome-Based Education" (OBE), the function of which aims to provide all students with the necessary tools for future success (see "NCTE Supports").

In 1991, I was introduced to the concept of outcome-based education, and I remember that as we sat in the audience, my colleagues and I had more questions than the presenters could answer. Basically, we were told that OBE was based upon the notion that "success breeds success" and that students should be given every chance possible to learn and progress (Nelson). Accomplishing goals and absorbing knowledge take precedence over grades. We all learned that OBE presented a positive approach and promised results that all of us were searching for in education. What was lacking at that time was the actual "nuts and bolts" for the classroom implementation. I still remember walking away thinking that OBE was a target for the long-distant future. Little did I know that soon trial and error and a little luck would bring OBE into my own classroom.

From my previous years with seniors in modern literature, I knew that a multitude of problems and solutions stood before me. First, and most important, being a proponent of the writing process, I had to come up with a way of evaluating papers that did not just stamp a grade on a paper. Next, I needed a method of testing that not only reflected acquisition of the material, but also ensured that all students had completed the required work. In addition, I needed to establish a way to force all seniors, especially the "at-risk" students (Morris), to finish the work necessary to complete the high school English requirements. The majority of these same students would be attending various colleges, while a small percentage would be entering the local job market. As if these were not steep enough goals, I had one last piece of personal baggage to rid myself of—eliminating the pressure of grades, one of a teacher's basic tools for motivation, and replacing that pressure with a thirst for individual success. My destination was set, but I had not yet decided upon my basic mode of transportation and delivery.

Writing Process: Accept/Revise Evaluation

For years, as a student, I had pondered the question "What is the difference between a B+ paper and an A- paper?" Of course, I was trying to find out because I seemed to be constantly receiving that B+ on my own papers. Just where was that fine line in subjective evaluation between a minus and a plus? In fact, in one of my own college classes, one of my English teachers gave percentage points as a grade on a subjective essay. It made me wonder if percentage points had been deducted because of poor voice, grammar, or theme statement. As I recall, no one in that class ever received 100 percent, proof positive that no paper was perfect.

This point bothered me throughout my schooling and into the eighth year of my teaching career, as now I had become the grade giver instead of the receiver. Certainly, I had my scoring rubric and constantly shared it with students, but the gray area of swaying to the minus or the plus side constantly plagued me. I truly enjoyed teaching each day, but putting on my grader's hat almost ruined teaching for me. It was not until I started to follow the implications of the writing process in my grading that I was able to overcome this obstacle.

The writing process, as articulated by the National Writing Project, emphasizes responses in the form of praising and questioning. Among the biggest bonuses that I found from this approach to writing was the positive psychological impact it had on the individual student. The strokes from peers and teachers, plus the freedom, enabled the student to feel a strong degree of success. That is, until a final grade was marked on the paper.

Then we were back to what every English teacher has experienced. The hypothetical, typical English teacher takes home the papers to evaluate over the weekend. Each paper is read once, twice, and sometimes three times, the teacher making as many corrections as deemed necessary along with praise and suggestions for improvement. Some papers may take as long as fifteen to twenty minutes to go through. Finally finished, they are handed back to the pupils on Monday, and the teacher stands back and watches. To his or her dismay, the students immediately turn to the last page, look at the grade, and put the paper away, never giving the comments a glance. As a result, the same mistakes that were noted on that piece of writing will undoubtedly appear in the following papers.

The writing process had produced positive self-esteem and optimism, but the grade, whether it be by letter or number, renewed the traditional feeling of either success or failure. By using a traditional grading method, I had further fed the notion that the grade was far more important than the paper or the author's growth in the writing of that paper.

In attempting to correct this notion, I stumbled upon another system in a Greater Kansas City Writing Project class that has produced some remarkable results. The facilitator, Dick Luckert, who teaches at nearby Olathe East High School, introduced the concept, and I eventually called it *accept/revise* grading. Essentially, after the students work through the process of possibly three or four drafts, including numerous revisions and editorial opportunities, they turn in all drafts and prewriting along with their final copies. I read through the material very carefully, making comments, asking questions, and suggesting corrections. At the end of the paper, I write a general comment to the student and then write one of three words:

- *Accepted:* If the paper is what I believe is the best product possible for this individual student and has no glaring errors, then it is accepted, and the student is finished with the paper. The student will receive all points possible (e.g., 100 points out of 100) in the grade book.

- *Revise:* If the paper is below average for this individual student, if it has numerous mistakes, or if a recurring problem from previous writings has not been resolved, then the student is asked to revise the paper and correct whatever is necessary as stated in the comments. The student will receive a deduction of 10 percent of the total points possible for each time he or she has to revise. Thus, it is very possible to be asked to revise a paper, get 90 out of 100 points (90 percent), and still receive an A. This is a positive outcome for those parents and students who are still motivated by a grade. Also, it tells the poorer writer that he or she can attain success both by comment and by a letter grade. [Note: Some teachers using this procedure choose not to lower points for each revision, giving 100 percent for all "accepted" papers, whether accepted on the first or fifth submission.]

- *Reject:* If the student has failed to follow the correct assignment or not completed certain required parts, then the paper is rejected, and the entire project, from prewriting to final draft, must be redone. This is rarely needed due to the continuous process of writing being performed in the classroom, but periodically, it is necessary to bring the student back on track. A rejection does not mean failure, but simply: "Let's do this one over and get it right." After a 10 percent reduction in the total points possible, the student's paper is now treated again to the same accept/revise process.

The results of doing this for the past two years have been outstanding in both the quality of work and the positive self-confidence that students exhibit in their writing. The responsibility for a grade has been partially transferred from the teacher to the student, while the teacher still holds considerable control within the classroom. In incorporating this method, the teacher can influence the individual student at all the various levels of her writing. The poorer writers can be brought along at their own rates; the strong writers can be further stretched and challenged; the recurring problems can be eliminated; and all students learn that they can write and fix their own miscues without penalties.

In addition, the grade-conscious pupils discover that they can make mistakes and still receive A's. Meanwhile, the less gifted or motivated students can also achieve a high grade. The feeling of success in student writing produces, in general, a very positive atmosphere within the classroom.

Normally, I allow three days for a student to return a revision. As a result, due to all the constant writing in the class, some students find themselves working on several writing projects simultaneously. It does not take very long for many of the writers to learn to produce a good product on the first final draft, so as not to be overly burdened with work.

I have found that the quality of writing in content and grammar has far exceeded my expectations. In fact, it has become invigorating for me. I have the renewed confidence to attempt all types of writing within the classroom because through this process, the students have developed confidence in their work and in themselves. One last benefit has been that the parents are totally in support of this because they realize where the responsibility for student writing success lies. Also, they see positive rewards for effort and work as their children become better writers.

Testing—Accept/Revise Style

Once my students and I were comfortable with the accept/revise process with papers, I focused in on testing of the material we covered. From my reading of various researchers in the area of human development, I uncovered one basic agreement. Except for innate and inherited functions, humans have to be exposed to an environment or stimulus to learn. Talking about how to swim or the pain of being burned does not teach a human to swim or to fear burns. People must be exposed to water and feel the heat of the flame before they can truly claim to have at least partial knowledge of the topic.

My problem in class mirrored that of almost every classroom since Plato hung out his school placard. Students cannot fully grasp material unless they have read, discussed, or experienced it. This might be in the form of homework, self-study, or classwork. In most cases, when it comes time to prove achievement or demonstrate a level of familiarity with the subject matter, students take tests. The preconceived notion that a high score means acquisition of knowledge and a low score means ignorance is usually the norm, but is not necessarily accurate. But many teachers would agree that low-score cases mean that the high school students either didn't read or study the material. Consequently, the student receives the low grade; the teacher then begins the next book or unit; and the same student will never go back to learn the missed material. Hence, both the student and the teacher accept the loss of information or performance.

Just as students are mainly concerned with their grades at the end of papers, so it is with tests. The average student would prefer just to get the low grade and proceed with the new material rather than to try to absorb and comprehend the old material. The blame frequently falls on the teacher for not reviewing well enough. The teacher must decide whether to reteach the material to a handful of unwilling students or to proceed and accept the losses. The student never experiences the nature of the material, and the teacher must fall back to the security of the low grade for punishment. Neither the student nor teacher has succeeded.

Also, I have become extremely frustrated with the failure of a few seniors in my classes to completely read the short stories or novels. They've guessed their way through verification exams and insightful essays. Obviously, in general they were satisfied with just receiving passing grades. The knowledge missed in no way bothered them, and they considered "getting by" as totally acceptable. The lesson they learned was that little or no effort in life is enough to survive. At the same time, I, as the teacher, became frustrated with the belief that these individuals were not reaching their full potential. Neither the teacher nor the student won.

One of the most striking aspects of OBE is that essentially it should reflect in certain respects "the real world." In the workplace, if an employee writes a bad report for any reason, it will usually be sent back to him to redo or else he'll be fired. The company wants the report done properly, and the last thing an employer would do would be to put a grade on it.

Fueled by these notions, I decided to attack my own testing procedures. I came up with a solution that seemed to complement what we had been doing with the accept/revise procedure with papers. In essence, all examinations became accept/revise tests, much like a pass/fail system. The difference centered on the fact that our school district system required a grade. To cover both grading and pass/fail standards, I initiated a system whereby all tests and quizzes must reach a score of 75 percent or better to be accepted. If the test is not accepted, a student must retest over the material until the score reaches above 75 percent. The highest score recorded on any of the tests would become the grade recorded in the grade book.

Of course, such action was certain to be protested by some students. In anticipation of cries of "unfair!" from the students who made excellent grades on the first try, I put certain requirements on retakes. First, before a test could be retaken, a "ticket" which proved that the student had restudied the material had to be completed before the retest could begin. This ticket could be in the form of a paper, a journal, a related project, or an oral report. In addition, no exam could be taken during class time. As in business, the pupils had to sign up for appointments with me before or after school or during lunch or planning periods. I shifted all responsibility for completion onto them.

At first, I found that I had to have two or three sets of exams available for retesting. Eventually, in the case of tests over novels, I started using the same tests, but made them open-book tests requiring the page numbers where the answers could be found. I discovered this to be most beneficial in allowing "at-risk" students who possessed little retention to prove that they had at least read parts of the book. Although open-book tests can be extremely difficult, they can serve as educational tools as well.

To date, the results have all been positive. I perceive fewer and fewer seniors failing exams because they do not want to retake the tests. The previously labeled "low achievers" are suddenly discovering success in the classroom and are more engaged in discussion. As the instructor, I can now emphasize many more important parts of the lesson being covered because all the students have reached a basic level with the material. And finally, there manifests in the room a feeling that the students and I are truly encountering academe on a positive note.

The Incomplete Grade

At Indiana University in June of 1992, George Gustafson spoke to Walden University doctoral candidates about his school district in Chicago, Illinois, and the trend toward OBE. To paraphrase one of his statements, "Students do not fail because of intelligence. They fail because of not doing the work."

Putting that statement into perspective—and into my classroom in particular—proved to be the necessary link in tying the accept/revise notion with papers and exams to OBE. In the past, when tallying up scores for semester grades, with some students I would come across quite a few empty spaces in the grade book. Normally, I would count these spaces as zeros. In fact, almost every student somewhere in the semester had not turned in an assignment or finished a revision. When I sat back and studied these missed assignments, I could not help but think about the lack of learning or writing that had taken place. Meanwhile, because of a lack of points, some seniors failed the modern literature course and ultimately did not graduate with their class, not because of ignorance, but because they had failed to do their work.

In 1992, I received permission to pilot a program at Blue Valley North High School (and the following year at Blue Valley Northwest High School) that allowed me to give an "Incomplete" (I) to any senior who did not turn in all assignments. The students were allowed to turn in assignments late with a percentage reduction penalty, but in all cases, no questions were asked as to why the delay. Any I not rectified within two weeks after issuing grades would turn into a "Failure" (F).

Letters and contracts about the program were shared with the students and parents, and I waited with anticipation of what would happen the few weeks before the end of the semester. As expected, the responsibility for learning and completion of work shifted from me to the students. Suddenly, the at-risk students were at my desk inquiring about which assignments were still needed. Even the better students were anxious to finish all of their work. I received papers from some seniors, almost a month late, that had needed revision work, as well as makeup exams for a novel we had completed five weeks earlier.

Out of eighty-three seniors and forty-seven juniors, I gave six incomplete grades, and within a week, only one senior had not finished his work. It was a remarkable achievement for the seniors who traditionally would have produced approximately a 5 to 8 percent failure rate. With this system, the low achievers and at-risk students did not see F's on their report cards—which reflected failure and closure—but instead saw I's—which presented hope and an opportunity for improvement. The program had acted as a deterrent, not as a punishment. As the teacher, I ended the semester with the feeling that, for the first time, all of my students had engaged in learning and had learned about life itself.

As far as the range of grades after using this process, I've found that the vast majority of the semester grades I've given have been A's and B's, with relatively few C's or D's, and an occasional F. At first I was concerned that the perception to an outsider might be that the class was easy and that everyone would automatically receive a high grade. But in their written responses, students have said that they were challenged more than they ever had been, that their writing and study habits had improved dramatically, and that they had left the class feeling confident that they could tackle writing and reading at the next level. The parents overwhelmingly approved because they personally experienced their sons and daughters not only improving their writing, but also working on their own to achieve success. Perhaps, the true bonus has been the success that the at-risk students have had as a result of this process. For many, this method has enabled them to believe that by taking responsibility for their own work, they can succeed. In many cases, they have proved even to their peers that their writing is as good and sometimes even better.

I did not seek out OBE—it just found me in my classroom. It was disguised in its philosophies and theories, and it repelled teachers with the fear of instructing without using grades as a lever. OBE has made me shed quite a lot of heavy, traditional educational baggage, while at the same time allowing me to retain some of the basics. But in my classroom—with the freedom of the writing process, the accept/ revise concept, and the allowance of the "Incomplete" grade as a backup—OBE has come to life. Sometimes, "doing it over and over and over again" does foster success.

Works Cited

Adams, W. Royce. *Think, Read, React, Plan, Write, Rewrite.* 4th ed. New York: Holt, 1986.

Beechhold, Henry F. *The Creative Classroom: Teaching without Textbooks.* New York: Scribner's, 1971.

Brookfield, Stephen D. *Developing Critical Thinkers: Challenging Adults to Explore Alternative Ways of Thinking and Acting.* San Francisco: Jossey-Bass, 1987.

Calkins, Lucy McCormick. *The Art of Teaching Writing.* Portsmouth: Heinemann, 1986.

Dowsett, Norman C. *Psychology for Future Education.* Pondicherry: Dept. of Educational Research and Development, Sri Aurobindo Society, 1977.

Gustafson, George. "The New Paradigm in Public School Assessment." Presentation. Indiana University. 28 June 1992.

Kirby, Dan, and Carol Kuykendall. *Mind Matters: Teaching for Thinking.* Portsmouth: Boynton/Cook, 1991.

Lindemann, Erika. *A Rhetoric for Writing Teachers.* 2nd ed. New York: Oxford UP, 1987.

Morris, Cecil K. "Giving At-Risk Juniors Intellectual Independence: An Experiment." *English Journal* 80.3 (Mar. 1991): 37–41.

"NCTE Supports 'Whole Language' but is Unfriendly with Standardized Testing." *Kansas Association of Teachers of English (KATE) Journal* 10.4 (17 May 1992): 1–3.

Nelson, Cary, ed. *Theory in the Classroom.* U of Illinois P, 1986.

Interlude

I was thinking about the way journalists like to use
metaphors of grading for schools, as in "schools don't
make the grade" or "local schools get failing grades
from parents, graduates." It happens so often that it
really is a journalistic cliche. I wonder if those
journalists are doing it to get back at teachers who
graded them down? Certainly, it has to give us teachers
a sense of how kids feel when all their work and effort
is reduced to a single grade: C-, C+, B+. Anything less
than an A hurts your feelings, and even an A (whether
applied to schools or kids) doesn't really tell you
much. A what?

—Will Heller
Internet communication

18 Portfolio Assessment as an Alternative to Grading Student Writing

Kathleen Jones
Lester B. Pearson High School, Calgary, Alberta, Canada

Kathleen Jones teaches humanities at Lester B. Pearson High School in Calgary, Alberta, Canada. She proudly counts herself as part of the alumni of the Calgary Writing Project, as it is through this association that she began to explore alternative possibilities for grading writing. She conducts workshops and writes extensively in order to continue to explore and make sense of alternative grading practices. She has previously published in English Journal, Teaching Today, *and* Alberta English.

In the wake of cutbacks and government intervention, the natural tendency may be to do less, not more, in our classrooms. I believe that the writing portfolio is a structure that will help simplify assessment and grading and at the same time help make learning meaningful in our classrooms. The National Council of Teachers of English has recently passed a resolution encouraging teachers to "refrain as much as possible from using grades to evaluate and respond to student writing." Using a portfolio approach can help us in this kind of assessment.

A portfolio can be many things, but for my purposes, ever mindful of the need to keep things simple, a writing portfolio is a collection of completed writing assignments. I want students to follow through on any writing they undertake, so every piece of writing, including the various drafts, self-assessments, peer responses, and teacher response is included in the portfolio. Revisions, rewrites, and false starts are also evident. This collection becomes a living, almost breathing, record of a student's thinking as well as his or her growth, through self-assessment, as a writer and learner.

For me, the issue of choice of writing topics is the first crucial component for meaningful writing to take place in the classroom. If the assignment is determined by the teacher, the students' stake in it will be guided by the external outcome of the teacher's approval, in many cases a grade. On the other hand, if students are given the opportunity and responsibility of finding their own topics and tasks, the outcome will be linked with what they have set out to accomplish and what they have achieved. I want the topics for writing to develop naturally from the reading and the discussion of ideas. I also want the form the writing takes to develop in authentic ways. The content or idea should suggest the form.

I believe this is true of the traditional, or literary, essay as well. I don't teach the five-paragraph essay; when students are writing about ideas in a genuine fashion, formula writing has no place. When we discuss an idea from a piece of literature that has affected us strongly, we may discuss how that idea was developed and the nature of its impact on us as a reader. This may mean we will deal directly with the literature, or it may mean we will use it as a springboard to something else, perhaps related to ourselves. It may even mean that we take the idea and develop our own story, our own literature—to explore the idea fully in a way that has meaning for us.

It is important, then, to encourage students to think in terms of the reader-writer connection. I think that when they begin to read as writers and write with potential readers in mind, they become their own best readers and learn to write for themselves. I have learned that I have to stay out of it. When I determine what it is that students write, the writing quickly becomes stilted. If the student has to jump through my hoops with regard to form, the writing deteriorates. When students are committed to writing—"This is my idea; now how can I best get it across?"—everything opens up, and the stage is set for portfolio assessment.

What does all of this have to do with the writing classroom and the grading or nongrading of papers? Every time we, or our students, sit down to write, we have myriad decisions to make. All of these decisions are part of the writing and the learning process. All of this leads to the quality of the end product. And it is the quality of the end product that we are concerned with. A single piece of writing is only a step along the way in that process toward a body of work which is the end product. If all of this ends in incomplete pieces of work, or numerous attempts that never get anywhere, then we are spinning our wheels. Quality counts. Getting finished and meeting some kind of deadline counts too.

In my classroom, the writing portfolio is placed within the context of a response-based program. Students do a great deal of writing in their journals in response to what they read. This writing varies, but can become the basis for a piece of writing that will be developed and polished for the writing portfolio. Writing is assigned at regular intervals. Depending on the class, my deadlines can be very definite, with built-in penalties for lateness, or fairly flexible, with target deadlines and a certain grace period. A student recently suggested that after the deadline has passed, I should speak to the student and together we should set a final deadline. The following description is given to students at the beginning of the term:

Writing Portfolio (30%)

You will be required to take ownership and responsibility for the writing you do in this classroom. You will come up with your own topics and formats from ideas found in your reading, your journals, and class discussion. From the basic topic through to the final polished draft, you will be responsible for revisions, peer editing, and responses, as well as a thorough self-evaluation of your work. Teachers will not edit work, but will be available for conferences to help with specific writing problems identified by the student or the teacher. It is expected that you will use the computer technology available to you, including spell checkers. Writing assignments handed in must include rough notes, drafts, peer comments, a writer's memo, and a cover page with the title, name, date, and class. Your final draft should demonstrate that you take pride in producing quality work.

Your portfolio should include a variety of formats each reporting period. Examples might include a short story/narrative writing, plays, TV scripts, poetic/descriptive writing, essays of all kinds—reflective, persuasive, opinion/viewpoint, position, letters. Completed work will be stored in a file folder in the room.

Individual writing assignments will *not* receive a grade. All work will require a self-assessment as well as comments from peers and teachers. All work will be shared, sometimes with the group and sometimes with the whole class.

The portfolio will be evaluated as a whole each reporting term in a conference between the student and teacher and according to the criteria provided. A grade will be assigned at that time.

Please note: *All assignments must be handed in to receive a passing grade on the portfolio. The portfolio grade is cumulative—each report-card period the portfolio is looked at as a whole.*

The issue of teacher editing comes up a great deal with regard to a portfolio approach. I used to do too much editing of student papers, and I may still do more than I believe we should. I have found that students get too dependent on teacher editors. Students need to be made responsible for revising their own papers. I agree that students need feedback during the process of writing, but the peer-response or writing group is the ideal place to train students to respond to each other's writing. We have to be careful that peers deal with more than surface errors. They have to learn to read each other's writing just as they would any author—with the intention of trying to understand—not just reacting, not just judging, but making an honest attempt at getting to the meaning intended or otherwise revealed by the author and the particular text. It becomes a transaction or dialogue between writer and reader just as with any literary text.

Depending on the experience and level of the class, I may structure the group process very carefully or just let them go at it and then make adjustments as I go. Students will already be familiar with their group and have some experience discussing literature in it. Looking at each other's writing is an easy transition. I have taken various approaches, especially when the class is starting up. Later they can decide which approach works best for their group. They may read their work aloud or pass it to the left. The expectation is that they will read the draft with the intention of understanding it. Sometimes I give them prepared questions; other times I ask them to respond to the writing just as they would to a piece of literature. This response is usually written, but later I allow students to do this orally if that approach works best for them. Sometimes I ask them to focus on a specific problem area such as great introductions; most often, I ask the student writer to determine the area of concern to be addressed. I discourage the actual correcting of a student's work, although students may bring errors to the attention of the writer.

Which brings me to a crucial point—students have to become their own best readers. And ultimately, they have to learn whether or not what they have written achieves the goal they have set for themselves. The assessment process begins with peer comments and continues with a self-assessment or a writer's memo that serves to open up a dialogue between the student and the teacher.

When the portfolio writing is ready for a response from me, it is always accompanied by evidence of the process. I want whatever there is: the concept maps, the outlines, the scribbles, the doodles, the drafts that were rejected, and the drafts that were responded to and sometimes corrected by peers. I want the written peer comments, as well as a brief summary of any discussion about the writing, with peers or with me, that has taken place. I also want a writer's memo (self-assessment) that chats with me about the writing, that tells me what the writer tried to do and whether or not the writer thinks his or her intention has been accomplished. I want writers to articulate their ideas very clearly. I want them to begin to recognize their strengths and weaknesses. This is crucial to the assessment process.

My response to this portfolio writing will be to this memo. I will agree or disagree with students' perceptions of their writing. I might make a suggestion or two. I might share my interest in their idea or I might share my pleasure in reading their work. I will read what they have written, certainly, and I may choose to make corrections in the first paragraph or even the first page of a longer piece. I may choose to zero in on one type of writing problem and ask the student to conference with me about it. Students always have the option of coming back to a piece of writing to revise or rework it. I might encourage a student to try another draft or just let it be. All writing doesn't have to be beaten to death or be perfect.

I don't put a grade on any of this writing. At first, students will ask for a mark, but I resist the urge to give them one. A grade is a final judgment, and any single piece of writing in the portfolio is only part of a process that should encourage risk taking and experimentation.

The assessment process continues with the first portfolio conference and is a learning experience for student and teacher. At this conference, the student and the teacher evaluate the portfolio and assign a grade. The grade reflects the work as a whole. Because you want to encourage risk taking, one poor showing shouldn't affect what is otherwise exceptional work. But you need criteria (mine are shown in Figure 1) that provide the basis for the discussion of the student's work. The set of criteria or the rubric should include completion, process, and quality of final product, and it should incorporate what you value. This should be spelled out quite clearly or conflicts will arise during the conference. Students need to be prepared to make a case (I like to receive this in writing at the time of the conference) for the grade they propose, and it must be supported by the criteria. It is important to listen; I have to guard against doing all the talking. Depending on the length between reporting periods, we may only have a couple of pieces of writing to look at the first time. The portfolio mark is cumulative, so that each time there is a larger body of work to look at. I use the time to talk about students' writing. I ask them which piece they are most proud of and which piece demanded the most work. During these conferences I get to know the student and the writing problems he or she may be having.

I hold these conferences at the end of each term to coincide with report cards. We offer a full-year humanities program, and report cards are issued four times each year. I have worked in a system where

---

Writing Portfolio Assessment and Evaluation Guidelines

A

The writer *extends and explores ideas and concepts* from the readings and discussion.

The writer takes ownership and responsibility for coming up with his or her own topics, establishing a personal focus, developing the idea, and seeing it through to the final finished *quality* product.

The writer deals with *complex ideas and issues.* Ideas are thoughtfully developed with carefully chosen support and detail. This expression of ideas is *fluent, thoughtful, and effective.* The writer takes *risks,* experimenting with a variety of formats.

The writer demonstrates a sophistication of language usage. Vocabulary is appropriate to the tone and topic of discussion. Terminology is discussed in a meaningful context.

The *writer's voice* comes through. The writer is *confident, insightful,* and *perceptive.* The writing demonstrates *confidence in control* of correct sentence construction, usage, grammar, and mechanics. The writing is *error free.*

The writer's memo (self-assessment) demonstrates a *growing self-awareness* and ownership in improving writing. The writer sets high standards and strives to meet them.

B

Topics are *related to the ideas and issues* that arise from the readings and discussions. *Understanding is evident.* The writer chooses a format that develops his or her idea. The writer considers his or her impact on the reader.

The writer has *met all deadlines.* Class time has been used well. Peer input is valued during the process of the writing. The writer uses feedback from peers to revise. The writer is committed to producing a polished final product.

A *clear focus is established* and thoughtful ideas are supported with appropriate evidence. The writing is *organized so that it has impact* on the reader. The conclusion is effective.

Vocabulary is clear and appropriate. Language used is *straightforward, clear, and fluent.* The writing demonstrates *competence in control* of sentence construction, usage, and mechanics. *Minor and minimal errors.*

The writer's memo carefully considers what has been accomplished in the writing as well as dealing with specifics of the writing.

C

Most deadlines have been met. *All writing assignments have been completed* (including revisions when asked to do so).

Topics are *related to the ideas and issues* that arise from the readings and discussions. *Ideas are dealt with simply but clearly and supported by/with some kind of evidence.*

continued on next page

Figure 1. Portfolio assessment criteria.

Figure 1 continued

The writer is focused and the introduction provides a general direction for the reader, but discussion of idea may be general or predictable. It may lack the specific detail needed to support ideas. The conclusion is functional.

Vocabulary is imprecise and/or inappropriate. The writing may be straightforward but limited to simple structures. The writer *demonstrates control of the basics* of sentence construction, usage, grammar, and mechanics. There may be *occasional errors*, but the communication of ideas is clear. The writer is aware of his or her purpose and audience.

The writer's memo is beginning to deal with specifics of the writing.

D

Deadlines have been missed/portfolio is incomplete.

Topics are *not related to ideas and issues* from readings and discussions in the classroom. The writer may be *confused or lack the background to deal with the subject chosen.*

The writer lacks a focus and/or is unable to develop an idea.

The writer may be unable to use paragraphing to organize ideas. The conclusion is not functional.

The writer *lacks control of conventions and language usage.*

The writer is *unable to write clearly* and/or effectively.

F

The writer has not completed any assignments or has made no effort in the assignments completed.

---

report cards were required two or three times in a semester. In order to prepare for the portfolio conference, I ask students to take a close look at the work they have completed, and they study the criteria and the comments they have received to see where their work fits. I ask them to make a case for a grade in writing and add notes during the conference. This then becomes part of their portfolio. Early in the year or semester, and depending on the level of the students, my emphasis is on process. As the course progresses, my emphasis shifts to product, with the final portfolio grade reflecting the overall quality of the product while acknowledging the process that went into it.

The discussion must relate to the criteria (see Figure 1). If the criteria state that all assignments must be done to get 50 percent, and the student hasn't done that, then the conference can focus on getting the student to realize that his or her goal is to get all the assignments in. If the criteria state that if any of these assignments are late, the maximum mark is 60 percent, that too is fairly nonnegotiable. If the criteria state that a B can only be achieved if there are minimal proofreading errors, then that too is quite straightforward. Yet, I have been known to fudge on my own criteria; flexibility is the key. Every conference is unique. A student may be an excellent writer in every sense of the word, but a terrible speller. Depending on what is most important to you and to the student, the mark assigned may be on the high side for the criteria. High standards are important, but the point of the conference is not just to assign a grade, but to help a student improve his or her writing. Most of the time students can determine their grade easily; sometimes they need your help. The goal is quality, and to the student whose effort is phenomenal, but whose work is still poor, I will often say I believe that in the long run the hard work will pay off.

This may sound like a lot of work when I could have just given them the mark in the first place and saved myself all this time and trouble. But more is at stake here. Ten minutes per student is about all the time I need. During this time, I also discuss the student's contribution to class discussion and briefly discuss any concerns I might have about the student's journal. You also need to post a schedule and make sure the students have everything they need for the conference: their portfolio and their report-card conference sheet (where they've made their case). In my experience, students feel better about their grades when they have had some kind of say in determining what they will be. But these are not grades that come out of thin air. The student understands the grades and the criteria because the student has been part of the process of assessing and improving the writing all along. This is time well spent because it puts assessment and evaluation in the context of the actual work of the writer.

The portfolio conference shifts the evaluation and assigning of grades from something done *by* the teacher *to* the student to the perspective of a *shared responsibility* in assessing what has been accomplished. It's one thing to fail a piece of writing because you couldn't figure out what the teacher wanted; its quite another to not quite reach the goal you have set for yourself. This kind of approach to writing allows an entry point for every student at whatever level of ability. Weak writers can still make gains when they choose to write a diary entry, while the stronger writer can try an interior monologue. And after a few diary entries, it is not amiss to suggest other approaches. Variety is written into my assessment criteria. It is also appropriate to be honest about a student's ability; we shouldn't need to hide behind numbers. It is okay to look at what a student has tried to do and see that it is simplistic in language, style, or idea, even if it is error free.

Conference time can be used to be honest and set individual goals with students. Each individual student should be challenged; and no one is in a better position than the students themselves to know whether they've been challenged and whether they've achieved their goals. This is possible in a classroom where students learn to write for themselves first, rather than for a teacher marker.

From a teacher's perspective, I look forward to what my students will write next. I enjoy watching them develop as writers and thinkers. And believe it or not, I even enjoy "marking" (or, more accurately, "responding") to their papers. A great deal of pressure is lifted when one can respond to genuine concerns of the writer and not worry about justifying a number at the top of the page. In the past, all the writing that students did in the classroom was an end in itself, and the teacher was the judge and jury. Portfolio assessment moves writing into a more open arena, a collaborative approach that allows for learning at all stages of the writing process.

In my effort toward simplicity, I have one portfolio grade that reflects their ability in writing, one journal mark that reflects their ability in reading, one oral participation mark that reflects their willingness to participate in discussion and presentation, and one category for tests and leftover stuff that doesn't fit into any other category. My report card clearly communicates to parents where there are strengths and where there are weaknesses. It also represents a commitment to working with students to determine where we go next. I leave you with a last word from one of my twelfth-grade students:

> The quality of the writing has improved....I worked harder on my assignments and tried to put more of my personality into the work....Self-assessment is very important. I didn't realize this before but I soon began to realize its importance. Looking at what you have just written and asking yourself questions about it really opens your eyes as to what you have done. It helps to develop your awareness of the writing process and shows you what you have really attempted and where you have succeeded....I became more interested in probing my ideas and developing them beyond just a simple exploration.

Interlude

A great way to send portfolios to the next grade level
is by having each child build his or her own Hyperstu-
dio portfolio. The students add their own pictures,
colors, text style, voice, sound, animation, etc. It is
much more interesting than looking at a folder.

> —Patsy Garcia
> Sunset Park Elementary School
> Pueblo, Colorado

19 Issues to Consider when Scoring Student Portfolios

Anne Wescott Dodd
Bates College

Anne Wescott Dodd, formerly a high school English teacher, currently teaches education courses and supervises student teachers at Bates College in Lewiston, Maine. She is the author of seven books and has written numerous articles on a variety of topics for general interest and educational publications, including English Journal *and* Teaching English in the Two-Year College. *In her own classes, she gives no grades until she is forced by the institution to submit one at the end of the semester!*

Even though reducing the assessment of any student work to a single grade or score always runs the risk of missing the mark for a variety of reasons, English teachers who use portfolios in their classrooms have the opportunity to get to know their students well. When they make decisions about scores or grades, they usually have the flexibility to figure out some way to accommodate the unexpected so that all students can be treated with a reasonable degree of fairness—or so they think.

Many of the issues raised when portfolios were scored by people who did not know the students may give some classroom teachers a new perspective on evaluation. Moreover, this experimental scoring session also raised other questions about the evaluation of portfolios on a schoolwide basis, especially if these become an essential part of a competency-based diploma. Some issues which might have been easily resolved at the classroom level by sensitive, knowledgeable teachers may become even more problematic.

Sally Mackenzie, formerly an English teacher at Freeport High School in Freeport, Maine, and now with the Department of Education at Bowdoin College, has been working with teachers at Freeport High School to develop a process for using portfolios to assess students' progress throughout their high school careers. To break the ice for four Freeport English teachers, who were very invested in the writing of their own students, Sally organized a fishbowl discussion. This activity gave the teachers a chance to see how "outsiders" would respond to Freeport students' writing and how a rubric might be used for evaluation.

I participated in this fishbowl activity along with two Bowdoin College students, two other members of the Bowdoin Education department, and the director of the Bowdoin Writing Project. As a result of our discussion, it became clear to me that there are several issues teachers need to consider in their own classrooms and in planning ways to extend portfolio evaluation beyond the classroom.

The Context for Our Fishbowl Scoring Discussion

Using a draft of a six-point holistic scoring guide (see Figure 1), the fishbowl participants scored and discussed six student portfolios selected by Sally as representative of the range of portfolios compiled by all of the seniors at Freeport High School. Although we looked only at senior portfolios, students at each grade level at Freeport High have been asked to compile portfolios. The requirements differ because the portfolios are tied to the curriculum at each grade level.

The seniors had been given the following definition of a portfolio by Freeport teachers:

> A portfolio is a collection of student work that exhibits to the student (and/or others) the student's efforts, progress, or achievement in (a) given area(s). This collection must include student participation in the selection of portfolio content, the criteria for selection, the criteria for judging merit, and evidence of student self-reflection.

They were told that "outsiders" would be looking at their work and were given a copy of the draft scoring guide which had been developed by the teachers using the Maine Educational Assessment rubric as a base. Students were asked to include the following pieces of writing:

- a business letter
- a job or college application
- a résumé
- an essay of self-reflection or self-regard (in many cases, students chose the "college essay")
- another piece of the student's choice

6 Excellent in overall quality
  Substantial in content (length and development)
  Mature in style
  Demonstrates ability to handle prose tasks successfully
  Uses language creatively and effectively
  Strong voice. Clear sense of audience and context

Often, there is a loose connection between the writer's sense of self and the writing. A "6" portfolio typically takes risks that work—either in content or form—and challenges the reader by trying something new.

5 Very good in overall quality
  Substantial in content, although pieces are not as fully developed
  Uses language effectively, but not as creatively as a "6"
  Demonstrates ability to handle varied prose tasks successfully
  Voice is clear and distinct, if not powerful. Sense of audience is clearly
      present, if not always firm

The "5" portfolio suggests the excellence that the "6" demonstrates. A "5" portfolio tends not to take as many risks as a "6."

4 Good in overall quality
  Competent in content and style
  Inconsistent demonstration of ability to handle a variety of prose tasks successfully and to use language effectively
  Sense of audience and task, but some of the writing seems formulaic or lacks a
      strong voice

There are more strengths than weaknesses, but there may be an unevenness of quality or underdevelopment in one or two pieces. There seems to be minimal risk taking or originality.

3 Fair in overall quality
  One or more pieces may be too brief or underdeveloped
  Some evidence of ability to handle prose tasks successfully and to use language effectively, but this is offset by recurring problems in either or both
      content and style
  Lacks both a clear sense of purpose and a distinctive voice

The "3" suggests the competence that a "4" demonstrates. Strengths and weaknesses tend to be evenly balanced either within or among pieces.

2 Below average in overall quality
  The writing may be clear, focused, and error free, but it is usually thin in substance and undistinguished in style
  Two or more of the pieces may be either short and undeveloped or abstract
      and vague
  Little evidence of ability to handle varied prose tasks

Weaknesses clearly predominate over strengths. The writer rarely takes risks, relying instead on formulas and clichés.

1 Poor in overall quality
  Characterized by brief pieces that are unoriginal and uncreative in style
  Major weaknesses and few, if any, strengths

The portfolio seems to have been put together with very little time and thought.

Figure 1. Freeport High School scoring guide.

As one might expect, students responded to the directions in very different ways. In some instances, these idiosyncrasies made it difficult for us to agree on a fair score for a student's portfolio. Before the fishbowl, we had been given the sample portfolios, so most of us had individually scored and noted comments on each one. As we shared our scores and the reasons for our decisions, we raised several issues regarding both the development of the portfolios and the scoring; these issues stemmed from differences in the content of the individual portfolios and the backgrounds of the students.

Questions Raised from Considering the Sample Portfolios

As teachers know, students do their best work when they feel some ownership of the task. Thus, an essential aspect of portfolio development has been to allow students to choose some of the pieces they include. Freedom to choose, however, can lead to problems in scoring.

The fishbowl group had to evaluate one portfolio that included a poem and others that contained writing from different genres. For example, while one student included an expository essay on *The Canterbury Tales*, another student chose a creative piece, "The New Canterbury Tales," written to imitate Chaucer's style. How does one evaluate such very different pieces? Some of us did not feel at all comfortable trying to assess the quality of writing of the poem, and we were not sure what to do with a portfolio that included only short pieces, most of which were personal and informal writing.

Another difficulty in scoring stemmed from our lack of knowledge about the context for inclusion of the pieces. For example, after some discussion about the lack of development in an essay about *The Scarlet Letter*, the teacher informed us that the class assignment from which the essay resulted had included a word limit. Perhaps knowing more about when and why the pieces were written would have made our scoring task easier. Should students be required to provide a brief introduction for each piece, telling when it was written, why, for what audience, and why they chose to include it?

Two other problems also stemmed from the choices students made. First, it was impossible for us not to be influenced by the order of the pieces in the portfolios. What we saw first influenced our overall responses. When students chose to put the weaker writing first, for example, we sometimes found it difficult to give full weight to the higher quality of writing that came later. Second, because some students chose to include extra pieces, we had to struggle with finding a way to "count" these in the scoring without being unfair to the students whose portfolios contained only what was required.

Finally, because these students had to include résumés and application forms, we could not help but be aware of differences in their backgrounds. These differences created problems. Such differences are likely to be apparent even when there is less direct evidence than we saw in the résumé and applications.

Because some members of our fishbowl group were not experienced teachers, this issue might have been exaggerated somewhat, but my own experience with high school teachers leads me to think that it will come up with any group of scorers. Some people, for example, value highly the kind of analytic writing that college-bound students are likely to include and tend to see pieces written by students who plan to attend a vocational school as superficial and undeveloped. In a more diverse community than Freeport, teachers may find that many students include writing which does not fit white mainstream middle-class standards. How can the scoring-process design deal with these disparities? Should students be penalized for having different socio-economic or cultural backgrounds?

Recommendations

On the basis of the preceding questions and other issues that arose during our discussion and scoring of this small number of sample essays, I offer the following suggestions for teachers who are planning to develop schoolwide evaluation of student portfolios. I believe that these recommendations are also important for individual teachers to consider as they grade portfolios in their own classrooms:

1. Decide up front the purpose of the evaluation, because those who score the portfolios will respond differently if their focus is to provide feedback rather than make a final judgment. If students compile portfolios each year they are in high school, for example, the first three may be considered as *formative assessment*, that is, a way of letting students know how they are doing so that they can work to improve their writing. In these portfolios, students might be asked to include pieces that focus on process. For example, students could include a "disaster" (an unsuccessful draft) and write a critique to show that they know how it might be improved. Or they might select one example to show the writing process as a whole: a series of notes and drafts of one piece, along with the final copy, as evidence of their ability to plan, write, revise, and edit.

At the end of the senior year, especially if the portfolios become part of a competency-based diploma, however, the assessment logically would be a *summative* one, that is, a means of rendering a final decision about whether students' work meets minimum quality standards for graduation. At this point, it makes sense for students to include such items as college or job applications, but they might also be asked to choose some pieces written during the previous years. These pieces could show their progress over a longer period and allow them to demonstrate their ability in a wider range of genres. The Freeport teachers, for example, noted that the curriculum prior to senior year included types of writing which would be considered more substantive than the job applications and résumés students do as seniors.

2. Think carefully about the core requirements and how these are described. The scoring will be easier and more equitable if students submit pieces in the same genres. Trying to evaluate apples (long research papers) and oranges (short personal essays written in class) at the same time can be problematic unless the scoring has been designed to accommodate a variety of student choices.

3. Ask the students to write introductions to their portfolios to tell readers what they think they do well and what they would like to do better. Some of the Freeport students did this even though it was not a requirement, and in each case these students correctly identified weaknesses we noticed in their writing. Perhaps the fact that students know what they need to improve on should count in the final score.

4. Ask students to write a brief introduction to each piece in the portfolio so that readers can evaluate the degree to which the writing is successful for its intended purpose. As I mentioned earlier, one essay had been assigned with a word limit. That piece, which seemed thin and underdeveloped on the first reading, actually seemed much better when we took into consideration the fact that for this assignment, the student had been asked to respond in no more than 200 words.

Because audience and purpose are essential considerations when anyone writes, no writing can truly be considered effective without taking into account the audience for whom it was intended and what it was supposed to accomplish. For example, the tone and content which would characterize effective writing in a personal response journal might be totally ineffective or inappropriate for an analytical essay or a business letter.

5. *Consider encouraging students to look beyond work done for their English class when they collect pieces for their portfolios.* Not only are the portfolios likely to be more interesting to readers, students will also get the message that good writing can be found everywhere. One of the Freeport teachers mentioned that a student had written a letter to the editor which had actually been published. Even though the letter was well written, the student had not chosen to include it in his portfolio. If students are so engaged with writing that they are doing it on their own outside of school, shouldn't that evidence be considered in an evaluation of their progress or achievement?

6. *Give students clear guidance regarding the development of their portfolios.* Give them copies of the scoring guide, tell them who will do the scoring, and explain the process. Discuss such factors as the possible effect the order they choose for presenting their work may have on their scores, the importance of carefully following directions about the core requirements, and the wisdom of carefully proofreading the work they submit.

Students should be reminded to make every effort to locate and correct typographical and other errors, i.e., to clean up their writing just as they would dress up for an interview for an office job, and to make sure everything they have included is complete. We read one essay with an ending missing due to a computer glitch and a job application with the personal statement section left blank.

7. *Thoughtfully develop the scoring guide to address specific issues that are likely to be problematic, but consider the guide as a draft which may need to be revised and reworked the next time.* Some issues which the scoring guide needs to take into account include the following:

(a) How will extra pieces count in the total score? One possibility is to establish a score for the core pieces and then to award a bonus if the quality of the optional pieces warrants one. (Students would be told that extra pieces can help but will not hurt their scores.) Another option would be to incorporate a descriptor in the guide that deals with this. For example, the 6 score might say: "Shows evidence of a superior interest in writing by providing optional pieces of high quality."

(b) How will you deal with pieces which do not fit the standards specified in the scoring guide or are expected by teachers? One way of handling the problem of differences that can occur in the level or types of writing done by college-bound and noncollege-bound students (or others) is to write some policy guidelines for scorers to follow. One possible statement: "When scoring, readers should forget their personal preferences for any particular type or characteristic of writing and evaluate a piece of writing solely in terms of whether or not it succeeds for the audience and task the writer has identified." Despite differences in diction, tone, and length, then, the business letter written by a student applying for a gas station job, for example, could be considered just as effective as one written by a student applying for admission to an Ivy League college.

(c) Should everything in the portfolio be considered in the final score? The fishbowl group found the job applications problematic because not all of them included writing. Filling in the blanks seemed to be a reflection of a student's ability to follow directions. Perhaps such items might not be scored at all, even though they are very appropriate to include in an exit portfolio at the end of high school.

Since I participated in this experiment, I have discovered another strategy for increasing student understanding of the evaluation criteria and also, perhaps, their scores. Instead of giving a final exam in my college classes ("Special Education" and "Gender Issues and Education"), I require students to compile portfolios which demonstrate their learning during the semester. One very important component is a list of "big ideas" or major concepts which students explain by integrating specific examples from the course reading, class discussions, field-experience placements in public schools, and their own prior experience and knowledge. To help students internalize the evaluative criteria, I ask them at midterm to write up one of these "big ideas" in essay form (as it would be done for the final portfolio). Each student is then given a scoring sheet and asked to evaluate a classmate's sample essay and provide feedback. I also score these sample essays afterward. This practice enables students to understand both the way a holistic scoring process works and a rating of their work in relation to the evaluation criteria, which is nonjudgmental at this point.

There is no doubt that portfolios are much better than on-demand, timed essays for evaluating students' achievement in writing and in other curricular areas as well. Portfolios give a much broader picture of what students know or can do. Teachers or others can see how students handle many different types of writing as well as varied aspects of the writing process or other topics of study.

But if students have some choices about their development, portfolios are perhaps most important because they can motivate students to take a greater interest in improving their writing skills. By collecting their work in classroom portfolios, students can see their progress over time. As their folders get fatter and fatter, they can also feel a sense of accomplishment.

If students also have to compile portfolios for schoolwide scoring, they will experience the pleasure, or maybe the pain, of going public with one's writing. Either way, they will get valuable experience for adjusting to real-world demands they will face when they graduate from high school. Because portfolios are personal, they can be very powerful for students, but as our fishbowl conversation made clear to me, they can also be very problematic for the teachers who have to score them. By being aware of potential problems and attempting to deal with them beforehand, teachers can help to make the scoring process smoother and more equitable. Because it is doubtful that anyone will ever be able to design the perfect scoring process, any process or rubric should be thought of as a draft, subject to future revision as knowledge increases with experience. Thus, portfolio evaluation in the classroom or in a school is likely to work best when reflective teachers make decisions thoughtfully and sensitively.

IV Faculty Workshops in Alternatives to Grading Student Writing

Developing Intrinsic Motivation for Students' Writing

Immaculate Kizza
University of Tennessee at Chattanooga

Immaculate Kizza received her Ph.D. in English from the University of Toledo and is associate professor of English at the University of Tennessee at Chattanooga. Her research interests in rhetoric and composition include evaluation strategies, placement tests, basic writing, minority writers, grammar, and technology.

Introduction and Aims

This workshop integrates our discussion of grading with the entire writing process. Often, students ignore our very comprehensive comments on their papers and instead focus on the grades, thereby doing very little to improve their writing but succeeding in disheartening us. One reason for the focus on grades may be a failure of the writing process itself: For response to be meaningful, students have to find the writing task itself meaningful. You can minimize your students' concentration on grades and maximize their involvement in and enjoyment of their writing by employing the concept of *intrinsic motivation*—that is, by helping students find the writing assignment significant and therefore worthy of assessment. This workshop will help you to

- reexamine the concept of intrinsic motivation and assess its role in student writing;
- explore ways to foster intrinsic motivation in the writing classroom;
- design intrinsically motivating writing assignments;
- link good assignment design to criteria for student and teacher self-assessment.

Resources

In This Volume

Bencich, Carol Beeghly. Chapter 4: "Response: A Promising Beginning for Grading Student Writing."

Guthrow, Mary B. Chapter 9: "Writing at Reading: How a Junior Year in England Changes Student Writers."

Holaday, Lynn. Chapter 3: "Writing Students Need Coaches, Not Judges."

Other Resources

Ames, C. "Motivation: What Teachers Need to Know." *Teachers College Record* 91 (1990): 409–21.

Raffini, James P. *Winners without Losers: Structures and Strategies for Increasing Student Motivation to Learn.* Boston: Allyn, 1993. Chapters 4–10.

Reid, Stephen. *The Prentice-Hall Guide for College Writers.* 2nd ed. Englewood Cliffs: Prentice, 1992.

Discussion Topics

- Talk over the concept of *intrinsic motivation*. What role can intrinsic motivation play in the composition classroom? How can we foster intrinsic motivation in writing assignments and activities? How is intrinsic motivation going to affect the way students perceive writing and the grades they get? How will intrinsic motivation affect the way we evaluate students' writing? How can intrinsic motivation be utilized to focus students' attention away from grades on their writing? (Raffini's Chapters 1 and 5 are particularly strong on this topic.)

- Share writing assignments that seem to have had the trait of intrinsic motivation, the ones where students took to the task eagerly instead of groaning or asking "How many words?" Once you have accumulated several of these assignments, analyze them and outline the basic elements of an intrinsically motivating writing assignment (see also Raffini 69–72).

- Consider how discussion of assessment criteria can be made a part of the assignment process. To what extent can students be made responsible for thinking of assessment criteria *before* they write? What effect will this have on the intrinsic motivation of the assignment?

Activities

- Working with fellow teachers, design what you consider to be several intrinsically motivating writing assignments. Compare these to the criteria you developed previously. Discuss the designed assignments as a group. (Also see Reid's writing assignments, especially his assignments for observing, remembering, investigating, explaining, evaluating, problem solving, and arguing. See also Raffini's "Family Biographer" 155–56 and "Headline News" 255–56.)

- Try out the designed assignments on your students, and ask them to comment anonymously after completing and getting back at least two of the assignments. Seek comments that will help you:

  1. assess whether your assignments were intrinsically motivating (basic elements as discussed above);

  2. evaluate the effectiveness of your intrinsically motivating assignments.

- Discuss the students' comments with your colleagues. Were you successful in engaging students in writing for the fun of it, as opposed to writing just for the grade? Did they pay more attention to your comments for improvement? Were their final products visibly better than their previous ones?

- Explore the effect of alternative grading systems on students' intrinsic motivation. Try portfolio grading or contracts; work with rubrics (teacher and student developed); try pass/fail or accept/revise and compare it with ABC grading. Cautiously evaluate student responses. Can the grading system itself influence how students perceive writing assignments and the quality of their work?

Follow-up

- Even if you do not get the results you are expecting with your first assignments, continue designing and assigning intrinsically motivating tasks for at least a term. Compile your experiences—the successes and tribulations—for an annual NCTE/CCCC Convention presentation (intrinsically motivating idea, wouldn't you say?). The resultant discussion might point you in new directions "to strive, to seek, to find, and not to yield."

- Interview (or have your students interview) people who write regularly: journalists, freelance writers in your community. Ask these writers about their own intrinsic motivation strategies. Also, have these writers discuss how they self-assess their own writing.

- Donald Graves and Nancie Atwell have argued that the best writing assignments are those which are student—rather than teacher—generated. Develop a series of trials in which students develop their own writing topics and their own assessment strategies. How do both the assignments and the assessment strategies differ from what a teacher might employ? What are the implications for teaching?

- Use brainstorming with students to compile writing assignments, first as individuals, then in small groups, then to a class list. Students can then choose assignments from that list, and as Raffini points out, allowing students to experience choice is one of the most powerful ways to enhance their intrinsic motivation. Choice leads to commitment and commitment of responsibility. You can also involve students in the structuring of the assignments; make them feel they are in control.

Weighing and Choosing Alternatives

Stephen Tchudi
University of Nevada, Reno

Stephen Tchudi (introduced on the Editor page) chaired the NCTE Committee on Alternatives to Grading Student Writing.

Introduction and Aims

This workshop will help you and your colleagues to evaluate your present grading system and to develop and evaluate alternatives. Because it's important to base change solidly in educational theory, I suggest that you read or reread the introductory essays in this collection to square away your pedagogical beliefs and commitments. Through this workshop you can

- examine your current system and assess its strengths and weaknesses;
- study alternative grading plans and assess their possible strengths, drawbacks, and implementation problems;
- create a series of trials to explore the effects of alternatives to grading student writing in your classroom, school, or district.

Resources

In This Volume

McDonnell, Charles. Chapter 14: "Total Quality: A Farewell to Grades."

Nelson, Marie Wilson. Chapter 2: "Growth-Biased Assessing of Writers—A More Democratic Choice."

O'Hagan, Liesel K. Chapter 1: "It's Broken—Fix It!"

Tchudi, Stephen. "Introduction: Degrees of Freedom in Assessment, Evaluation, and Grading."

Other Resources

Kirschenbaum, Howard, Rodney Napier, and Sidney B. Simon. *Wad-Ja-Get? The Grading Game in American Education.* New York: Hart, 1971. [A must-read classic in the field.]

Knowles, Malcolm S. *Using Learning Contracts.* San Francisco: Jossey-Bass, 1986.

"Reporting What Students Are Learning." *Educational Leadership* 52:2 (Oct. 1994). [An entire issue devoted to a discussion of alternative grading and reporting systems.]

Discussion Topics

- What grading systems do teachers currently use in your school or district? What dissatisfaction is there with them? In what ways do they satisfactorily serve your needs? Why, in the end, do teachers want to explore alternatives to grading student writing?

- Review the research on grading (see both O'Hagan and Nelson). To what extent do your experiences support, extend, or run contrary to the research?

- Have the teachers in your school or district explored alternatives to grading? Has anyone worked with variations of pass/fail? Contracts? Point systems? Rubrics and scoring guides? What do they find to be the strengths and weaknesses of each?

- Discuss grading alternatives in terms of current composition theory. In what ways are the current systems (both traditional and alternative) consistent with what your group takes to be the best current knowledge about writing? Which systems provide the greatest number of degrees of freedom for teachers to be consistent with the research and helpful to students?

Activities

- With courage and caution, bring in student papers that teachers in your group have responded to and/or graded. Carefully study the comments. What are their purposes? What sort of instructional philosophy do they reveal? Study the link with grades. Is there a correlation between instruction and grading? (With even greater courage, supplement this activity by having students write about what they learned from those particular comments and the grade.)

- Review the articles in Part II of this book to create a list of grading alternatives that seem interesting or attractive to your group (see also the summary chart in the introduction to this volume). What problems does each of these systems purport to solve? What do you anticipate to be the practical problems with each?

- Then design a series of trials of alternative systems. Members of your group might each agree to try a system for, say, one marking period. Or individual teachers might want to try a different system each marking period for a semester or a year. Of course, people should only test out systems that they see as particularly interesting or attractive.

In the spirit of the teacher as researcher, keep accurate data on these trials. In a logbook, each teacher might write

- *Preliminary aims and reflections.* What do you want to learn from this trial? How do you think the new system has potential for solving traditional grading problems?

- *The plan.* Document the design and implementation of the system: introducing it to the students, the ground rules and mechanics (how papers are collected, marked, returned to students—don't trust this to memory).

- *Reflections on various efforts.* What happened the first, second, or fifth time you used this system? What seemed to work well? What were the problems? In particular, what were the unanticipated (Murphy's Law!) side effects or complications?

- *Comments on sample papers.*

- *Assessment of student responses and reactions.* Ask your students to write about the new system. Does it seem fair and equitable to them? Did it give them the kind of feedback they needed? How would they change or modify it?

- *Reflections and recommendations.* If you were doing the trial again, how would you modify it? Is this a system that could work broadly in your school or district? What advice would you give to teachers implementing it? (See especially Charles McDonnell's report of how he developed, implemented, and evaluated his "total quality" assessment system.)

Follow-up

- Continue the grading trials for a reasonable time period. Continue to meet to discuss the strengths and weaknesses of each alternative approach.

- Discuss grading alternatives with teachers at the grade levels above and below you. To what extent do grading systems represent and accurately describe student achievement? What sorts of grading alternatives could lead to improved articulation and reporting among levels.

- Explore combinations of grading systems. Develop and give trial runs to these new systems. Could you, for example, combine a pass/fail writing system with graded work in other areas of the language arts? Can contract learning be done pass/fail? Can point systems be combined with rubrics and scoring sheets? Remember that no alternative system is a panacea to the problems induced by the grading system. Keep on searching!

- Write an account of your grading trials and submit it to *Language Arts, English Journal,* or *College English.*

Contract Grades: An Agreement between Students and Their Teachers

Lynda S. Radican
California State University–Sacramento

Lynda S. Radican currently teaches freshman and sophomore composition at California State University–Sacramento. She specializes in working with students who experience learning difficulties in their reading and writing. She has taught English at both the middle school and high school levels and conducts inservice workshops for high school- and college-level teachers. Additionally, she is a consultant for the California Highway Patrol Writing Competency Exam. After receiving her M.A. in literary drama from CSUS, she continued her education as a teaching fellow in rhetoric and composition at the University of Nevada, Reno. At present, she is working on a case study that focuses on home schooling children with learning challenges.

Background

Contract grades essentially transform the grading process from teacher-developed criteria into an agreement between teacher and student, with considerable freedom for students to propose and assess work on their own initiative. Like the related concepts of point systems, achievement grading (Adkison and Tchudi), total quality assessment (McDonnell), and outcomes-based grading (Pribyl), contracts eliminate highly subjective and pseudoscientific gradations (O'Hagan) and link grades to the quantity of high-quality work completed. I was first introduced to contract grades several years ago during my graduate studies and felt a tremendous amount of freedom because I could write for myself, rather than for my professor or for a grade. Having been liberated from my own phobia of the "bad grade," I implemented contracts in my own freshman and sophomore literature and writing courses. My initial concerns were as follows:

- to ensure quality controls within the contract to make certain students were producing good work, not just lots of work;

- to deal with the objections of students who were opposed to having to work harder for an A than students who earned B's or C's and those who operated under the assumption that A's are awarded simply for not doing anything wrong, rather than for showing an ability beyond the minimums.

I had students maintain a portfolio, and if their portfolio contained the core assignments to satisfy basic course requirements, they were guaranteed a C, provided they had attended class and participated actively. Students were then allowed to contract for a B or an A on the basis of their willingness to add high-quality work to their portfolios, work such as additional readings and writings, with a range of possibilities that I outlined in class. Students needed to turn in their contract proposals for their chosen project by the fifth week of the semester and complete drafts by the twelfth week. To ensure that students understood that quantity does not replace quality, I included a statement in the contract that established my right to ask students to revise assignments that did not demonstrate competent writing skills, including originality of thought, clarity of focus, depth and detail of development, precision of language, and control of mechanics and usage. To deal with the objections of being forced to work harder, I reminded students that those who earn exceptionally high grades should and often do work harder than others. (Not every student has been convinced by this argument.)

Several years later, after numerous personal comments and class evaluations from my students, I conclude that at least 90 percent of my students like the freedom of the contract grade. They feel secure knowing that if they "don't get it right" the first time, they can revise. As the teacher, I enjoy the freedom of not having to include grade justifications in my comments and responses. I praise what they do well, focus on areas that need improvement, and request revisions when necessary. For those students who are less trusting of contract grades, I offer the choice of waiving the contract and opting for a traditional grading system. Interestingly enough, even those who complain about the contract system seldom choose to forgo the opportunity to control their grade.

I highly recommend this alternative to grading and maintain that teachers at any level, in any subject matter, can successfully implement such a strategy either for individual units or entire semesters.

Introduction and Aims

This workshop will help you determine, first, whether a contract-grading system is a viable alternative and beneficial to both you and your students and, second, how to implement such a system. Through this workshop you can

- examine where such a system would be beneficial, i.e., the grade level and subject matter;
- devise various strategies for incorporating contract grades into your current grading practice;
- develop satisfactory contracts for both individual units and entire courses;
- create a contract-grading policy statement or set of guidelines for your faculty interest group;
- develop strategies to deal with objections from other faculty and administrators.

Resources

In This Volume

Adkison, Stephen, and Stephen Tchudi. Chapter 13: "Grading on Merit and Achievement: Where Quality Meets Quantity."

McDonnell, Charles. Chapter 14: "Total Quality: A Farewell to Grades."

Nelson, Marie Wilson. Chapter 2: "Growth-Biased Assessing of Writers—A More Democratic Choice."

O'Hagan, Liesel K. Chapter 1: "It's Broken—Fix It!"

Pribyl, Rick. Chapter 17: "Unlocking Outcome-Based Education through the Writing Process."

Other Resources

Courts, Patrick L. *Literacy and Empowerment: The Meaning Makers.* South Hadley: Bergin & Garvey, 1991.

Elbow, Peter. *Embracing Contraries: Explorations in Learning and Teaching.* New York: Oxford UP, 1986.

Kirschenbaum, Howard, Rodney Napier, and Sidney B. Simon. *Wad-Ja-Get? The Grading Game in American Education.* New York: Hart, 1971.

Knowles, Malcolm S. *Using Learning Contracts.* San Francisco: Jossey-Bass, 1986.

"Reporting What Students Are Learning." *Educational Leadership* 52:2 (Oct. 1994).

Smith, Frank. *Insult to Intelligence: The Bureaucratic Invasion of Our Classrooms.*
    New York: Arbor House, 1986.

Discussion Topics

- Review the recommended essays in this book and discuss or outline the traits of contract grading, including:

    1. How work is "graded" pass/fail or accept/revise;

    2. How work is credited or translated into report-card grades;

    3. How various systems are designed and implemented in the classroom.

- Consider how contract grading attempts to solve the following problems:

    A child who has learned that something is worth doing only for a grade has learned the wrong thing. (Smith 183)

    [Students] write in order to evidence that they have listened to what the teacher said.…The student's language and thought is directed at getting through the day…and achieving success (good grades, promotion), and almost none of it is directed at the…expression of one's ideas, at the process of assimilating and/or wrestling with what is being learned. (Courts 83)

    When they trust the teacher to be wholly an ally, students are more willing to take risks, connect the self to the material, and experiment. Here is the source not just of learning but also of genuine development or growth. (Elbow 144)

- Consider the following arguments that are frequently raised against contract grading:

    1. Contract grades would replace quality with quantity.

    2. Traditional grades are needed to maintain control.

    3. Students need the threat of grades to do high-quality work.

    4. Such systems would result in everyone receiving A's and B's, leading to grade inflation.

- Consider ways in which contract grades could be linked with other kinds of grading alternatives and writing practices, such as pass/fail, accept/revise, point systems, and portfolio grading.

- How can contract grades satisfy university, district, or school grading policies and restrictions and requirements while supporting current composition theories such as student ownership, collaborative writing, peer-group analysis and discussion, multiple drafts, and teacher as collaborator, not judge?

- What benefits do contract grades afford students at all ability levels? What benefits do they afford teachers?
- What happens if students fail to meet their contracts?

Activities

- Hold discussions with students in which you introduce the contract-grading system. What are their positive and negative responses? What can you do to deal with each kind of response in designing a system?

- Discuss the grading systems currently being used in the classes at your school (not only for English, but for other disciplines, as appropriate). Consider how you could develop contract approaches in those courses by

  1. specifying the quantity and quality of work required for a base grade of C;

  2. detailing the options for students to earn B's or A's;

  3. using the portfolio or other system to document work completed;

  4. engaging students in self-assessment of their work.

- Design a series of trial contracts. Start simple. The first contract might simply be for a B or an A in a single unit of work or as part of a unit. You might want to make contract grading optional the first time around so that students who are distrustful of the system can continue with familiar grading practices. Treat your trials as an action-research project. Keeping accurate data is a must, especially when dealing with the reservations of students and even opposition from administrators or parents. (See also the material on "Weighing and Choosing Alternatives" by Tchudi, this volume.)

- Consider developing a set of guidelines for contracting in your interest group, grade level, or department. What are the elements of a good contract? How can those elements vary? Begin conducting trials of a variety of systems. Include samples in your guideline publication.

Follow-up

- After completing trials, ask students to comment again on the contract system. How has their attitude changed?

- Discuss the claims of contract grading. Does it seem to relieve grade anxiety for students? Does it free up the teacher to teach? Does the quality of student work improve or get better?

- Hold a workshop on contract grading for parents, to show them how this system makes both teachers and students accountable.

- Hold a contract-grading workshop for teachers at other levels.

- Solicit teachers from different grade levels and/or content areas who are interested in contract grades in their classes. Encourage these teachers to keep logbooks and later to compare the results of student growth and performance in, for example, math, science, physical education, and social studies.

- Hold an exhibit or exposition of student work completed under contracts, along with a display of the contracts themselves, students' ancillary work (notes, drafts, etc.), and the final products, with self-assessment showing how the work fulfilled the contracts.

Using Rubrics and Holistic Scoring of Writing

Jean S. Ketter
Grinnell College

Jean S. Ketter (introduced earlier) served on the NCTE Committee on Alternatives to Grading Student Writing.

Introduction

A number of writers in this collection discuss the use of rubrics or holistic scoring for classroom, schoolwide, or even districtwide assessment. In this workshop, you will examine and test an approach to evaluating student writing that you can use in your classroom as an alternative to placing letter grades on student papers. Although using holistic scoring as "high-stakes," large-scale assessment is a contested practice, its use at the classroom level holds possibilities as a means of providing quick and informative feedback to students and of training students to evaluate their own and their peers' writing. You will explore several topics that will help you make an informed decision about when and how to use holistic scoring in your teaching of writing.

Resources

In This Volume

Bauman, Marcy. Chapter 11: "What Grades Do for Us, and How to Do without Them."

Blumner, Jacob S., and Francis Fritz. Chapter 16: "Students Using Evaluation in Their Writing Process."

Young, Gail M. Chapter 15: "Using a Multidimensional Scoring Guide: A Win-Win Situation."

Other Resources

Hourigan, Maureen M. "Poststructural Theory and Writing Assessment: 'Heady, Esoteric Theory' Revisited." *Teaching English in the Two-Year College* 18 (1991): 191–95.

Huot, Brian A. "The Literature of Direct Writing Assessment: Major Concerns and Prevailing Trends." *Review of Educational Research* 60 (1990): 237–63.

———. "Reliability, Validity, and Holistic Scoring: What We Know and What We Need to Know." *College Composition and Communication* 41 (1990): 213.

McKendy, Thomas. "Locally Developed Writing Tests and the Validity of Holistic Scoring." *Research in the Teaching of English* 26 (1992): 149–65.

Prater, Doris, and William Padia. "Developing Parallel Holistic and Analytic Scoring Guides for Assessing Elementary Writing Samples." *Journal of Research and Development in Education* 17 (1983): 20–24.

Purves, Alan. "Reflections on Research and Assessment in Written Composition." *Research in the Teaching of English* 26 (1992): 106–22.

White, Edward M. *Teaching and Assessing Writing: Recent Advances in Understanding, Evaluating, and Improving Student Performance.* 2nd ed. San Francisco: Jossey-Bass, 1994.

Williamson, Michael M., and Brian A. Huot. *Validating Holistic Scoring for Writing Assessment.* Cresskill: Hampton, 1993.

Discussion Topics

- On the basis of your reading, what is holistic grading/scoring of writing or scoring using rubrics, and what do you see as the advantages and disadvantages? How does developing a scoring guide or rubric provide assessment information for both students and teachers?

- Many schools and districts collect a writing sample on a common topic or prompt and have faculty members score it with an agreed-upon holistic scale or rubric. Consider the advantages and disadvantages of such a program for your school or district. What could be learned by having students write on common topics and having teachers compare holistic scores? What would be the logistical problems? How much time would be required, and does your faculty think the results would be worth it? How would a discussion of holistic scoring help you think about issues in grading student writing?

- Discover the students' perspectives. In class, talk to students about what they think one of your assignments means. Show them the teacher's scoring guide or rubric. Since we can't assume that the students' interpretation of a prompt/assignment is the same as ours, ask students to discuss what they think the criteria mean. If you don't have time to interview each student, ask students to write a short note about what they think is expected of them with an assignment/prompt.

Have the students describe the criteria they think ought to be employed by a teacher who'll be judging the writing. How closely do their perceptions coincide with yours and those of your fellow faculty members? Honor unexpected but plausible constructions of meaning. Adopt a constructivist approach to assessing writing. Because students are stakeholders in assessment, they should be involved not only in a discussion of the technical aspects of writing assessment, but also in the metadiscussion of how criteria are constructed.

Activities

This activity has you take part in a simulated training session for raters, one in which you can test your assumptions and come to your own conclusions about whether and how to use holistic scoring in your teaching:

- First, *gather some student writing on a common theme*. Here is a prompt that has been used successfully with students from many different age groups[1]:

  Write about an incident or event when you had a strong feeling. It might have been a time when you were very scared, angry, embarrassed, or excited. Include enough details so that your readers can understand what happened and how you felt. Try to make your readers understand why you felt such a strong emotion at this moment in your life.

- Second, *develop a scoring rubric*. (Sample scoring rubrics are presented at several places in this volume; see pages 95, 227, 230, 237, 260–61, 267, and 303.[2]

- Third, *score papers*. Taking into account the grade level of your sample, take about fifteen minutes to score four or five papers.[3]

- Fourth, *look at the results*. If the scores cluster, discuss why that might be (similar educational backgrounds, experience as teachers, shared discourse community, experience scoring/grading). If the scores do have a wide spread, theorize why this might be true:

  1. Where do our ideas about what good writing is come from?

  2. What qualities of writing tend to either turn us off or impress us personally?

  3. How comfortable are we with asserting that our grading of writing is impartial and objective?

4. What happens in a setting where raters are "trained" to assign reliable (consistent) scores to essays? Does consistency mean validity?

■ *Discuss the assumption that students understand prompts similarly.* Think for a minute and then discuss how this topic might have been misconstrued by your students. What words or phrases might mislead? What range of responses might you get? How might you prevent misunderstandings if this is a class assignment? How might a person from another culture respond differently to this assignment? What circumstances might exist that would cause resistance in students?

■ *Reflect on the assumption that a single writing performance is a valid measure of a person's writing.* Consider whether you believe that the scores you gave the papers have predictive validity and should therefore be used as part of a portfolio passed on to the next grade or to inform any placement decisions.

Ending Questions

■ Why might holistic scoring be preferable to letter grading?

■ When could it be used in the writing process?

■ How might it be used to communicate with parents?

■ How might it be used to "grade" writing portfolios?

Follow-up

Start simple: Implement holistic or rubric assessment for one assignment:

■ Make the class assignment, and then ask the students to discuss or write about what they believe is expected. If interpretation of the assignment varies widely, come to a class consensus about the assignment through discussion. You might provide models of appropriate and inappropriate responses and discuss why each model does or does not represent an appropriate response. You could also allow more leeway, encouraging students to interpret the assignment differently, but you will have to account for these differing interpretations in the criteria.

■ Have a classroom discussion about criteria for the assignment; then, design a classroom rubric by which to judge this particular assignment.

- Provide students with anchor papers (student papers from past years will work) and have them practice scoring using the class-devised criteria. Then have them meet in groups of three to confer on their scores and clarify their understanding of the criteria.

- Assign writing (to be completed in class).

- Have students share their writing with a partner and instruct them to score each other's paper.

- Have students rewrite papers using peers' suggestions and then have them score their own papers before they submit them to you.

- Ask students to write a reflection on their experience. Did they find the holistic scoring process useful? Ask them to explain what they did and/or did not like about the process and make suggestions for improving it.

Reflect: How did your students perform on this task? Did you learn anything about them as writers, learners, or readers? Do you believe this method of assessment aided your students in providing peer feedback? Do you believe this method of assessment was superior to letter/number grades? In what ways will you adapt this process if you decide to use it again?

Compare: Discuss with students how they perceive grading and its alternatives and ask them to explain their preferences for either approach.

Share: Share your successes and frustrations with other faculty who are concerned about improving their teaching of writing. Discuss the possibility of creating departmental criteria for certain major assignments at each grade level.

Notes

1. If the workshop participants teach in districts that already have a state writing assessment in place, I would suggest that you investigate the prompts already in use in their districts.

2. Again, I would suggest that the workshop participants use rubrics currently in use in their districts or state, but it is also very useful to go through the process of developing your own.

3. If your state or district already uses some type of holistic scoring, it might be useful to bring in sample papers for discussion.

Alternative Assessment Methods across the Disciplines

Pamela B. Childers
The McCallie School, Chattanooga, Tennessee

Pamela B. Childers has been interested in alternatives to grading student writing since she began teaching in the sixties. Currently, she is Caldwell Chair of Composition at The McCallie School in Chattanooga, Tennessee, where she directs the writing-across-the-curriculum program and works with teachers from all disciplines to find alternative assessments for writing.

Introduction and Aims

The purpose of this workshop is to help you and your colleagues across the disciplines to consider the "hows" and "whys" of assessing writing in all subject areas. The workshop also focuses on the importance of real audiences in the assessment methods. For a good background in educational theory, I suggest that you read the introductory essays in this collection to consider the pedagogical beliefs and commitments of the authors. Through this workshop you can

- examine your current writing assignments and their assessments across the disciplines, considering strengths and weaknesses;
- study alternative grading methods that have worked;
- design a series of writing activities directed at different audiences and with alternative assessment methods.

Following are some caveats about assessing writing assignments across the disciplines:

- Use an assessment tool appropriate to the purpose of the assignment.
- Consider allowing the students to determine the assessment tool.
- Give the students a checklist to help them revise the assignment before you read it.

- Consider using another evaluator. For instance, if students are writing to another audience, then publication or a letter of response may be enough of an evaluation.

- Try peer editing for assessment of grammatical and structural considerations, and then you can focus on content.

- Consider giving several sequential assessments that are prerequisites for the next part of a sequential, long-term assignment.

Resources

In This Volume

Adkison, Stephen, and Stephen Tchudi. Chapter 13: "Grading on Merit and Achievement: Where Quality Meets Quantity."

Bauman, Marcy. Chapter 11: "What Grades Do for Us, and How to Do without Them."

Chandler, Kelly, and Amy Muentener. Chapter 12: "Seeing How Good *We* Can Get It."

Robbins, Sarah, Sue Poper, and Jennifer Herrod. Chapter 10: "Assessment through Collaborative Critique."

Other Resources

Farrell-Childers, Pamela, Anne Ruggles Gere, and Art Young, eds. *Writing across the Secondary School Curriculum.* Portsmouth: Boynton/Cook, 1994.

"Reporting What Students are Learning." *Educational Leadership* 52:2 (Oct. 1994).

Tchudi, Stephen, and Stephen Lafer. *The Interdisciplinary Teacher's Handbook: Integrated Teaching across the Curriculum.* Portsmouth: Boynton/Cook, 1996.

Discussion Topics

- Why have alternative assessments? What's wrong with the current grading methods? How will alternative assessments help our students learn more than they're learning now?

- What kinds of alternative methods have worked? How have they worked in other disciplines?

- What audiences are your students using other than the teacher? What audience might you have for writing other than the teacher? Why have real audiences for real assessment?

Activities

- Team up with a teacher from a another discipline. Each of you bring a writing assignment that you've graded. Discuss why you gave the assignment (purpose), and what you intended the students to learn in the process. As a team, design a new assignment that focuses on a different audience and uses an alternative assessment tool.

- Consider the link between the assignment and the assessment. Determine the relationship between what you, the teacher, want and what you want the student to learn—that is, what you want the student to remember and apply long after the assessment has taken place.

- Work with another teacher through e-mail. Consider a college education instructor as a partner. Examine the possibility of having his or her future teachers respond to the writing of your secondary school students. The college students would gain experience preparing them for classroom teaching, and your students would have a real audience responding to their writing in a much more objective way (Sam Robinson, University of Saskatchewan, and Michael Lancaster, The McCallie School).

- Try portfolio evaluation in a science, math, or history class.

- In order to practice using technology, have students subscribe to a listserv, focusing on a particular topic from a list of possibilities in a particular course. For instance, in a biology course, some of the topics might be air pollution, water pollution, rain forests, endangered species, ecosystems, conservation issues, orphan diseases, etc. Have students participate in the discussion online. By saving and printing their involvement in the discussion, they are proving their study of the topic. Response from the teacher could be nothing more than pass/fail for demonstration of knowledge of their topic. Students will have found audiences with common interests, knowledge, and the ability to respond to their ideas.

- Design a set of holistics and rubrics for a writing assignment that reflects humor and demonstrates a knowledge of content. At my school, for instance, in chemistry, students wrote a one-page story on an element, written in the first person. Students received an A for "very creative stories full of wonderful information" (Cissy May, The McCallie School). In an economics class, the teacher determined evaluation criteria with 75 percent focusing on content and 25 percent focusing on structural considerations (Skeeter Makepeace, The McCallie School).

- Have students write a letter to you at the beginning of your course. Ask them to describe their history with the subject, what they liked and disliked about it, and what they would like to do in class this year.

  Also, ask them to share anything they think you should know about them to help you as a teacher and learner. Respond in one letter back to the class that reflects ideas voiced in specific letters.

  Additionally, let students know that you will try to use some of their ideas to help you design some aspects of the course. You may even want to use the letter at the end of the year to evaluate what happened with learning during the course. A letter response from you, even a class letter, is a good alternative to a grade.

- Try a journal writing activity that either helps students reflect on what they have learned or becomes a response to a prompt. Rather than grade, count the number of entries per marking period only to meet a minimum requirement. Since these journal entries may lead to classroom discussion, the goal is to get students to write and allow their ideas to flow. Allow students to highlight anything they want you to read and respond to (Michael Lowry, The McCallie School).

- Try an interactive journal assignment that focuses on writing to think, responding to a topic, and demonstrating critical thinking (David Hall, The McCallie School).

- Try having students describe, in a letter to their parents, a concept or idea they have learned in a particular course. Then ask the parents to respond as to whether they understood the concept or idea.

Follow-up

- Make a list of possible alternatives to grading student writing for the activities suggested.

- Also, make a list of possible real audiences to use in responding to student writing.

- Involve parents in their children's learning by informing them of some of the ways that you are improving learning without always putting a grade on a paper.

- If you have two sections of the same course, use writing-to-learn activities in one class (experimental group) and your old methods only in the other class (control group). Give a pretest at the beginning of the year, and then a final test, and compare the results of the experimental and control groups. In two algebra classes, we discovered the experimental group improved much more than the control group (David Perkinson, Charlotte Country Day School).

- Keep a journal of what you try in your classes. Include the learning activities, what was successful, and what failed. This kind of classroom research will be valuable to you and to others.

- Correspond through e-mail with a partner. Sometimes it is easier to tell a real audience what you are doing and how it is working. You also have someone to ask questions of. Your partner may do the same with you, and both partners will learn from the experience.

- Ask students to evaluate the assessment methods you have used. You could revise something you tried earlier in the year and use the revised method (on the basis of student evaluations) later in the year.

- Save copies of significant data that you may want to use in an article or in a presentation you make before parents, the school board, administrators, or colleagues.

- Collaborate with colleagues, either within the same or different disciplines, to write an account of your study or to make a presentation before your department or at a professional conference.

- Collaborate with students to write an article or to make a presentation. If you have a writing-across-the-curriculum program, keep files of alternative writing assessments that have worked. If you don't have such a program, request a faculty file or notebook as a resource for your colleagues to record alternative writing assessments in all disciplines.

Communicating with Parents and the Public

Marilyn M. Cooper
Michigan Technological University

Marilyn M. Cooper is associate professor of humanities at Michigan Technological University, where she also directs graduate teaching assistant education. She writes about composition theory and practice, environmental rhetoric, and technical communication.

> Nothing in the preceding discussion should be taken to mean that assessment of learning is not an important aspect of teaching and learning. The uncommonsense approach to assessment has several significant differences, however, which can be briefly sketched. Among the most important is that uncommonsense assessment is based on positive achievement rather than on deficiency identification. Uncommonsense assessment is, further, individual, holistic, and cumulative, and although it is criterion rather than norm referenced, the criteria used must be based on explicitly negotiated standards.
>
> The importance of the last point that the criteria must be understood by all concerned—students and parents as well as teachers and administrators—can't be overstressed.
>
> —John S. Mayher, *Uncommon Sense* 261

Introduction and Aims

In any attempt to change the way in which students' writing is assessed, the importance of discussion and negotiation among teachers, students, administrators, and parents cannot, as Mayher stresses, be overemphasized. Not only must everyone understand the criteria, everyone must understand and accept the principles on which the proposed assessment system is based. One goal of alternative means of assessment, too, is to give students, parents, and administrators more information about students' writing abilities and to involve them more in the process of assessing and encouraging those abilities.

In this workshop, participants (teachers, parents, administrators, students) will discuss applications of the strategies to their particular situations.

Discussion Topics

- A useful opening activity is to discuss the four sample student reports presented in Figures 1–4. Distribute photocopies of these figures to your group and explain that if the students' writing had been assessed by means of a grading system, each of these students would have received a B.

  1. Have each participant write a description of each of these students on the basis of what can be inferred from the report card.

  2. In groups of three, discuss your descriptions: How similar are they? Why? How do they differ?

  3. Discuss the results of your discussion with the whole group. What did you learn from each of the different reporting methods? What *didn't* you learn?

- Have group members reminisce about grades in their school careers. Was grading a pleasant or an unpleasant experience? Did it lead to improved learning? Compare notes on the range of experiences reported by the group members; typically, you'll have some people (often high achievers) who think grading was helpful and some who report a range of bad experiences, even traumatic ones, that resulted from negative grades.

- Ask the group to discuss the function of reporting. What do parents want to learn from it? What should students learn from it? In what ways do grades interfere with communicating the kinds of information both groups want to acquire?

Activities

- Involve the workshop group in the process of planning a new assessment system. Discuss the goals of writing assessment and evaluate the ability of various assessment systems to meet these goals (see the summary chart in the introduction to this volume). Discuss the effects of the systems on students' learning and on teaching practices. Discuss, too, the resources needed to implement the various systems.

- Integrate student writing and community and school activities. The more parents and the public see and use the writing students do, the more they appreciate and understand students' writing abilities. And, of course, writing for the community is also quite rewarding for students. Interdisciplinary projects—such as an adopt-a-stream project that involves students in cleanup, pollution research, writing a newsletter, or producing a video—integrate learning and skills development and produce results beneficial to the community.

Report			
Name: Joe Kelley			
Writing			
	Low	Average	High
Focus			x
Organization			x
Clarity		x	
Grammar	x		
Spelling	x		

Figure 1. Joe Kelley's report.

REPORT					
Name: Eric Young					
Writing					
	Not a priority				Strength
	1	2	3	4	5
Has creative ideas			x		
Analyzes ideas		x			
Connects ideas to make a point			x		
Uses information	x				
Uses personal experience					x
Uses descriptive detail		x			
Experiments			x		
Organizes				x	
Expresses opinions				x	
Writes clear sentences					x

Figure 2. Eric Young's report.

- Ask students to write progress reports and the parents to respond. Instead of one-way communication—from teachers to students and parents in teacher-written progress reports—this strategy encourages students and parents to think about what the students are learning about writing and what they need to learn. It also helps teachers.

- Revise report cards. Different educational situations need different reporting methods. Together, students, teachers, par-

---

Report

Name: Jody West

Jody is anxious about her writing—she says it doesn't "sound right"—and she works hard at it. She is eager to receive feedback from the instructor and class-mates (she solicits feedback from her friends too), and she puts the advice she receives to good use. She is also able to decide for herself what she needs to do in her writing. She shows a great deal of initiative not only in attacking the process of writing but also in finding information about her topic (she decided to inter-view friends about how they felt about educational technology and to interview a counselor at counseling services about tips for dealing with stress in college). She is willing to express her own opinions and to listen to the opinions of others. She organizes her papers in a straightforward fashion and her ideas are clear and make sense.

Figure 3. Jody West's report.

Report

Name: Fred Carney

Writing

Student's report: I like writing and I want to be a good writer. I have a hard time staying interested in the ideas I write about, though, maybe I'm, just not smart enough.

Teacher's report: Fred poses interesting questions in his writing and writes with a great deal of passion about personal experience. He does not like to revise his writing.

Teachers aide's response: Fred is an enthusiastic participant in class discussion and does a good job of facilitating the work of his group.

Figure 4. Fred Carney's report.

ents, administrators, and the public at large need to think about what methods of reporting might work best in their sit-uation.

Follow-up

- Once an alternative system of assessment is in place, writing teachers and their students need to continue to communicate to the public about how the system is working, what goals it achieves, and how it affects their classroom work. They should report to school boards/boards of control and the media on their assessment system. They should also write letters to administrators and local newspapers. And they should give presentations to administrators as well as on local television and radio programs to keep everyone up-to-date on the reasons for and achievements of their assessment system and to remind them of the principles that underlie the development of writing abilities.

Work Cited

Mayher, John S. *Uncommon Sense: Theoretical Practice in Language Education.* Portsmouth: Boynton/Cook, 1990.

Editor

Stephen Tchudi is professor of English at the University of Nevada, Reno, where he teaches and writes in the composition and rhetoric program. He is co-director of "Reading and Writing in the West," a summer institute for teachers, and is coordinator of UNR's University Seminar program, which offers interdisciplinary experiences for first-year students. He previously taught at Michigan State University, where he received the Distinguished Faculty Award in 1990.

He is the author of some forty books for the general public, teachers, and young adult readers. Among his recent books are *The Interdisciplinary Teacher's Handbook* (with Stephen Lafer); *The New Literacy* (with Paul Morris); and *Change in the American West: Perspectives from the Humanities.* His young adult books include three novels, *The Valedictorian, The Burg-O-Rama Man,* and *The Green Machine and the Frog Crusade* (published in French as *La Croisade des Grenouilles*). His most recent nonfiction book for young adults is *Lock & Key: The Secrets of Locking Things Up, In, and Out.*

He is a past president of the National Council of Teachers of English and former editor of *English Journal,* and a past president of the Nevada State Council of Teachers of English and the current editor of their newsletter *Silver Sage.*

The Committee on Alternatives to Grading Student Writing was established in 1994 by a decision of the Executive Committee of the National Council of Teachers of English. Its charge was to study alternatives for evaluation of student writing in ways sensitive to the needs of students as well as institutions; to organize the results of the study through manuscripts that help teachers understand alternatives to grading; and to develop these manuscripts into a book to be proposed to the NCTE Editorial Board. Members of the committee were Stephen Tchudi (Chair), University of Nevada, Reno; Lynda Radican (Associate Chair), California State University–Sacramento; Robert Baroz, Ripton, Vermont; Nick Carbone, University of Massachusetts at Amherst; Mary Beth Cody, University of Nevada, Reno; Marilyn Cooper, Michigan Technological University, Houghton; Alice Cross, Horace Greeley High School, Chappaqua, New York; Dallas Davies, Fremont High School, Sunnyvale, California; Carol Dietrich, DeVry Institute of Technology, Columbus, Ohio; Pamela Childers, The McCallie School, Chattanooga, Tennessee; Elizabeth Hodges, Virginia Commonwealth University, Richmond; Gwendolyn Jones, Tuskegee Institute, Alabama; Jean Ketter, Grinnell College, Iowa; Immaculate Kizza, University of Tennessee, Chattanooga; Terri LeClercq, University of Texas Law School, Austin; Marie Wilson Nelson, National Louis University, Tampa, Florida; and Joe Strzepek, University of Virginia, Charlottesville.

This book was typeset in Palatino and Helvetica.
The typeface used on the cover was Lithos Bold.
The book was printed on 50 lb. offset paper.